GROW
RICH
WITH
YOUR
MILLION
DOLLAR
MIND

THE AUTHOR

Brian Adams' career reads like a page from his own book: at age 19, he was editor-publisher of *The Western Examiner* in Sydney. At age 23, he was editor-publisher of a chain of newspapers in Toronto in addition to heading a radio-television production company, an advertising-press consultancy and a retail enterprise in Canada. He is an accomplished and successful actor-writer-director, an international platform speaker and has been voted one of the world's Ten Best Dressed Men.

Born in Australia, his career began as an advertising copywriter. He became a radio announcer then a columnist for *Tempo* magazine before starting his own newspaper.

In 1953 he toured the world as a freelance journalist. Settling in Toronto, he formed Canadian News Publications and consolidated other successful business enterprises. In 1960 he sold his Canadian interests and moved to New York to further his studies at New York University.

Setting up residence in Los Angeles, he formed Briad Productions, producing the 'Starlight Mystery Theatre' series and the Los Angeles stage production of 'See How They Run'. He was placed under contract by CBS to host a daily TV show 'Adams At Noon'. He has appeared in countless TV and film shows in Canada and the USA.

In 1967 he was brought back to Australia by Channel 10 to host the 'Tonight Show'. He also conducted a nightly talk-back radio show, hosted 'Adams After Noon' and 'Around The World With Brian Adams' for Channel 10 and has appeared as an actor in numerous Australian drama series and films.

As a lecturer he is named in the top ten motivational speakers in the USA. His dynamic platform presentations are given to companies, organizations and training institutions in Australia, Canada and the USA. His material centers on self-image, motivation and success development, sales-marketing procedures, media communications, TV-Film production methods and principles of negotiation. He has made a serious study of metaphysics, psychology, comparative religions, philosophy and communication-motivation principles. Drawing from his own personal and business success, he has formulated a practical and workable approach to the attainment of a worthwhile lifestyle. Much of his outstanding lecture material is included in this book.

GROW RICH WITH YOUR *MILLION DOLLAR* MIND

BY
BRIAN ADAMS

Melvin Powers
Wilshire Book Company
12015 Sherman Road
North Hollywood, California 91605

Copyright © 1991 by Brian Adams.

All rights reserved. No portion of this book may be
reproduced, stored in a retrieval system or transmitted
in any form or by any means, electronic, mechanical,
photocopying, recording or otherwise without the prior
written consent of the copyright owner. A reviewer may
quote brief passages in a review for a newspaper,
magazine, radio or TV program.

National Library of Australia ISBN 0-95895-12-3-3

Books by Brian Adams ...

How To Succeed*
Sales Cybernetics The Psychology of Selling*
Screen Acting
Grow Rich With Your Million Dollar Mind

*Available on audio tapes and in home study programs.

Printed in the United States of America

Gratefully dedicated to *Sunita*,
who has enriched my life . . .

*Our affections are our life. We
live by them; they supply our
warmth.*
—CHANNING.

HOW THIS BOOK
CAN MAKE YOU RICH

This book is for every person desiring high achievement, lifestyle enhancement and the accumulation of wealth. It is for every man and woman determined to stop struggling and start living a meaningful, creative and outstandingly-successful life. To those who follow the techniques and concepts offered, it is a practical and helpful guide to the *riches* of this magnificient universe.

Grow Rich With Your Million Dollar Mind reveals the principle of psycho dynamics — *thought force* — and how to release this subconscious power to quickly change the direction of your life. The *million dollar* formulas enchance personal effectiveness, expand inward perceptions which guide you in decision-making, problem-solving and action-taking. You will discover how to tap your personal ideas source to attract opportunity resulting in guiltless prosperity. The power that controls your destiny is part of you and can be used to turn adversity and failure into challenge and success. With *thought force* working for you, nothing can stop you from experiencing the things you've always wanted — health, happiness, love, a beautiful home, luxury car, travel to exotic lands, a successful career, your own business and financial independence.

Thousands-upon-thousands of men and women from all parts of the world have amassed wealth by applying specific techniques, by thinking, feeling and believing in a certain way and by learning and applying the laws of mind. I have taught these cosmic laws to great numbers of people in the United States, Canada and Australia and have witnessed and been told of the amazing changes in lifestyle to those who have diligently applied them. The strategies and tactics to change *your* life are revealed in this book. They are explained in a concise and simplistic way so that you can use them for immediate results. Apply the techniques as instructed and you will entice into your life everything you require to live joyously, creatively and abundantly.

Presently, the world faces difficult economic and social challenges which reveal themselves in mounting unemployment, see-sawing inflation, increasing personal-business bankruptcies and community unrest through soaring crime. Millions of humans are locked into a seemingly-limited income potential and frustratingly-restrictive lifestyle. For these people, the highly competitive, volatile and depressing complexities of our times have brought personal empire-building to a standstill.

Though many people are stagnating within this negative lifestyle environment, others are not. Today's successful entrepreneurs are amassing larger-than-life fortunes and achieving where so many are failing because, whether they know it or not, they are tapping the extraordinary power of the deeper human mind — the *same* power that *you* can use to uplift the experiences, conditions and events of your life.

Grow Rich With Your Million Dollar Mind teaches you how to become a scientific thinker, a shaper of your own destiny, a winner. It is a blueprint for personal victory in the 21st century. The easy-to-apply techniques help to raise your self esteem and expand your desire and capacity to achieve. The formulas reveal how to greatly improve your personal presentation skill which, in turn, elevates your social and business status. With your conscious and subconscious mind operating at peak efficiency, your dreams and aspirations become a reality, you become a *wealth-creator*.

With each reading of this book, you will discover how to release more and more of the imprisoned genius within you. It doesn't matter *who* you are, *what* you are or *where* you are, provided you apply the intelligence you were born with and work *with* not against the cosmic laws, you cannot help but succeed in life. You were born to be rich and you can *be* rich through the scientific use of your faculties. This book shows you the way.

With greater knowledge and wisdom, you will become a highly-motivated person eager to pursue goals you previously thought were beyond your reach. You will be ready to grasp opportunities, to attract life's glories and luxuries, to *grow rich* each exciting new day with your highly-creative *million dollar mind.*

— **BRIAN ADAMS.**

FORMULAS FOR THE
RICHES OF LIFE

HOW TO ACQUIRE A MILLIONAIRE MENTALITY TO GROW RICH

FORMULA 1

WHY IT IS YOUR RIGHT TO BE RICH

You were born into this world to be rich. It is your *birthright* to receive riches as a perfectly normal way of life. The material riches of the universe are at your disposal. They are life's gifts to those who desire them, seek them, strive for them, share them and intend to do good with them. The fountain of life's luxuries, glories and beauties never runs dry. There is more than enough to benefit all humans. The source of supply is inexhaustible. Recognize and take up your inalienable right to a fair share of nature's bounty.

UNIVERSAL RICHES ARE WITHIN YOUR REACH

Your desire to live in a luxurious home, drive a prestige car, operate a successful business, travel to interesting countries, paint a beautiful picture, compose wonderful music, dress elegantly, become financially independent, experience a happy family relationship and to lead a more lavish lifestyle can be fulfilled. Your very first move is to condition your mind to accept the possibilities and opportunities which are within your reach, ready for you to extract everything you need to live productively and affluently.

RICHES HAVE THEIR BEGINNING IN YOUR MIND

Wealth is a state of consciousness. Riches begin to accumulate from desires and ideas resident in your mind. The more you stretch your imagination, expand your desires, skills, talents and ideas, the easier it becomes to attain wealth and success. It is through an habitual use of prosperous thinking that you grow rich. It is through your mind that you can claim the prosperity you desire.

WHY IT IS IMPORTANT TO BECOME SUCCESSFUL

You are here to fully express your creativity—talents and skills—to benefit the world around you. You are here to discover your true place in life, to grow mentally, emotionally, spiritually and physically as well as financially. You have been blessed with everything necessary to experience a joyful, beneficial and self-satisfying lifestyle. You are in this world to make the most of yourself, to fully exploit your potential as a highly-creative human being. You owe it to yourself and to the Giver of Life to use the creativity bestowed upon you to become an outstandingly-successful person.

YOUR PERSONAL USEFULNESS IS ENHANCED THROUGH WEALTH

There is no merit in poverty, no usefulness whatsoever in coasting through life subjecting yourself to lack, limitation, poorness and displeasure. You are not here to fail, to live in a hovel, to be unproductive, uncreative and unfinancial. You entered this world with the blessing, power and majesty of your Creator. You have been gifted with the power to create and to experience life through your magnificent mind. You have been given freedom of thought choice along with the freedom to act in any way you choose. *You* determine which turn of the road to take—mediocrity or achievement. Your usefulness to the world is enhanced when you determine to succeed, to accumulate and dispense riches honestly, productively and beneficially.

EXTRICATE YOURSELF FROM RACE-MIND THINKING

Generally speaking, the world is made up of pessimistic thinkers, backward thinkers, unscientific thinkers and mind wanderers. Collectively, they are called race-mind thinkers. The *race* mind is in-tune with things negative. Fortunately, not all people fall into this category. Forward-thinking people become leaders, winners and *high* achievers. If you wish to join them, jump out of race-mind thinking. Become a *possibility* thinker. Vision success rather than failure. Contemplate wealth rather than poverty. Imagine career advancement rather than creative limitation. When you move up to scientific thinking, your intellect is illumined, motivating you to exploit your potential, to go after and achieve success.

BECOME ILLUMINED THROUGH TRUTH

Your personal success and desire for financial security will be determined by your thoughts, feelings, beliefs and actions. If you are a *low* thinker you are likely to miss out on much of what life has to offer. Get in-tune with truth. Raise your level of consciousness. Seek the knowledge of who you are, what you are and what you can become in this life. Cease living in ignorance of your true worth. Stop forfeiting your true place in this world. If you fail to use the power at your command, it is precisely the same as if it were not there. The *power* is in your thoughts, your feelings and your beliefs.

WHY THE WORLD'S FIRST AFFLUENT MAN LOST THE RICHES OF LIFE

In the early chapters of Genesis, Adam is presented as an affluent person. He had been granted dominion over his environment—the garden of beauty, plenty and good. The story of Adam is a story of prosperity as well as creation. It reveals that humans are born into limitless opportunity, creativity and vast riches with the choice to accept or reject them, to use them wisely or wastefully.

Adam fell from grace because he chose to misuse that which had been gifted to him. He chose to be negative thinking, to believe in lack, limitation and the power of evil, even though he was surrounded by riches and beauty. Adam was banished from the Garden of Good and through 'painful toil' and the 'sweat of his brow' made to tend the ground from where he was taken. There are millions-upon-millions of similar Adam-style thinkers struggling through life by the sweat of their brows today, even though they are living amid a universe of opportunity, beauty and prosperity.

ALL HUMANS ARE PART OF THE ONE LIFE FORCE

There is one Universal Mind and all humans are part of it, regardless of race or religion. This Spirit or Infinite Intelligence created the universe and everything and everyone in it. If we desire to reside in the Garden of Eden, to take up our share of life's riches, we must unite with the Source of our beginning. Adam chose separation and suffered. When the Life Mind and the human mind are in harmony, riches flow from One to the other.

YOU DO NOT NEED TO SUFFER PAIN TO SUCCEED

Humans are created out of the same rich substance of which the universe was formed. The 'dust of the earth' from which Adam was created is symbolic. All holy books are psychological textbooks exploring and explaining life and offering a sensible path to follow. The Garden of Eden is where we can reside if we so choose. However, we must abide by the terms of entry. The riches of our beginning are in plentiful form for all to use and share. It is not necessary to experience the painful toil Adam experienced unless we choose to do so. We are at liberty to think sensibly and to act honorably which is our passport to a rich, joyful and beneficial lifestyle.

WHEN YOU LEARN HOW TO THINK YOU LEARN HOW TO SUCCEED

Adam and Eve represent every man and woman who, by choice, may enter the Garden of Good and experience a marvellous lifestyle or, through separation and misuse of the mind, suffer and struggle through life by the 'sweat of the brow'.

Wealth comes through the logical and achievable concepts developed in your conscious mind which are then acted upon in an affirmative way. You don't have to necessarily work harder than is comfortable to grow rich. You have to learn how to *think*. When you learn to think constructively, you become a confident person, a self-motivated person and a director of your destiny.

HOW TO TAP THE SOURCE WHICH GENERATES RICHES

Life's riches enter your life through your mind. They begin as seeds—ideas, desires, concepts, beliefs—which motivate you to take certain courses of action to make them a reality. When you tap the true power source of riches—your mind—through inspired, bold thinking, you create an affirmative consciousness and this is your stepping-stone to success and wealth accumulation.

In its early form, the word *man* represented mind. The *power of man* translates to mean the *power of mind*. It is through the mind that humankind lives. All things are experienced through consciousness. All action is determined by attitudes which pass from the conscious to the subconscious mind for processing. Because thought *precedes* action, the key to controlling your life is to take firm control of your thoughts.

YOUR POWER SOURCE HAS TWO DISTINCT INFLUENCES

It is important to understand that there is only *one* power of mind, not two. However, this power source when activated is capable of producing either negative or affirmative events, conditions, circumstances and results depending upon *how* it is used. The power to attract misery, suffering and failure is the *same* power capable of attracting happiness, peace of mind and success. The former is the result of negative mind application, the latter is the result of affirmative thought force. Eliminate destructive thinking. Replace it with constructive, power-laden concepts which, unleashed, fulfill your desire to overcome problems, to expand creativity and to attain wealth.

DISCOVERING THE WEALTH SECRETS OF THE BABYLONIANS

In ancient times, the wealth-gathering philosophy practiced by the earliest-known money creators was taught secretly. The affluent Babylonians—pioneers of clever business and financial systems still applauded today—passed their success formulas on to their descendants. In later times, these same principles were taught in Alexandria at the School of Philosophy. Bible historians refer to them and we are told that Abraham, Isaac, Jacob and Joseph passed them along to succeeding generations resulting in the Hebrews becoming an outstandingly-wealthy group.

The Babylonians believed in the power resident within the human mind. They recognized the benefits which could accrue from confident thinking. They taught their people to discipline their thoughts, feelings and actions and to look upon happiness, creative achievement and financial security as attainable goals. The Babylonian teaching centered on humans being given dominion over their personal environment. It was ignorance of this truth that kept humans poor they said. The Babylonians were the first people to develop a riches consciousness.

LOOK UPON WEALTH ACCUMULATION AS INTRINSICALLY GOOD

It is not a sin to become rich and successful. Even in this day-and-age there are people who look upon wealth accumulation as wrong and evil. This is ignorant thinking. Material wealth in the pockets of right-thinking individuals is capable of great works. If from day one the populations of the world had lived poorly, lacked ambition, had no potential to grow rich, there would not have been the amazing lifestyle developments we humans experience and enjoy today. Life would be a meaningless, unproductive and miserable existence.

When you establish a proper relationship to money it will flow to you more easily, compounding its value and benefit. Also, any fear you may have of losing it once you have acquired it, will diminish. If you pursue money in an honest way, you need not have guilt feelings about accumulating it. Look upon wealth creation as intrinsically good.

APPRECIATE THE VALUE OF MONEY

Don't be guilty of squandering money or of hoarding it. Either action will prove detrimental. Give thanks each time you receive money. When you pay a bill, express appreciation for the goods or services received. Thank those who pay your salary or customers who support your business. Praise the success and financial achievement of friends, relatives or business associates. If you have earned money honestly, you are entitled to enjoy the benefits which come from its use. You are also entitled to be proud of your financial achievements. A healthy and sensible attitude to riches will keep them flowing to you. Money blessed attracts greater benefit than money condemned.

THE RICH CAN PLAY A BENEFICIAL ROLE IN SOCIETY

The marvellous inventions, discoveries and developments in this electronic space age are due to men and women of vision thinking and acting in a purposeful and generous way. Medicine is one area of development which has greatly benefited humankind through the generosity of the rich. Money pays for the products and services we enjoy. Money helped to develop the motor car, airplane, computer technology. It paid for our exploration of space. It has brought us time-saving and useful household appliances, fashion garments, entertainment films, video recorders, telephones and fax machines, office buildings, hospitals, libraries and a host of benefits we humans desire and demand. In the right hands, money plays an essential role in society. A role which can benefit *every* living person.

RICH AND SUCCESSFUL PEOPLE CAN CHANGE THE WORLD

High-achievement people are applauded for their knowledge, cleverness and ability. Pity is seldom offered to failures. More often than not, scorn is heaped upon them. I do not feel it is wise to ignore the plight of those persons unfortunate enough to fail in life. They should be encouraged to try again, to alter their thought processes and taught to tap the subconscious power resident within them. Young people should be taught to look upon success as a good thing and to view wealth accumulation as necessary and beneficial, not only for themselves, but for society in general. The better-off humans are, the better world we will live in. The less we will experience misery, suffering and social unrest.

GO FIRST CLASS

Your aim is to become wealthy. Therefore, you must begin to *think* and *act* as a person of wealth. The way you present yourself must change so that you appear to be a person of good character and financial substance. Toss out old-fashioned ideas. Think boldly and positively. Wear your best clothes. Give yourself a 'look' of success. Don't be satisfied with second-class thinking, a second-class appearance. Go first class. Accept the abundant life, the opulent life in your mind and you will not only look rich you will become rich.

All it takes to expand your life is a simple redirection of your attitudes. Your true richness consists in identifying yourself with opulence and success—thinking, feeling believing and *acting* as a person of fame and fortune. Become a walking, talking symbol of beauty, luxury, well-being, self assurance, power and wealth.

> *Begin to be now what you will be hereafter.*
> —St. Jerome.

YOUR FIRST STEP TO WEALTH CREATION

Your ascent to wealth accumulation is governed by the *level* of your consciousness. It is imperative that you develop a *superior* level of consciousness which will lead to strategic action-taking to manifest all that you desire in life. A low-level state of mind impedes creativity, dulls enthusiasm, thwarts ambition and destroys your ability to make sensible decisions. It places you in the position of being slave to your mind instead of master of it. Wealth-creators need to be in control of the mind to determine *what* they think.

The first step to attracting the riches of life is to *cleanse* the mind. This process incorporates the removal of self-limiting concepts—negative beliefs about who you are and what you can become. Constructive thoughts must fill your consciousness which imply that you are born to succeed, to triumph over personal and career impediments and your fortune begins with *you*. Instill into your deeper mind that the power within you *can* and *will* lift you up and set you on the path to life's treasures. Mentally rehabilitate yourself and riches will flow to you without obstruction and undue hardship.

HOW TO AVOID THE PITFALLS OF WEALTH ATTRACTION

The thinking of some humans is illogical, irrational and unscientific. Far too many people believe that life is unfair to them. They blame circumstances and others for their failure. They condemn the rich and successful, envy them and even hate them. People who are selfish, envious and covetous have no chance of becoming rich, no matter how much they desire wealth. Their enmity produces a contaminated consciousness which blocks the flow of life's pleasures and fortunes to them.

Your thoughts, feelings, beliefs, create your destiny. The key to your success lies within your mind. You are responsible for what you think and how you act. This is the justice of the law of mind which is the law of *belief*. You follow your beliefs. The circumstances, experiences and events of your life are an exact reproduction of your beliefs. If your desire is to be rich and famous, you must *believe* in your desire, ability and right to wealth and fame. This is logical, rational and scientific thinking and it is the fastest, safest and surest way to *self* mastery, outstanding achievement and prosperity.

A SIMPLE FORMULA FOR RICHES

Whatever is impressed on your subconscious mind as a *dominant* idea is expressed in your physical world. Be on your guard as to what you allow to penetrate your deeper mind. Neutralize a negative concept before it becomes dominant in your thinking and is passed to your subconscious for processing. Keep your thoughts centered on what you *want*, not on what you lack or seemingly cannot get. Take control of your ideas. Guide your thoughts, feelings, beliefs, images in the direction you desire to go. Command your mind to give proper attention to the wants, needs and objectives you set in life. Your future resides as a yet unborn child in your present ideas and beliefs. *Tomorrow, is today's thought grown up.*

HOW TO SWING THE SUCCESS PENDULUM IN YOUR FAVOR

The majority of the world's population suffers from thought imbalance. All of us have our ups and downs, our anxieties and excitements, our failures and successes. These *swings-of-life* very quickly settle into a routine, a *pattern* and become firmly attached to us until we decide to recondition our thinking and take charge of our lives.

Thought imbalance occurs when the mental pendulum swings too far to the negative, sabotaging our ability to think clearly and constructively. Well-being, vitality, poise, enthusiasm and happiness are replaced by depression, anxiety, fear and loss of self esteem. The vision of victory, triumph, wealth and success rapidly diminishes.

The cure for thought imbalance is to move the attention away from destructive feelings and imagery and focus it on your positive power which awaits your direction. Tap your power source. Command your thoughts to lift you triumphantly above the consciousness of negation. You can think whatever you *choose* about your life. You can allow your thoughts to drop you into the gutter of your mind or you can direct them to pick you up and thrust you into a world of beauty, wholeness, peace and prosperity. Your personal swings-of-fortune can be better-balanced and tilted in your favor for success by giving *positive* attention to what you want, what you dream about and what you *can* attain if you become master of your thought processes.

HOW TO UNITE WITH THE GIFT OF LIFE TO INSPIRE YOUR THINKING

The tree of the knowledge of life as exposed to Adam and Eve is the knowledge of good and evil, right and wrong, affirmative and negative. The Serpent encouraged Adam and Eve to be disobedient and eat from the tree of knowledge. Both wilfully misused mind power and suffered accordingly. They were given *freedom of the will*, a wonderful gift all of us have received. We know the difference between good and evil and we know the consequences we must face if we choose to adopt a wasteful, dishonest existence.

Don't misuse your freedom of thought choice. Unite with the 'gift of life' by choosing *good* thoughts which heal, bless, dignify, illumine and prosper your being. Do not be swayed by the Serpent mentality of others who, through envy, jealousy and covetousness, try to mislead and detract you from the lifestyle you desire. Rise majestically in mind. Think good and you will lead a balanced, creative and prosperous life.

> *Some people study all their life, and at their death they have learned everything except to think.*
> —Domergue.

HOW TO GAIN LIFE'S RICHES THROUGH THOUGHT CHOICE

Man and woman can become what they determine to become. It rests with each person whether he or she becomes wealthy or remains poor, becomes a leader or is led, succeeds or fails. The gift of life is freedom of thought choice—to choose what you want to *be*, *do* and *have*—and it should not ever be misused or wasted.

Your mind works to attract what you choose. When you choose good, good follows. When you select evil, evil follows. This basic law of mind applies to every thought you produce. The responsibility for your thoughts and actions rests with you. Your relationships, experiences, circumstances and events are a duplication of your thinking. Your day-to-day state of mind sets the degree of your affluence, your physical well-being and the level of your success.

Use thought selection wisely. Steer your mental images—*dreams*—in the direction you want them to go. Become a selective *affirmative* thinker and automatically you will become an affirmative action-taker destined for a revitalized, exciting, creatively-rewarding and highly-beneficial lifestyle.

THE PRIZE YOU RECEIVE MUST EQUAL THE PRICE YOU ARE PREPARED TO PAY

Some people choose to believe that the riches of life can be gained without undue effort. There is no such thing as something for nothing. It is a myth. In life, the prize and the price are always equal. The input and the output must match. If your input to achievement and wealth accumulation is minimal, your gain will be minimal. What you give to life and what you take from life require balance and fairness. When you determine what you need to live freely, joyfully and beneficially, decide what you are prepared to give in return and in what proportion.

GIVE GENEROUSLY WITHOUT STRINGS ATTACHED

Laziness, greed, selfishness and wrongdoing are not fair exchange for high achievement, community respect and rich living. The price does not equal the prize. There are numerous ways to give thanks for your good fortune. Perhaps you might choose to donate a portion of your accumulated funds to a charity or give of your time to a community aid group, charity organization or church. It might be a promise to be a better husband or wife, a more caring parent, teacher, leader or just being a better friend and helper to others.

Don't look for special thanks when you go out of your way to do good. Attach no strings to the material possessions you give to others. Your willingness to give *freely* brings you in harmony with the Creative Power of the universe. Your selflessness helps to increase your own well-being. Your acts of charity bless you in countless ways. There is multiplication of your good and you attract the life more abundant.

A POSITIVE WAY TO INCREASE RICHES IS TO APPLY THE GOLDEN RULE

Remove from your mind any idea that you can steal from others or from life and get away with it. You must treat others and life as *you* wish to be treated—fairly and honestly. This is simply practicing the *Golden Rule*. Correct expression of your ideas and ambitions pays handsome dividends. If you are an honest person, a loyal person, a generous person, you will prosper in all of your undertakings.

It is a good practice to show gratitude for your personal enrichment. Do not take life for granted, expecting it to continually bow to your demands. Share with others the knowledge, wisdom, truth, intelligence, creativity and material riches you acquire. Greed and selfishness will not enhance your lifestyle. Your appreciation of life's gifts and your sharing of them with the world around you, will attract even greater good fortune. The more freely you give, the more freely you receive. *Do good unto others.*

THE GOLDEN RULE

Christianity: Therefore all things whatsoever ye would that men should do to you, do you even so to them: for this is the Law and the Prophets.

Matthew 7:12

Judaism: What is hateful to you, do not to your fellowmen. That is the entire law; all the rest is commentary.

Talmud, Shabbat 31a

Confucianism: Surely it is the maxim of loving-kindness: Do not unto others that you would not have them do unto you.

Analects 15, 23

Islam: No one of you is a believer until he desires for his brother that which he desires for himself.

Sunnah

Brahmanism: This is the sum of duty; do naught unto others which would cause you pain if done to you.

Mahabharate 5, 1517

Buddhism: Hurt not others in ways that you yourself would find hurtful.

Udana-Varga 5, 18

Taoism: Regard your neighbour's gain as your own gain and your neighbour's loss as your own loss.

T'ai Shang Kan Ying P'ien

ESTABLISHING THE RIGHT MOTIVES TO MULTIPLY YOUR GOOD

The development, expansion and achievement of your goals must be coupled to proper motives—reasons *why* you desire them. Forthright motives for achievement will never harm you. If you embark upon a brutal attack on others to succeed, success, if attained, will be shortlived. Consciously setting out to hurt others, to obstruct their progress and livelihood, to steal from them, clearly denotes dishonest motives.

Write down your goals and the reasons for their attainment. Do not waste time and energy on worthless pursuits or on goals motivated by dishonesty, envy, jealousy, or greed. Pursue ambitions that add to your stature, test your skills, challenge your creativity, bring satisfaction, financial gain and benefit without hurting others. You can be a determined, ambitious, shrewd and clever person in your business dealings, provided you are honest, fair, just and honorable in your thoughts and deeds.

The riches of life available to you are in unlimited supply. You can have all you want without taking anything away from others. Be a person of unyielding integrity as you go forth and conquer and you will multiply the good you seek as it flows to you freely, endlessly and rewardingly.

> *However brilliant an action, it should not be esteemed great unless the result of a great and good motive.*
> —Rochefoucauld.

HOW YOUR MENTALITY CAN LIFT YOU FROM MEDIOCRITY TO SUCCESS

It has been estimated that of the 5 billion or so persons on this earth, 96-percent are followers and only four-percent leaders. The majority, it seems, are content to be *average* in what they accomplish and what they have. Generally speaking, average people are poor people.

It isn't difficult to recognize average persons. They *look* average because they *act* in a standard, unexciting and conformist way. Material possessions are few and usually far less than they desire. Creative talents are seldom fulfilled, career aspirations rarely accomplished and monetary expectations often compromised. Being 'average' has little going for it.

Average persons miss out on the riches of life through ignorance of their true worth, fear of failure, laziness, superstition and often, stupidity. No one decrees that you make a career out of being average. It's a decision you make on your own behalf. Your true worth will expose itself when you rise in consciousness, eliminate race-mind thinking and identify yourself with high desires and affirmative actions. Your good fortune will magnify and your mediocre lifestyle will expand and progress into a new, exciting and creatively-rewarding pattern of living.

HOW TO DEVELOP A MILLIONAIRE MENTALITY

No matter how average or poor you may seem to be, you have the power to turn your life around, to become an extraordinary person, an affluent person experiencing and enjoying the treasures of life. The power is in your thought. What you think all day long shapes and dictates the events and circumstances of your tomorrow. Your present mental world is the key to the successful fulfillment of your ideas, plans and objectives. You live in your mind. It is from *within* that you succeed or fail, experience health or sickness, become rich or remain poor. Your thoughts are creative. They create according to your beliefs.

Your intelligence is wasted if you do not know *how* to apply it or are too lazy to apply it effectively. Like the success-minded Babylonians and Hebrews, you must cultivate an *affirmative consciousness*, whereby your thoughts, feelings and beliefs are powerfully-directed through positive actions. A millionaire mentality is the result of thinking about wealth as a reality and believing that you *can* and *will* become rich. You use the power of your thought projections to push aside impediments and meet all challenges to create what you desire in life. A riches mentality is simply a determined and positive pattern of thinking which lifts you from the slums of your mind into a vital, confident and dynamic consciousness. Use the power within your command to expand your knowledge, improve your skills and develop your creativity and you will automatically rise from mediocrity to success.

HOW TO USE YOUR MILLIONAIRE MENTALITY TO PROSPER

Change in a positive way, development and increase, are what all people throughout the world are seeking. Lifestyle enhancement, wealth accumulation, creative fulfillment and worthwhile personal and business relationships begin as ideas and ideals in your conscious mind. If you focus your attention on happiness, wealth and achievement, your inner power goes to work to attract to you these benefits. You reap riches by depositing in your subconscious *ideas* of riches. Attached to your ideas must be immovable faith and confidence in your ability to reap them. Also, your ambitions will need to be attached to an achievement strategy—a practical plan of action you intend to follow.

When you establish a riches mentality, a clearer picture emerges on how to go about advancing in life. Your imagination, mental discipline and enthusiasm, turn the seemingly-improbable situation into the possible, enhancing your capacity and will to win.

Empty your consciousness of impurities—negative concepts. Restore your mind with high ideas and ideals which bless, inspire, strengthen and enrich your entire being. Use your new millionaire mentality to open the doors to opportunity, personal and business advancement and the inward flow of life's riches. The degree of your prosperity increases or decreases according to the degree of your vision—your thoughts, feelings, imagination and concepts.

A TECHNIQUE TO USE FOR RICHER LIVING

Meditating upon positive statements—*affirmations*—is a beneficial way to initiate positive change in your life. Write down on 3 × 5 cards your personal thoughts on the lifestyle you desire. The ideas you deposit in your deeper mind, when supported by faith, help to quickly transform your experiences and circumstances and attract to you the prosperity you seek.

WEALTH AFFIRMATION

The wealth of the universe is before me. I have been granted free will to accept or reject the riches of the universe. I am born to succeed. I attract wealth in accordance with my desires, ambitions and needs. I use it wisely and beneficially. I am rich now. Rich in health, happiness, personal accomplishment and human relationships. My power and riches are used to benefit the world around me. I give thanks for my continually-improving lifestyle and future achievements.

FORMULAS TO GROW RICH

- You were born to be rich. It is your birthright. Claim your share of nature's bounty. The gifts of life await you. But *you* must claim them.

- You are on this earth to express your creativity. Make the most of *who* you are and what you can become.

- Riches or poverty are your choice. You have the power to choose and win the lifestyle most beneficial to you. What you *think* dictates your actions. It controls your destiny.

- You live and have your being through your mind. It is possible to change negative circumstances and conditions by changing your attitudes. Become an affirmative thinker.

- Seek the knowledge of *who* you are. Immerse your mind in truth and release yourself from race-mind (negative) thinking. Remember, Adam was banished from the Garden of Eden (riches) because he was disobedient and misused his mind. Adam was a negative thinker and suffered because of it.

- The Babylonians were the first people to develop a success consciousness. They knew that the riches of nature were freely available to those who claimed them. You have been given dominion over your environment to achieve whatever you desire.

- Look upon riches as beneficial. See money as a medium of exchange rather than evil. Do not experience any guilt feelings about becoming wealthy. Be proud of financial achievement.

- Develop a superior-level of consciousness which leads to strategic action-taking. Cleanse your mind of negative concepts. Think scientifically—*rationally*. Avoid the swings-of-life by balancing your thinking. Depressed thoughts produce unhappiness. Think good and good follows.

- If you want to take from life, be prepared to *give* something. There is no such thing as something for nothing. Be sure your motives for success are good and honorable.

- Meditate on success affirmations. Impregnate your subconscious mind with ideas of *good* and you will transform your life.

HOW TO COMMAND
THE POWER OF YOUR
MILLION DOLLAR MIND

FORMULA 2

HOW TO STABILIZE AND TAKE CHARGE OF YOUR LIFE

All humans have a deep-seated desire to control the conditions, events, circumstances and *direction* of their lives. It is perfectly natural to want to be in charge of personal creativity, health, personality, career and financial resources. The success or failure of personal destiny-control is determined by the state of consciousness each person develops and nurtures. States of consciousness *manifest* themselves.

You are here to play the game of life. The standard of game you play is up to you. You are free to choose your thoughts, feelings and beliefs just as you are free to choose your friends, the car you buy or the clothes you wear. If you choose to fill your mind with false ideas, superstitions and preconceived notions, the standard of your consciousness is lowered and this has a direct bearing on the quality of your lifestyle.

You are capable of improving the quality of your life by improving the quality of your attitudes and by applying the principles of mind which govern your everyday actions. When you unite with the principles of life, you set into motion the intelligence and power within you which is capable of achieving all that you seek. Your happiness, achievement and prosperity require a special way of thinking and believing. An habitual pattern of *affirmative* thinking is a powerful internal movement of your mind which stabilizes your life, allowing you to take control and shape the lifestyle you desire.

THE NATURE OF MIND

Human beings are life expressed. Life is experienced through the mind — *awareness* and *perception*. This 'experience' is transmitted to the mind via the senses, allowing us to 'see' and 'feel' our environment. We live within a state of consciousness: thoughts, feelings, memories, emotions. Through the mind, we experience an *inner* and an *outer* world. The inner life takes precedence over the outer life because all things have their beginning *within* before manifesting as circumstances, conditions and events in the material world.

You are the center of your own universe. You cannot lead any other life than the life you lead *within* your mind. The pattern of your existence is determined by the pattern of your consciousness — attitudes, feelings, beliefs. The power to control your existence comes from within. The outside always exhibits what the inside creates: *as a man thinketh, so is he.*

HOW YOUR MIND WORKS

There is no device made by man or woman to compare with the majestic workings of the human mind. The mind is a complex and highly-creative mechanism. We humans use only a minor portion of its potential, mainly because we have not been able to fully understand what it is and how to harness its awesome power.

What we do know is that the mind has three separate divisions, each working with a specific purpose. These divisions function according to principles or *mind laws.** These laws are much like the laws of physics or chemistry. They are impersonal. The laws of mind respect no particular race or religion. They are not subject to any creed, dogma or tradition. They change not for the royal person or the pauper, the holy person or the evil person. No government can legislate against them, no court can change them.

The mind has the faculties of will, reason and memory. The inner life receives feedback from the outer life via the central nervous system as it passes continuous messages to the brain. The mind is the source of images, sensations, feelings. It puts life into gear through thinking and feeling. Behavior is a reflection of these thoughts and emotions. All our events, conditions and circumstances of life are the manifestations of powerful thoughts, feelings and beliefs emanating from the human mind.

THE THREE DIVISIONS OF MIND

All humans are linked to *Infinite Mind*, the Creator of the cosmos and the source of our visible and invisible supply. Within the personal mind

*See *How To Succeed* by Brian Adams (Image Book Company).

26

there are three divisions: *objective, subjective, superobjective*. Each of the divisions is endowed with specific powers and each operates according to laws and principles which are timeless, ageless and unchanging.

There are principles and laws by which the universe operates to bring order and control over the elements. Nature strives for balance and stability. In order to work *for* humankind, nature must work via principle *through* the mind. The Life Principle is constantly seeking expression through you so that you might experience more *richness* of life. When there is separation from Infinite Mind, as Adam and Eve chose, the quality, order and balance of life deteriorates.

OBJECTIVE MIND

This division is also known as the *conscious, thinking* or *male* aspect of mind. It is the *reasoning* power which makes constant decisions after receiving information from the various sensory organs: touch, taste, smell, hearing, sight. The objective mind is bestowed with free will to choose *what* it will think and decide upon. It is the pilot of your desires, the guide and master of your affairs and environment.

The objective mind operates according to the universal law of *belief*. You think and believe with your conscious mind. You argue and rationalize with the conscious mind, form views, opinions, prejudices in order to arrive at decisions which are then passed for processing to the subjective division.

The objective mind does not have the power to retain information once it has let it go. It must rely on the subconscious to store information. The primary purpose of the objective mind is to *reason*, form impressions, create ideas and make decisions. It is not subject to hypnosis.

SUBJECTIVE MIND

This area of mind is known as the *subconscious, instrument of memory, emotion mind, responsive* or *female* aspect. It is the *memory* vault for thoughts, feelings, beliefs and knowledge passed to it by the objective mind. It does not have the power to decide. It deals with all information given to it in an unbiased manner. It does not separate experience from imagination. It accepts everything at face value. A lie is as readily accepted as the truth, a negative concept is given equal status with an affirmative one. Its power acts in exactly the same manner toward negative thoughts as it does toward positive concepts.

Your deeper mind has the task of taking care of you, even while you sleep. It keeps your heart beating and your lungs breathing. It constantly regulates all of the natural functions of your body. Whenever you cut yourself or damage your body, the subsconscious immediately triggers an internal healing process. It has complete control over the conditions and sensations of your body. Its goal is self preservation.

The subjective mind operates without self-conscious awareness. It can only reason deductively. Once an idea is accepted, it begins to bring it into existence regardless of the nature of the idea. It acts *compulsively*. Your past and present conditions and events are the reactions of your subsconscious mind to your beliefs.

The subjective mind operates according to the universal laws of *belief* and *cause and effect*. Every thought implanted into the subjective mind is a cause, every condition and event, *effects* which mirror the cause. When you think good you produce good. When you think evil you attract evil. The pattern of your day-to-day thinking determines the pattern of your day-to-day living.

REVEALING THE GREAT SECRET OF THE SUBJECTIVE MIND

The subconscious or subjective mind is a goal-striving mechanism and being amenable to suggestion will work to bring about the desires and beliefs you feed it. Your subconscious never argues with you. Program sensible, solid concepts and it will bring them to pass just as easily as it will produce negative circumstances and conditions if your mental programming is negative based. The subsconscious has the capacity to achieve goals for you, improve your personality, uplift your confidence, increase your income, find a marriage partner, select a business associate, write a novel, compose music, paint a picture, maintain good health and make you a happy, well-adjusted and prosperous person. The only impediment to these things. is the *type* of program you give your subconscious to work with.

Negative concepts (programs) are obstructions to success and financial security. They set the goal-striving device in the direction of failure, unhappiness and poverty. The secret of the subconscious is to program it into success mode and it will automatically bring forth desirable and beneficial results.

The truly successful are those who understand and use the creative power of thought to program the subsconscious mind with concepts and beliefs of health, achievement and prosperity. Start doing this today. Get into harmony with your subjective mind and your life will be renewed and uplifted, blessed and benefited. The creative power within you is unlimited. You don't have to brow-beat it or bribe it. You only have to program it correctly and it will set you on the way to victory and riches.

THE SUPEROBJECTIVE MIND

This area of mind is a direct link to Infinite Intelligence. It is recognized as the *high self, psychic mind, spiritual mind* or *superconscious*. This higher form of cosmic consciousness represents both the male and female principle. To be in harmony with this powerful form of intelligence is to experience liberty, beauty, tranquility, coupled with a capacity for creative genius and high achievement. It is to enter into the kingdom of perfect health, happiness, peace, abundance, inspiration, guidance and true expression. The superconscious unites us with the true Spirit of Life.

Whenever we are in harmony with the superconscious sphere of mind we are free of earthly limitation and released from negative influence. We enter into a superhuman state, exhalted, illumined and immersed in truth. We are able to rise in consciousness, separating from the race mind and the forces which keep it poor, sick and unhappy. The superobjective state allows us to be Divinely guided in thought and action. We become a true expression of the Intelligence which created us.

The desire of Life is to manifest itself through each of us in order that we might grow and enjoy the riches which surround us. There is a need within all races of people to better understand life so that it might be experienced more abundantly. When the desire of Life and the need of humans meet, there is *oneness* with the Source of Life, resulting in human stability, creativity and prosperity.

HOW TO HARMONIZE WITH THE SUPEROBJECTIVE MIND

The mind requires training and discipline to ready itself for superconsciousness. Spend 15 minutes every day disciplining your mind to release itself from fear and negative influence. Find a quiet place in your home, office or a tranquil setting outdoors where you will not be distracted or disturbed by others. Sit comfortably. Close the eyes and focus the attention on an inner light which radiates from the center of the forehead. Release all thoughts. Quiet the mind. Be still. Meditate on the concepts of beauty, peace, wholeness, joy and perfection of mind, body and spirit. Feel your mind releasing your body weight allowing you to float completely free of muscular tension.

You will need practice to sever current stress, anxiety, fear, frustration and past negative influences. The more time you spend meditating and elevating your consciousness, the sooner you will experience a union with the Spirit of Life. You will discover that following each personal consciousness cleansing, you will become a fountain of inspiration with increased energy, more accurate, *affirmative* thinking and acting enabling you to experience radiant health, happiness and self control. The Cosmic Intelligence which created you will release *through* your mind ideas, opportunities and challenges leading to a rewarding lifestyle.

LIFESTYLE AFFIRMATION

I am One with the Intelligence which created me. I am endowed with the qualities and attributes capable of expressing creativity, health and happiness. I am at peace with the universe as I seek out my true place in life. Love, truth and beauty fill my life.

HOW TO USE THE SUPEROBJECTIVE THROUGH SELF REALIZATION

Getting to know your inner power of mind is called *self realization*. The greater your understanding of *who* you are enables you to draw closer to the Source of life through your superobjective channel. The more you *unify* with nature the more you may draw from it. The answers to life are *within* you and *around* you. The comprehension of your being unfolds as you open your mind to new ideas, ideals and visions. Establish a close relationship with your Source and you will discover the great secret to creative self expression, health, success and wealth creation. The following suggestions get your started:

1: Identify your present personality and character. *Why* are you as you are? *What* has shaped your thinking, feeling, believing and acting? *Who* has most influenced your life and why?

2: What have you achieved of value to this present day? Are you proud of your success? What circumstances, events and persons helped you to succeed?

3: Assess your failures. What brought them about? What have you learned from them?

4: What is your present relationship to life and your *Source* of being? Do you understand *why* you are here and your position in the great scheme of things?

5: Read and discover how your mind works. Through self analysis discover your weaknesses and strengths and how to correct weaknesses through positive application of your mind.

FOLLOW THE PATH OF THE ANCIENT MYSTICS TO CONTROL YOUR MIND

In early times, the great teachers of life taught that prosperity could be experienced through a creative consciousness, a special way of using the mind. They spoke against a 'sweat-of-the-brow' mentality, attempting to force life into submitting to demands through mental intimidation. Some so-called 'positive thinkers' still use this method in their desire to succeed. They brainwash themselves into thinking that repeated demands — positive statements — are the answer to wealth accumulation, health and success. New ways of living require new methods of thinking. Positive thinking does not stand alone. It requires not only words but *beliefs* and *acts* of an affirmative nature to produce success.

Abraham 'pictured' wealth in his mind, established *belief* in his visualization process and soon manifested the prosperity he desired. Abraham's secret is revealed as a strain-free, faith-inspired manner of thinking, believing, picturing and *acting*. Abraham developed a prosperity consciousness which brought rich results. And so too, can you, by believing in and *utilizing* the miracle power resident within your mind. It is your attitude toward your personal capabilities that determines the degree of your prosperity and success. Give proper mental attention to your ideas and ideals. Picture the end result in your mind and your subconscious will respond, bringing your desires to pass.

CONSTRUCTIVE MIND USE MOTIVATES SUCCESS

Professor Gavriel Saloman of Israel's Tel Aviv University holds the view that: 'Life is little more than a mindless exercise for most people.' I support his contention. Far too many people wander through life passively accepting failure and a less than rewarding lifestyle when, with constructive thinking and performance, they could experience health, happiness and prosperity. *The harvest truly is plenteous, but the labourers are few.*

Famous American author Christian Bovee observed more than a century ago: *Mind unemployed is mind unenjoyed.* Wake up your thinking.

Put your mind into high gear. Steer it in a positive direction. Cease accepting whatever comes along. Place absolute trust in the principle of your mind. When you *think* right you *act* right. Impregnate your subconscious with the concept that *you* are the master of your destiny and according to your thought and belief is it done unto you. When you take charge of your mind and control your actions, life ceases to treat you badly. It stops being a 'mindless exercise'. Instead, it becomes an exciting experience, challenging you to go after and achieve those things you desire to enrich your life. You become the *King* or *Queen* of your private universe.

UNDERSTANDING YOUR MIND ELIMINATES FEAR OF THE MATERIAL WORLD

Knowledge of the way your mind works and how to direct it, eliminates fear, frustration and anxiety about the future, the economic situation, stock market drops, business bankruptcy, monetary devaluation, inflation, high taxation, unemployment, etc. You know that the real power to change and control the conditions of your life is within *you* and not resident in events, others, governments or institutions. Your conscious mind makes the decisions and your subconscious carries them out according to your directions. Your superconscious acts when it is acted upon. Your life is the sum total of your thinking and your beliefs. To live harmoniously and beneficially, follow implicitly the law of mind which, simply stated, is the law of belief. *As thou hast believed, so be it done unto thee.*—MATT. 8:13.

Discover the stress-free way to the attainment of riches. Think scientifically. Think rationally, creatively and enthusiastically about your aims and build into your consciousness the belief that you are destined to succeed with or without the assistance of others. Rid your mind of passive thinking. Lift your ideas and ideals to the highest level and you will attract the best life has to offer and rejoice in harmonious and useful human relationships. Resist caving in to personal and business pressures. Rise to each new challenge, confident in the knowledge that within your mind — conscious, subsconscious, superconscious — is the extraordinary *power* to demolish obstacles and produce riches from life's bountiful storehouse.

YOU ARE RESPONSIBLE FOR BECOMING PRINCE OR PAUPER

Psychologists maintain that everything is done by choice, that humans fail or succeed by virtue of the thoughts and actions they choose. Your mind operates through your selection of ideas and ideals — the attitudes you construct and *cling* to. It is your responsibility to select what you want to achieve, what you want to have and what you wish to become. Your actions are motivated by your attitudes. It is essential to select and adhere to affirmative attitudes if you desire to bring about affirmative actions and thus success.

Select ideas and ideals which bless and prosper you in every way. The laws of mind are impersonal. They respond to your beliefs. *Believe* that it is spiritually right for you to achieve and prosper. Whatever is blessed increases.

PROSPERITY AFFIRMATION

I choose to prosper in every way. I use my mind constructively, believing that life responds to my thoughts. I am blessed in all ways. Every day my prosperity increases.

HOW TO ACHIEVE WHAT YOU WANT VIA MENTAL CO-OPERATION

Your desires and aspirations are best served when they are supported by confidence, a strong *feeling* that you have the ability to achieve them. Your affirmations for success need the co-operation of your conscious and subconscious mind. Both divisions of mind must be in agreement that you *can* and *will* win. You destroy any chance of success if you feel that you cannot attain your dreams. A lack of self assurance neutralizes any affirmation you make and sets your conscious and subconscious on a collision course. Your subconscious always wins because it accepts and acts on what you *believe* to be true. It reacts to the dominant idea.

Your source of prosperity lies within your inner feelings. Consciously affirm and believe without wavering that it is your right to be rich, happy and successful. Bring your conscious and subconscious into agreement. Where there is internal harmony there is no fear, frustration, anxiety or worry. Prosperous thoughts produce prosperous deeds. Remember: prosperity and achievement are created mentally *first*.

YOUR CONSCIOUSNESS IS THE DIRECTOR OF YOUR FUTURE

The main function of your objective (conscious) mind is to prepare a direction for your life and it accomplishes it through thoughts, feelings and beliefs. It deals with the outer world via the five senses. They supply vital information concerning your environment, enabling the conscious mind to formulate attitudes and make decisions. The day-to-day working of your conscious mind is therefore devoted to reasoning, deciding and planning. This first level of mind is the *planner* of your future.

THE SECOND LEVEL OF MIND IS AN AUTOMATIC GOAL-STRIVER

The subconscious mind perceives via intuition and does not need to rely on information from the five senses to operate. It can depart from the body, comprehend the thoughts and feelings of others, retain information and produce amazing personal benefits and results when it is given affirmative programs to work with. The subconscious mind is an automatic goal-striver. It seeks to achieve whatever program it is offered.

Your subconscious mind never sleeps. It is on the job 24 hours a day, 7 days a week. Because it is subject to the conscious mind, takes its orders and directions from it, be careful what ideas you give to it. When the thoughts and beliefs deposited in the subconscious are constructive, the deeper mind responds in a positive way. When there is no division, no quarrel between the first and second levels of the mind, the desires, prayers, dreams and aspirations for a better, happier and more prosperous life are answered.

PROTECT YOURSELF FROM SUBVERSIVE THINKING

You must protect yourself from subversive concepts — attitudes which undermine your objectives. Because the subsconscious acts compulsively rather than reasoning through actions it is to perform, establish the habit of thinking in an innovative, rational, practical and self-encouraging way. Reject fear thinking. Concepts backed by fear and anxiety are morale depressants. When the subconscious mind is programmed with concepts that suggest, 'I will fail, I am broke, I am unhappy,' the motivation to alter these ideas and conditions is strangled.

Neutralize pessimistic beliefs by swamping them with spiritually-uplifting ideas. Regularly and systematically exorcise your consciousness with constructive patterns of thought and feeling. Through a process of mental cleansing, your deeper mind is protected against subversive programming. You will be pleased with the results: new-found enthusiasm, greater stimulation to take on challenges, grasp opportunities and a determination to win and prosper.

HOW TO CONTROL THE DYNAMICS OF YOUR MIND

Disciplined thought expression is the key to your prosperity. It is just as easy to think of yourself as an achiever as it is to think of yourself as a failure. Don't bother with failure when you can, by raising your concepts, start propelling your way to the success you desire. The thoughts you entertain and the beliefs you support contain TNT. They are all powerful. They reign over your life to either enslave you or free you. Don't allow your life to take the wrong turn. Take control of your *power* and direct it for beneficial results. Use the following affirmation whenever your thoughts are challenged by negative situations, events or conditions.

MIND CONTROL AFFIRMATION
My thoughts and beliefs are of my making. I am in control of my mind. Therefore, I control the power to overcome obstacles and to shape the lifestyle and success I desire. I now unleash this power to raise myself to great heights of personal achievement and financial security.

FORMULAS TO GROW RICH

- States of consciousness manifest themselves. To improve your lifestyle, improve your attitudes. An habitual pattern of affirmative thinking will help to stabilize your life allowing you to better control the conditions, circumstances and events of your world.

- Your mind is a magnificient, highly-complex mechanism. Its potential remains dormant if you are ignorant of what you can accomplish by applying the law of mind, which is the law of belief.

- There are three divisions of mind: conscious, subconscious and superconscious. Your mind is part and parcel of the Creator of the cosmos, the Source of all visible and invisible supply. When you separate yourself from Infinite Wisdom, the quality, order and balance of life deteriorates. Purify your consciousness. Uplift your thinking. Harmonize with things noble, just and good.

- Your subconscious mind is an automatic goal-striving device. Program into it strong belief in the success, creative achievement and financial security you desire.

- To overcome stress, fear, frustration and negative influences, spend time each day meditating on *peace, beauty, wholeness, perfection.* Get in touch with your superconsciousness. Separate yourself from the race mind. Go within. Join with the Spirit of Life.

- Abraham pictured wealth in his mind. He established belief in the *visualization* process and manifested the prosperity he desired. Believe in your mental picturing. *See* yourself as prosperous and as you work toward the accomplishment of your goals their acquisition will come to you without anxiety and stress.

- For some people life is little more than a mindless exercise. Take on more life. Don't be afraid of tackling challenges. Use your mind constructively to open up opportunities which put you in the running for high achievement and financial success.

- Success or failure are your choice by virtue of what you choose to think, what you choose to feel, what you choose to believe and how you choose to act. Give yourself a break. Choose health, happiness and wealth and believe that they are your birthright.

HOW TO LOCK INTO
THOUGHT FORCE
FOR IRON-GRIP CONTROL
OVER EMPIRE-BUILDING

FORMULA **3**

HOW TO UNLEASH THE POTENCY OF THOUGHT FORCE

Simply stated, *thought force* is a powerful way of striking attitudes. It is the super-charged energy resident in needs, wants, desires, ideas and ideals once they have been emotionalized and passed to the subconscious for processing. Energized thought patterns have the power to make or break you. When these thought forms are affirmative, they boost your morale, stimulate self assurance and motivate you to take on challenges. They not only make you feel great, they create greatness within you. Negative thought forms lower your morale, strip you of self confidence and play havoc with your emotions and actions. It is the *directional* flow of this energy which must be controlled and guided.

Thought force is unleashed in an affirmative way when you discipline your thinking, eliminate inner conflict and remove obstructionist beliefs. This action brings the conscious and subconscious into agreement.

Where there is mental harmony there is no conflict, no impediment to the use of your mental power in a positive way and therefore no obstruction to your aims and objectives.

HOW TO GAIN IRON-GRIP CONTROL OVER YOUR RISE TO THE TOP

Iron-grip control over your efforts is necessary if you desire to empire-build. The first step is to become a personal-power strategist, totally in command of all actions you take. Your personal power-base will depend on your level of self reliance. Self dependency gives you control over what you do and how you do it which in turn controls circumstances and events related to your actions.

Self reliance is determined by the strength of your thoughts and the degree of *control* you have over your thinking. It is imperative that you be a *self* manager, a person who does not have to rely on others to make decisions, take actions or offer support on your behalf. Naturally, there will be times when you will need others to assist you, but you cannot afford to lose control of your rise to the top. *You* must be in charge every step of the way.

Self management and *self* assertiveness generate genuine power, influence and control over empire-building activities. When you take charge of your thoughts, consolidate your beliefs and regulate your feelings, you automatically instigate iron-grip control over your actions. Thought force is unleashed in a positive way, attracting to you the success you desire.

HOW TO WRITE YOUR OWN EMPIRE-BUILDING GUARANTEE

It is no secret that life offers no guarantee of success. A guarantee that you will be happy and successful rests with you. It depends on how you play the game — the goals you set and what you contribute to achieve them. The best success guarantee you can give yourself is to become self reliant, determined and hard working. Do not seek handouts or rely on the promises of support from friends, associates or relatives. Never abrogate your personal power. Hold onto it. Control over your life by others robs you not only of opportunity but enslaves you to their viewpoints and directions.

Life is too short to waste time waiting on others to elevate your personal and career positions. Meet the challenge of everyday circumstances, conditions and events via the potency of your powerfully-creative mental faculties. Positive use of thought force is a firm guarantee of rich living.

HOW TO DIRECT THOUGHT FORCE IN A POSITIVE WAY

Failure-prone individuals do not control their thought processes. Their thinking revolves around lack, limitation, resentment and failure. With them, pessimism runs rampant. This negative consciousness drives thought force into negative gear, producing negative circumstances, conditions and events in their lives.

Your thoughts are a never-ending stream of activity working for or against your good. As a working principle, your mind produces outward things according to the mental images and beliefs it holds. You are a living expression of your concepts. Where you stand tomorrow is determined by what you think, feel and believe today.

Now that you have decided to claim the riches of life, you must come to grips with who is to control your thinking — you, others or circumstances. Placing thought force under your personal command will immediately bring balance, harmony and a positive sense of direction into your life. The medium through which you succeed or fail is *your* mind. Therefore, you must be captain of your ship, director of your progress and master of your destiny.

HOW TO AVOID NEGATIVE USE OF THOUGHT FORCE

The power of your thinking remains constant whether you think in an affirmative way or a negative way. Negative thinkers unleash this power which attracts negative conditions. It is the same power which, if used constructively, can bring about life's fortunes. It is commonsense to align yourself with *positive* use of thought force.

Some corrupt, greedy, dishonest persons use the power of mind to hurt others, demean them and take advantage of them. It is an act right-minded persons should avoid. In life, humans become more prosperous and happy by entering into a spirit of *co-operation* rather than confrontation and questionable competition with others.

The motion picture *Wall Street* was an entertaining and enlightening one. Two of the central characters, Bud Fox and Gordon Gekko, became powerful and wealthy through greed. Their modus operandi was to step on people, take advantage of them and without conscience destroy them if necessary. According to Gekko, 'greed is a good thing'. Acts brought about by greed seldom, if ever, produce good. Generally speaking, greed breeds meanness, envy, selfishness and corruptness. Momentary gains eventually turn into losses as the law of cause and effect comes into play. This cosmic law is one of justice. It is universal and applies to *all* men and women throughout the universe. It is wrong to knowingly and willfully cause distress and harm to a fellow human. Do the right thing by others and you will have no one to avoid, to fear or to fight with on your way to empire-building.

HOW TO REMOVE MENTAL TOXINS WHICH OBSTRUCT YOUR WAY TO RICHES

Envy and jealousy are mental toxins. They poison the mind and are capable of bringing about physical illness. Those who seek to share the riches of life must see negative thinking as a disease which can be cured by reversing attitudes. A negative thought can be neutralized by a contrary thought. A thought of envy must be grounded. It is capable of poisoning rationality which hampers your ability to make sensible decisions and take rational actions. Fill your consciousness with thoughts of the highest and the best in life. Be generous in your praise, your gratitude and your thankfulness for the life you've been given and the benefits awaiting you. Keep in mind that you become happy by making others happy. You attract wealth by helping others to become rich and you expand your wisdom and personal strength by lifting your mind upward in close harmony with the Creative Force of the universe. Purity of mind will open your life to infinite riches within and without.

HOW A BUSINESSWOMAN REMOVED MENTAL TOXINS TO SUCCEED

A businesswoman attended one of my success seminars. She told me that over a two-year period her management consultancy had been operating at a financial loss. During the course it became evident that she was an envious person. She spoke critically of friends, business associates and competitors who were doing well. She suggested that some persons she knew had acquired wealth by dishonest means. Her attitudes were pockets of poison.

This woman desired success for herself but not for others. I explained to her that she had to change her warped concepts and envious nature if she wanted to get her business working successfully and her life in balance. I told her that the power of thought force was operative and working against her, souring her disposition, alienating friends and losing clients. The cure was to start blessing others rather than cursing them.

About a year later, I received a letter from her which read: 'My life and business are on an upswing. I took your advice and stopped seeing others as crooks and wasters just because they were wealthy and successful and I wasn't. Now when I meet people socially and in business, I silently bless them. I offer words of praise and encouragement. I go out of my way to be of assistance whenever I can. I feel much more comfortable and confident in the presence of others. My business has expanded and is now making money. I am thankful I learned how to control the direction of my thoughts and to use my mind power beneficially.'

HOW TO EMPIRE-BUILD VIA GENEROSITY OF THOUGHT FORCE

Use the power of your thought to bless others, to help them rise, shine and win. A major human weakness today is the reluctance of some successful people to assist others to victory. What you hoard, you lose. What you give, you get back. Mental and physical misers display a visible negative personality. They are suspicious and secretive, envious and greedy. These are traits which spoil their ability to fully enjoy and properly use the benefits of their accomplishments.

Be a generous person of thought and action. Inspire others through your words of kindness. Cease using the mighty power of your thoughts and words against others which, in reality, you are using against yourself. Use thought force to help make rich all those with whom you socialize and do business with.

HOW TO THROW THE SUCCESS BOOMERANG

Remember, the thoughts you release — affirmative or negative — act like a boomerang. They return to you. Second-class concepts return as second-class results. Let your thoughts flow from the standpoint of rightness and truth and you will receive countless blessings including well-being, happiness and contentment. Say to yourself: 'My thoughts center on infinite riches, not only for myself, but for all those I come in contact with'.

THOUGHTS TO GET YOUR EMPIRE-BUILDING UNDERWAY

An early lesson a fledgling entrepreneur needs to learn is to attach a visible and an invisible display of faith to personal ideas, ideals and career objectives. Unleashing thought force through faith is a key factor in attaining success. Faith, as the wise say, *moves mountains*. It is a wonderful incentive to make your marriage work, build your business, develop your skills and attract happiness. Get acquainted with what faith can do for you. It is an invisible force capable of manifesting the glories, beauties and riches surrounding you. Follow these three important steps:

1: *EXHALT* and have faith in what you seek.
2: *DWELL* on and have faith in your success capabilities.
3: *ACT* in a fearless, relentless but faithful, loyal and honest way.

HOW TO USE THE BOSS TECHNIQUE TO INCREASE YOUR SUCCESS POTENTIAL

While on a wonderful cruise through the Panama Canal, I had an interesting conversation with a fellow passenger about success techniques. He told me that a couple of years ago, his business suffered a serious sales and profits downturn until he *retrained* his attitude to success. 'Whenever a business problem came up, I buckled under the stress of it. I worried about it, became frustrated and feared the outcome. Sales dropped, staff morale was low, an increasing number of customers bought from my competitor. My attitude was hooked on defeat. I told myself I was on the way out. My mind was divided against itself. I wanted to succeed, but feared I would fail. I enlarged my problems by focusing on defeat. In desperation, I decided to turn my attitude around by reversing negatives into positives. After two months of believing in and accepting the inevitability of success, business increased dramatically. I'm celebrating my good fortune by taking this cruise,' he said.

This now successful businessman told me that he uses what he calls the 'boss technique' to keep his attitude centered on success. Each morning before commencing work he sits in his office and meditates on this statement: *I am boss of my life. I alone control my personal destiny. I have the wisdom, knowledge and skill to make my business an outstanding success.* It's thought force in action and it works.

HOW TO DEPOSIT IN YOUR MENTAL BANK EMPIRE-BUILDING STIMULATORS

Wealth accumulation is a subconscious conviction which requires your support without wavering. Get into the habit of convincing your subconscious that wealth and success are yours for the asking and doing. Think of your subconscious as a bank. Deposit into your mental bank ideas which inspire you to take on challenges and opportunities. Raise your expectation of what you can and should achieve. Don't short-change yourself. The knowledge and skill you already have can be turned into compounding dollars.

Open your success bank account today. Deposit into your account these beneficial ideas: *happiness, faith, confidence, love, health, creativity, advancement, luxury, personal power, influence, action control, energy, perseverance, wealth, affluence, achievement, success.* Your mental bank and the power of your ideas will give you the returns you seek.

THE REASON WEALTH CREATORS AMASS FORTUNES

Wealth creators think alike. Their eyes and minds are always open to possibilities and opportunities. They know that money accumulation requires strong conviction, rock-solid determination and positive action. They view money as beneficial. They do not envy other wealthy persons. They see money as a means of personal development and security. They want to live the life more abundant. They believe it is their *right* to do so.

Wealth creators are lateral thinkers. They sweep aside directionless, wishful thinking. They smash down seemingly-impenetrable walls by locking into mind power and using this energy to get them up on their feet and running. Wealth creators think big, are assertive, dynamic, persuasive and persistent in their pursuit of excellence. They speak confidently without faltering and via impressive communication-motivation are able to win others to their aims, objectives and causes.

Wealth creators take steps others are afraid to take. They do not surrender to fear, setbacks or temporary failure. It is not money alone that motivates them to achieve but the added comfort, creative expansion and the good it can bring through proper use of it. Empire-builders amass fortunes because they are grateful for the work they have been given to do and for the ability to do it. They love their work. They thrill to victory. And so will you if you build a spiritual bank of high thoughts, emotions and ideals and then channel them constructively via thought force.

MOVE TO THE OPPOSITE WHEN DOWN AND YOU WILL AUTOMATICALLY PICK UP

Do not allow past mistakes and failures to stop you taking a chance on a new idea or venture. Use defeat as an excuse to rise up and begin again. View failure as a lesson to be learned and use the knowledge to find new and better ways to do things. Do not accept material loss as anything other than temporary. Don't allow your thoughts to dwell on self pity. Immediately you start feeling sorry for yourself, *dump* the emotion. Move to the opposite. Give yourself a dose of mental medicine. Rejoice in the idea that the abundant life begins in your imagination. All that is required of you is to *feel* happy and prosperous and when you move to this pattern of thought your feelings manifest themselves.

CLAIM YOU CAN AND YOU WILL

The secrets of health, wealth and happiness are not somewhere outside of you. They reside deeply *within*. You are a repository of knowledge and wisdom. You must use these personal assets constructively, not destructively. Because your concern for survival and lifestyle excellence is paramount in your thoughts and emotions, it is your responsibility to take charge of your thoughts and emotions and direct them beneficially. If a problem is upsetting you at this moment, affirm the following statement: *If I say I can't, I won't. If I claim I can, I will.*

HOW A BUSINESSMAN LOST A FORTUNE AND REGAINED IT QUICKLY

I knew a businessman in Toronto, Canada, who told me during dinner at his fabulous home how he had lost everything during an economic downturn. 'I lost four million dollars. My friends thought I was finished. The loss bothered me for a short period but I quickly recovered and began re-building my empire. I looked at money as a symbol, numbers printed on small pieces of paper. I had made money through the proper use of my mind. Having made money once, I knew I could make it again. What set me going was my determination not to let myself down.'

Although this businessman has now retired, his story is worth reporting. He read an advertisement in a newspaper calling for tenders to manufacture an automobile part. He called the company and got the necessary specifications and requirements. He took them to a retired friend who had been in the toolmaking business. Together they worked out a costing and submitted it. They won the order. Within a month they both set up a small plant, leased the necessary machinery and went to work 14 hours a day manufacturing the part. Within six months they were producing parts for other companies. Within 18 months the business was grossing $6 million.

'I could have packed it in and applied to the Government for the dole. But that's not my nature. The power within the human mind is greater than the power in an atomic bomb. I used this power to stimulate my mind and motivate my actions — all that is necessary to produce success,' he told me.

THE OPPORTUNITY TO EMPIRE-BUILD RESTS WITH YOU

The achievements you desire and the financial riches you seek already exist. Others are claiming and receiving them and so must you. Don't let opportunity pass you by. Get your mind and heart set on what you want and track it down. Focus your thoughts and the *power* they contain on a practical and acceptable achievement formula. Affirmative thought force moves you forward, advances your cause, enlarges your awareness and manifests your dream. Don't strangle this power. Give it the freedom it needs to transform your life. Apply your skills. Don't waste time and energy chasing unrealistic goals that are out of sight. Go after goals that are at the moment slightly out of reach. The opportunity to empire-build challenges you now. Take up this challenge and you will win.

FORMULAS TO GROW RICH

- Thought force is your passport to wealth accumulation and achievement. It is a powerful way of striking attitudes which stimulate personal action. Energized thought forms have the power to make or break you. Select affirmative thoughts and the super-charged energy they contain will support your quest for success.

- Gain iron-grip control over your life if you have a desire to empire-build. You must develop self reliance. It is your personal power-base. Become a *self* manager. Choose your own way of thinking, prepare your own success plans and act on your own decisions. Command every thought, feeling and belief and you will move up from follower to leader.

- Life offers no guarantee of success but you can write your own personal guarantee for empire-building via self reliance. Do *not* pass control of your personal power to others. Don't allow your thinking to be manipulated by others. Don't rely on the promises of others. Take charge of your life.

- Establish a visible and an invisible display of faith and loyalty to your aims. Have faith in your ability to succeed. Dwell on good fortune. Exhalt what you seek.

- Act in a fearless, relentless but honest way and you will have no one to avoid, no one to fear and no one to fight as you empire-build.

- Thoughts boomerang. Don't project negative ideas, feelings and beliefs. They will haunt you on their return.

- Deposit in your mental bank ideas of happiness, health and wealth. Your deposits will compound and make you happy, healthy and rich.

- Wealth creators think alike. They refrain from envy and jealousy. They sweep aside directionless thinking. They are self assertive. They think big.

- Do not allow past mistakes to stop you taking a chance on new ideas, undertaking new ventures or risking your time and energy on new challenges. Give yourself a dose of mental medicine. Pick yourself up from depression and self doubt. Become boss of your life.

- The success you desire awaits your call. The opportunity to empire-build rests with you. Harness the power of thought force and get it working in a positive way to ride you to the top.

HOW TO INCREASE
PERSONAL ASSETS

FORMULA **4**

PERSONAL ASSETS REFLECT YOUR LIFE-LONG ACHIEVEMENTS

Personal assets can be separated into two divisions: *self* assets and *material* assets. Each is representative of your achievements. The legacy you leave this world will reflect the self values you established and whether you were an industrious, forthright person or an indolent, disreputable person.

Charles Simmons (1798–1856) an American clergyman and litterateur, claimed: *Industry keeps the body healthy, the mind clear, the heart whole, and the purse full.* For the entrepreneur, that statement says it all. One of your major goals should include the strong desire to become successfully industrious so that the legacy you leave reflects a person who was hardworking and *decent* in all respects.

TAKE STOCK OF WHAT YOU HAVE AND VALUE IT CORRECTLY

A personal assets inventory is the best way to take stock of your real worth. It may surprise you as to what you have achieved. Some people undervalue and fail to appreciate their good state of health, employment position, acquired skills, excellent family relationships, personal friendships and business associations. Give yourself credit for scholastic, sports, creative, professional and business achievements. Don't undervalue what you are and what you can become with added knowledge and effort. See yourself as a *worthy* human being and expand your life from this solid foundation.

PERSONAL RESOURCES HELP YOU TO GET WHERE YOU WANT TO GO

Taking on new opportunities, challenges, career projects and tackling a new approach to life require you to have on hand specific resources. Discovering at a critical point in your life that you lack some or many of the essential ingredients to succeed could prove to be frustrating, depressing or downright disastrous. This is why it is wise to take stock of your current resources and where necessary add to them or improve them. The stronger your assets the easier and quicker it will be for you to reach your objectives.

Self assessment, feedback from friends, relatives, teachers, business associates or psychological testing will assist you to get a good overview of your present resources status. If you need to boost your knowledge or purchase equipment, do it *now* to give yourself the support needed to succeed. Worthwhile objectives nearly always have a price tag. They cost you something: money, time, energy. If your wardrobe isn't up to scratch, change it. If you need to purchase business equipment or pay for specialized training, commit yourself to it.

IDENTIFYING RESOURCES

Personal resources include: intelligence level, attitudes, prejudices, self assurance level, personality appeal, character traits, talents and skills, leadership ability.

Material resources include: cash on hand, investments, access to credit, business and professional contacts, equipment or tools necessary to operate a business, profession or trade, wardrobe of suitable clothes, automobile.

SO YOU WANT TO MAKE A MILLION — WHAT'S STOPPING YOU?

Sometimes, healthy desires and good decisions never come to pass for want of proper *self* support. Many people have a wish to be wealthy but take the desire no further because they feel they do not possess the necessary talent or confidence to become rich. Clarifying your personal state-of-affairs helps to remove some of the mystique from empire-building. It boosts your confidence level and gives you the *urge* to succeed.

The only person standing in your way to success is *you*. If you want to increase your skills, build a bigger bank account, expand your career, then go to it. Begin your ascent to fame and fortune this very minute. Make a success covenant. Vow to take on the challenge of starting your own business, rising to executive level, becoming an outstanding achiever and growing rich through your efforts. Opportunities are all around you, *waiting* for you to take advantage of them. Harness the forces at your command and jump into the business of winning.

HOW TO REAP DIVIDENDS FROM THE MOST VALUABLE ASSET YOU POSSESS

The most priceless asset you have is your mind. It gives you the ability to think, to rationalize and to decide before you act. The cause of so much unhappiness, loss, unproductivity and poverty in the world is mental indolence. Far too many people fail to use the mind in a sensible way. They are mentally restricted through ignorance of what the mind can accomplish.

Scattered through many of the offices of IBM Australia's headquarters are small desk plaques urging employees to *THINK*. The trouble with many people is their willingness to let someone else do their thinking for them. Mental laziness is an international disease which should be stamped out if we are to make the world a better place in which to live. You can readily improve your lot-in-life by tapping into the powerful resources resident in your *million dollar mind.*

DON'T DEPOSIT PENNIES IN YOUR MILLION DOLLAR BANK

Your mind is your bank. The returns you get are determined by the deposits you make. Penny deposits return penny gains. Material assets have their beginning in the vault of your mental bank. They begin as ideas, needs, wants, desires and motives for acquiring a better lifestyle. When they are attached to faith, belief, confidence and positive action, they give compound interest — *success* and *wealth*.

From your personal bank you are able to draw an unlimited supply of opportunity. You are advanced a chance to grow mentally, emotionally and financially. It is also made available to you to open the door to a self-determined existence. Don't be mean. Deposit *big* ideas. Expect *big* results. Work your mental bank for all it's worth and your returns will rise from pennies to dollars.

DYNAMIC PERSONAL ASSETS TO INCREASE YOUR POTENTIAL

Set your mind to achieving greatness in a trade, business or profession of your choice. In the process, determine to earn the praise, admiration and respect of those you do business with. Strong character and always acting in a forthright way mark you as a person worthy of respect. The following list of strong character traits should be adopted by those seeking a *respected* position in life.

- IMPECCABLE MANNERS
- DECISIVE ATTITUDE
- TRUTHFUL

- RELIABLE
- HIGHLY MORAL
- COURAGEOUS

IMPECCABLE MANNERS DRAW ATTENTION TO YOU

Entrepreneurs are acutely aware that they must get others to see them as intelligent, *powerful* persons. They recognize the value of developing an impressive, highly-magnetic presentation manner. It is the key to making people instantly aware of their importance. A display of courtesy, respect for the position of others, politeness and manners, all contribute to the power-base of those desiring to empire-build and grow rich.

A display of common courtesy when dealing with others simply means being considerate of their views and position, their needs and desires and doing it pleasantly, not impatiently or grumpily. Politeness is the mark of a well-bred person, a considerate and cultured person. Rudeness, especially where there is no cause to be rude, is the mark of an ignorant, generally low-thinking person.

Good manners are indicative of good breeding — a person who is kind and considerate. A high-thinking person. Through a display of superior manners, your self-power base is strengthened, bringing you greater recognition, respect and admiration. Good manners play an important part in empire-building.

In the changing business world today, it is surprising how many executives display rudeness when approached by persons desiring to do business with them. Some managers refuse to return phone calls or answer correspondence. It is frustrating for those on the other end and the quickest way to get them off-side. A non-response to a phone call or letter builds resentment and the insult is often long-remembered. It is well to remember the axiom: *today's rooster is tomorrow's feather duster.* If you are on the way down, it is surprising who you meet on the way up. A display of courtesy to someone of less importance than yourself today, could pay dividends should you meet that same person in the future and find he or she is in a position to do you good.

HOW TO BE DECISIVE

Generally speaking, worry, fear, frustration and fatigue are brought about because of an inability to make decisions. A decision is a choice of alternative means to move *toward* an objective. The outcome of a decision is either direct action by the decision-maker or a statement of intention to commit others to a course of action. Leadership demands good decision-making ability.

Lack of information or wrong information results in poor decisions being made. Gain as much information as possible. Listen to the opinions of others but weigh them against the facts at hand. Business leaders need to call for information from *every* available source before deciding on a course of action. The best plan to follow is: *be sure you are right, then go ahead.*

Important decisions require analysis. This does not mean that they should be given a lengthy investigation period unless it cannot be avoided. Taking too long to make a decision could result in lost opportunity. *Define* the problem. How critical is it? When does it require solving? What will be gained by solving it? Are there alternative solutions to the problem? Is a decision being arrived at via guesswork, a 'gut feeling' or by logical thinking? The basic rules of good decision-making are:

1: Identify and define each decision to be made.

2: Write each decision to be made on paper.

3: Weigh the pros and cons. Study the result of each.

4: Review all information gathered and come to a conclusion.

5: Convert the decision into *action*.

HOW TO GAIN THE RESPECT OF OTHERS THROUGH TRUTHFULNESS

A truthful person is an honest person. There is no substitute for forthrightness. An individual who has high ideals, speaks the truth and practices personal integrity, instantly strikes others as a person worth knowing, associating with and doing business with. Being truthful is a very necessary ingredient for those desiring to rise to the top and stay there.

Don't be a liar. Design your character to include truthful thoughts, feelings and actions. Do not compromise personal integrity. It is your *real* strength. It will bring the respect of your peers, even your enemies. When you abide by truth, you have nothing to fear. Thomas Carlyle, English philosopher, more than a century ago wrote: *I have always found that the honest truth of our own mind has a certain attraction for every other mind that loves truth honestly.*

RELIABILITY IS A DEMAND SUCCESS MAKES ON YOU

There is nothing more frustrating and disappointing than being let down by those you have relied upon to fulfill a request or promise. Dealing with unreliable people can be time wasting and costly. I make it a business practice to steer clear of persons I have found to be unreliable. Unreliable persons usually have another negative character trait, they aren't truthful. Your reputation in business will sour if you do not fulfill your promises. Stick by your word. Carry out your obligations to others, even though you may temporarily lose in some way.

It was said of the film star, the late Errol Flynn, 'He could always be counted on for his unreliability.' Whether the statement is a true one reflecting Flynn's character, I do not know, but it made the rounds and ended up in a book on his illustrious life. As an entrepreneur, the last thing you want is a negative reputation making the rounds of your friends and business associates. Play it straight. Play it right. Be a person others can count on and you will be applauded.

YOUR STANDARD OF MORALITY CAN RAISE OR LOWER YOUR CHANCE TO SUCCEED

Webster's New World Dictionary describes morality as: *the character of being in accord with the principles or standards of right conduct; often, specifically, virtue in sexual conduct.* Our social system today has gone haywire. Free sex has brought many problems. It has destroyed relationships and marriages. It has spread disease. Individuals, intentionally or not, hurt others by their 'do as I please' attitude to life. In recent years, we have witnessed so-called religious persons getting involved in immoral practices — financial as well as sexual.

Practice moral honesty. Be true to the self and in turn you will be true to others. It may be pleasurable to cheat on your wife but when you do so, you lose part of your soul. More than ever before, there is a real need for *morality* in people. Don't give in to what you know is wrong and situations you know will hurt others. Keep in mind that all successful personal and business relationships rest on the foundation of proper moral conduct.

HOW TO BECOME A STRONG AND COURAGEOUS PERSON

It takes mountains of courage to overcome problems, tackle challenges and make it to the top. It has been said that a man or woman of courage moves *forward* while a man or woman lacking courage flees *backward* in a cowardly fashion. True courage requires coolness and calmness under all situations. Courage dissolves fear. It is through fear that humans buckle at the knees and take flight when meeting obstacles. By facing up to an obstacle, fear is subdued, allowing an opportunity to rationally plot a course of action or find a solution.

Have faith in your internal power to solve problems and meet all level of obstacles which may confront you. Stiffen your backbone. Face up to all confrontation. Elevate your consciousness and get control over circumstances. There is a solution to every problem. Contemplate the happy and successful ending you want. Cast out of your mind false beliefs and superstitions. They are the breeding ground for fear and defeat. When you stand up for what you want, the door will open and show you the way to reach your dream. Courage stands behind you, supports your desire to do what you wish to do and be what you long to be. Wear a badge of courage and nothing will move you, affect you or destroy your opportunity to succeed.

HOW TO BENEFIT FROM A PERSONAL RESEARCH OF ASSETS

Study the *Personal Assets Inventory* and the *Material Assets Inventory* charts and when you feel you can complete them satisfactorily, fill them in and go to work improving your position. It may be necessary to alter your attitudes to people, places and things or you may need to revise your investments, change them or cash some of them in. Perhaps you should act on your desire to run your own business or change your job. *Now* is the time to *think-through* your present position in life and to take steps to bring about the changes and improvements you want.

The benefit of seeing personal and material assets in written inventory form is that it helps to clarify what *has* been achieved and what *needs* to be achieved to expand your worth. A clear picture is revealed allowing you to devise strategies and tactics to move onward and upward in life.

WHATEVER YOUR PRESENT WORTH YOU SHOULD AIM FOR THE SKY

When you have tagged your personal and material assets, don't allow yourself to become depressed if you feel you haven't accomplished much to this day. While you may feel it could be difficult adding thousands of dollars to your bank account, there are others who are at this moment adding millions and even billions to theirs.

The world's richest man, Mr. Yoshiaki Tsutsumi of Japan, amassed $US20 billion into his bank account by age 54. There are thousands of persons who are millionaires *plus*. Many started with little more than dreams, ambitions and strong belief in their right to be rich. Don't undersell your ability, your present worth or your capacity to grow rich. Aim your sights high. You have nothing to lose but much to gain. Riches begin to grow from the ideas in your imagination. From the tiny acorn springs the giant oak. From the depth of your imagination emerges opportunity and the where-with-all to grow rich in every aspect of your life.

> *There is no thought in any mind, but it quickly tends to convert itself into a power, and organize a huge instrumentality of means.*
> — Emerson

PERSONAL ASSETS INVENTORY

SELF ASSETS	GOOD	IMPROVE
ABILITY TO THINK AFFIRMATIVELY		
ABILITY TO MAKE RATIONAL JUDGEMENTS		
ABILITY TO GENERATE WORKABLE IDEAS		
ABILITY TO SPEAK WITH AUTHORITY		
ABILITY TO PERSUADE EFFECTIVELY		
ABILITY TO MOTIVATE DYNAMICALLY		
ABILITY TO IMPRESS WITH DRESS–GROOMING		
ABILITY TO CONTROL REACTIONS		
ABILITY TO LISTEN PATIENTLY		
ABILITY TO HARMONIZE WITH OTHERS		
ABILITY TO HUMOR OTHERS		
ABILITY TO EXPRESS CREATIVITY		
ABILITY TO OVERCOME DEPRESSION		
ABILITY TO PRAISE OTHERS		
ABILITY TO VISUALIZE AIMS AND OBJECTIVES		
ABILITY TO BE TRUTHFUL AND RELIABLE		
ABILITY TO BE SELF RELIANT		
ABILITY TO BE RADIANT–ENERGETIC		
ABILITY TO DISPLAY EMPATHY TOWARD OTHERS		
ABILITY TO OVERRIDE OBJECTIONS AND CRITICISM		
ABILITY TO IDENTIFY OPPORTUNITY		
ABILITY TO EXHALT AND BELIEVE IN THE SELF		
ABILITY TO BE TRUSTWORTHY		
ABILITY TO BE CHARMING–AFFABLE–SOCIABLE		
ABILITY TO STEM ENVY AND JEALOUSY		
ABILITY TO FORGIVE AND FORGET		
ABILITY TO GROW MENTALLY AND SPIRITUALLY		
ABILITY TO RELAX AND THROW-OFF STRESS		
ABILITY TO EXPERIENCE INNER PEACE		
ABILITY TO FACE UP TO OTHERS		
ABILITY TO BE GENEROUS AND SHARE WITH OTHERS		
ABILITY TO SUCCEED		

COMMENTS:_____
_____
_____

MATERIAL ASSETS INVENTORY

MATERIAL ASSETS	VALUE	OWING
CASH IN HAND		
BANK DEPOSITS		
TERM INVESTMENT DEPOSITS		
SHARES VALUE		
OTHER FINANCIAL INVESTMENTS		
BUSINESS NET VALUE		
HOME OWNERSHIP EQUITY		
OTHER PROPERTY INVESTMENTS 1: 2: 3:		
RETIREMENT BENEFIT		
INSURANCES		
YEARLY SALARY		
AUTOMOBILE NET VALUE		
BOAT NET VALUE		
SPORTING GOODS		
COMPUTER		
TYPEWRITER		
VIDEO GEAR		
ELECTRONIC GEAR		
COIN–STAMP COLLECTIONS		
TOOLS OF TRADE		
LIBRARY OF BOOKS		
RECORD LIBRARY		
MUSICAL INSTRUMENTS		
FURNITURE		
ANTIQUES–PAINTINGS		
CLOTHING		
JEWELLERY–WATCHES–CAMERAS		
OTHER PERSONAL ASSETS		
TOTALS		

FORMULAS TO GROW RICH

- Your personal assets can be separated into two divisions: self assets and material assets. Each is representative of your life to this day. One of your major goals should be the desire to become a successfully-industrious person, a person of forthright character so that the legacy you leave this world is an honorable one.

- It may surprise you to learn your real worth. Many people undervalue what they have accomplished and what they have the potential to become. A personal inventory of assets can establish what needs to be done to make your life happier and more financially-rewarding.

- The only thing keeping you from high achievement and a rich lifestyle is your *attitude* to these things. Marshal your personal and material resources. Reach for opportunity and get started on your road to empire-building.

- The most valuable asset you possess is probably undervalued. It is your mind; your capacity to *think*. Tap the resource that can elevate your position. Give it value.

- Don't deposit penny concepts into your mental bank if you want to reap millions of dollars. Deposit *big* ideas. Expect *big* results.

- Set your mind to achieving *greatness* in a trade, business or profession of your choice.

- Determine to earn the praise, admiration and respect of those you do business with. Genuinely-earned popularity is a must for the empire-builder.

- Entrepreneurship requires strong character: decisive, truthful, reliable, moral and courageous. These attributes pave the way for your success.

- Study the assets charts and fill in appropriate sections. You will have a clearer picture of what steps need to be taken to help you realize your goals.

- Whatever your present worth you can improve it. Don't stand still. Move forward. The world's richest person amassed a $US20 billion bank account by age 54. You have the same right to wealth as this billionaire. Don't live within a compromise mind. Reach for the sky. From your imagination comes the where-with-all to grow rich in every aspect of your life.

HOW TO GAIN
RECOGNITION THROUGH
PERSONALITY APPEAL

FORMULA **5**

WHY PERSONALITY APPEAL IS IMPORTANT

Many of the beneficial things you receive in life come directly from others or via the help you receive from others: friendship, encouragement, love, loyalty, happiness, employment, business opportunity, investment opportunity, tuition and skills training. People are important to you. You do not have to turn your life over to them, but you do need to enlist their assistance in order to achieve many of your goals. Therefore, it is vitally important that those you need to court see you as a person of *high* status, an impressive, dynamic and likeable personality who can be trusted. The greater the impression you create, the more effective you are as an entrepreneur.

WHY YOUR PERSONALITY MUST STRIKE OTHERS QUICKLY AND DYNAMICALLY

When people meet you for the first time, they quickly pass judgement on you. They *see* you, *listen* to you and then *appraise* you as being unimpressive, neutral or dynamic. This is the reason your personality needs to strike others in a positive way *instantly*. You have no more than a couple of minutes to establish your presence and have it *felt* so that others are drawn to you, impressed by you and want to associate and do business with you. A highly-individual personality presentation can have a profound effect, an hypnotic effect on those you meet. When this occurs, you are in a strong position to influence them.

HOW TO SEE YOURSELF AS OTHERS SEE YOU

It has been suggested that personality appeal is social seduction. It can be employed in an effective way to enhance your present social appeal and to entice others to enjoy a healthy business relationship with you. In order to arrive at a clear picture of how others see you, it is necessary to arrive at a reasonably-accurate appraisal of the image qualities you are exposing. Your initial step is to tag your plus and minus personality factors. This is easily accomplished via self appraisal and through questioning of family and friends as to your good and bad points. Assemble a profile of *you*. Assess it, then make the necessary changes.

THE FIVE FACTORS ON WHICH OTHERS JUDGE YOU

Ascertain the degree of excellence you present via the following five factors. If you discover you are weak in any one of them, begin an immediate program of self improvement. For the empire-builder, personality development should have high priority on the goals list.

1: THE WAY YOU *THINK*.
2: THE WAY YOU *LOOK*.
3: THE WAY YOU *TALK*.
4: THE WAY YOU *LISTEN*.
5: THE WAY YOU *REACT*.

HOW TO APPEAR INTELLIGENT WITHOUT BECOMING A BORE

Throughout this book, I have suggested that far too many people do not know how to think in a constructive and rational manner. With regularity, I meet people who expose their stupidity: store and bank personnel, public servants, politicians, tradespersons, businesspersons. Mostly, this is due to mental laziness and ignorance. Doing business with a thickhead can be frustrating as well as time wasting and often, costly. Sydney's University of Technology conducted a survey in 1989 to discover the level of adult literacy in Australia. Astonishingly, the report revealed that a third of those questioned were unable to use the Yellow Pages of the phone directory correctly. Twelve-percent were unable to find a specified intersection on a street map and 57-percent couldn't work out a 10-percent surcharge on a bill. If you desire important people to take notice of you, it is essential that they see you as *intelligent*. You must possess critical thinking skills.

Your display of intelligence is governed by your capacity to think rationally. It rests on your knowledge and how you apply it. If you want to be recognised as an intelligent person, apply the basic rule: *think first, then act.*

HOW TO IMPROVE YOUR INTELLIGENCE AND INCREASE YOUR APPEAL

The fastest way to improve your ability to think, to rationalize and to decide, is to expand your *information* base and your life experience. Embark upon a solid reading program. Start with newspaper editorials, magazine articles, progress to self-improvement books, then biographical and historical works. Read good novels and books on the arts. Expand your vocabulary. Take on new words and their meanings and inject them into your daily conversations. Visit art galleries, museums, places of historical and architectural interest. Attend concerts, plays, worthwhile movies. Travel within your own country and overseas. Study people, cultures and religions. Apart from self improvement, the added knowledge and experience will give you a great deal of enjoyment.

THE SECRET APPEAL OF SCREEN STARS

The great motion picture stars of the 40s, 50s, and 60s, displayed an appealing 'presence' which had a highly-hypnotic effect on the millions of fans who flocked to see them. Clark Gable, Humphrey Bogart, Cary Grant, Joan Crawford, Bette Davis, Ingrid Bergman, were professional performers who exuded a special *radiance*, an *individualism* which touched others immediately. It may not be your desire to become a screen star, but you do wish to become a star within your own personal and business circles. You want to be seen as an exceptionally-bright and appealingly-different person. You must work toward this goal.

Screen stars need personality appeal to stay at the top. Their success rests on an ability to develop acting talent and to make that talent 'felt'. Entrepreneurs become successful by using particular skills effectively and winning the confidence and assistance of others via personality appeal. The rule to follow is: if you want to be seen as a successful person, you must *look* and *act* like a successful person. When you exude success, you will build a legion of fans who flock to become part of your cause. These admirers will want to court you, enjoy a bond with you, help you and share your lifestyle.

YOUR PERSONALITY APPEAL MUST HAVE A RING OF SINCERITY ABOUT IT

'Projecting sincerity,' Kirk Douglas said to me, 'is essential if an actor is to be believed in the roles he or she plays. An actor cannot fake sincerity.' Sincerity comes from belief. Actors must believe in the roles they perform. They must 'see' themselves as the character, take on the personality of the character and then act out each situation as if it were really happening. Your desire to be liked, admired, respected and helped will find acceptance or rejection according to how you 'sell' yourself to others. If you appear to be insincere, others will shy away from you. You must exude a strong presence with a ring of sincerity about it. An actor must *appear* to be another character. Your role is not only to appear to be a person of sincerity, you must *be* a sincere person.

SELF ASSETS MUST INCLUDE A HEALTHY SELF IMAGE VALUE

Unless you are free of fear, anxiety, frustration and stress, your influence over others will be negligible. Your self assets must include a healthy value of the self which is the basis upon which self confidence is developed. Your self image is the sum total of what you conceive yourself to be. If you have poise, mental and emotional balance and self trust, then you are a person with a healthy state of mind and therefore, an adequate self image. This affirmative *presence* creates an aura which others see as personality appeal.

Get in-tune with what you are and what you can become. Place a high value on *you* as a creative human being, capable of great and wonderful achievement. Inject into your image value a sense of loyalty to your ideals which others see as strong character. Before you can become great, you must impress your subconscious with the *idea* of greatness and your *desire* to be great. Whatever is impressed will be expressed through your personality.

HOW TO PROJECT YOUR IMAGE VALUE TO IMPRESS OTHERS

When you have established in your mind that you are a person of *value*, a person worthy of achievement and success, your self assurance, vitality and strength of character will automatically be exposed to others in a dynamic way. The selling of your personality will come naturally, easily and forthrightly. It won't be necessary for you to oversell yourself, to force your personality on others causing them to shy away from you.

Your self image is your silent partner, either working for or against you. Size yourself up. Make whatever changes are necessary to alter what you are into what you wish to become. If you are moody, self centered, argumentative, lazy, envious, unreliable and see yourself as unworthy and a loser, then this image is projected for the world to see and it does you immense harm. Change these negative states into desirable personality assets which reflect a new, positive and vital you.

HOW TO USE YOUR IMAGINATION TO ADD TO YOUR APPEAL

The 'inner' picture you hold of yourself comes from your imagination. Hebrew mystics, revealed that, 'Man is what he *imagines* himself to be.' From your imagination spring ideas about yourself, people, places and things. These ideas shape your life, influence your judgements, decisions and reactions. Use your imagination to shape a picture of the ideal man or woman and then step into this portrait. Visualize yourself as intelligent, honest, confident, dynamic, charming and successful. *You go where your vision is.*

HOW TO ELEVATE YOUR SELF ESTEEM

I was in my office when the secretary announced that a relative was on the phone requesting to speak to me. When I picked up the receiver she said: 'It's only me.' 'Don't say that,' I reprimanded her. 'You are important in your own right and a very important part of my life. I'm pleased when you call.'

People unconsciously put themselves down. They demote and undervalue who they are and what they are. Take pride in *you* as an important human being. Whenever you are required to give another your name, speak it with confidence and pride. Raise your self esteem by raising your *self* value. See yourself as an important part of the human race. If you desire to rise above mediocrity, jump out of race-mind thinking, of seeing yourself as second-best, of little value and small potential. Become fired-up with the truth of your being, with your creative potential and the opportunities that exist for you to *be*, to *do* and to *have* everything that is worthwhile in life.

HOW TO GET ALONG WITH OTHERS

Until you learn to get along with yourself, chances are, you won't find it easy to get along with others. If you resent what you are, constantly blame yourself for errors in your lifestyle, then you need to do some soul-searching and make changes to the estimation you hold of yourself. An inferior self concept attracts an inferior lifestyle, creates emotional disability, harms friendships and smothers ambition. If you want to establish lasting, *quality* friendships and business relationships, develop a healthy respect for yourself. See yourself as a worthy human being. *Know thyself.* Praise the self. When you feel comfortable with yourself you will have no trouble getting along well with others.

HOW BETTY RAISED HER SELF ESTEEM AND SNARED A PARTNER

Betty attended one of my media presentation seminars. She told the group that she saw herself as a 'plain, everyday-type' devoid of personality. 'No man would want to marry me,' she said. 'I'm too drab and ordinary.'

Actually, Betty was attractive with charm and intelligence. Her problem grew out of her low self esteem. I suggested to her that she write down a list of her positive attributes as she saw them, then add to it comments on her personality as seen by her friends.

Much to Betty's surprise, the plus factors she assembled far outweighed the numerous negatives she imagined she possessed. 'I was astounded to hear my friends tell me that I displayed good dress sense, that I had a nice personality and was striking to look at. For years I had denigrated my importance as a human being. It's no wonder I couldn't find a good marriage partner,' she said.

Some months later, I received an invitation to Betty's wedding. She told me that she had formed a new image of herself which had boosted her self confidence when meeting people. She took on a position as a sales representative and it was while calling on a client that she met the man she has now married. 'The biggest mistake any person can make is to demean the self. Internal attractiveness produces external beauty. In my case, I changed my sour thoughts about myself into beautiful ones and because of it, I attracted the man of my dreams,' Betty told me.

HOW TO TURN YOUR IMAGE FROM VICTIM TO VICTOR

You are a victim of your thinking. Because your subconscious mind is responsive to your ideas, you must ever be alert to the concepts you allow it to take on. If you dwell on imperfection and on physical ugliness, your personality becomes soured and you outwardly appear unattractive. Do not indulge in unattractive thinking. Never imagine yourself as unpopular, ugly in appearance, unintelligent or unworthy. When you change your opinion about yourself, you change conditions. See yourself as attractive, popular, charming and talented. Be a beautiful thinker and others will see you as a striking, interesting and appealing personality.

HOW TO DEVELOP A PLEASING DISPOSITION

Negative concepts of the self reflect in the eyes, mouth, posture, walk and general disposition. Affirmative concepts of the self produce an attractive countenance. The 36 muscles of the face reflect the exact image of your thoughts. A flabby, lazy mind produces a flabby, down-at-the-mouth facial expression. Unattractive thoughts produce an unattractive disposition. Refined thoughts create a refined disposition and facial expression. An affirmative self image enhances the expression of your posture, walk and general manner. *As within, so without.*

HOW TO GET RID OF AN INFERIORITY COMPLEX

Author Lawrence Brennen, points out that: *An inferiority complex never was and never will be taken for modesty. An inferiority complex is read by others as a cheap label.* Eliminate any cheap labels you have attached to your character, personality and talents. People see and *react* to what you present. You cannot expect others to raise your sights for you, to enhance your value where you see yourself as valueless.

You must cast from your mind pre-conceived ideas which destroy your self confidence. Cast your own mould with the right thoughts and correct self image values. Destroy any concept which smacks of inferiority. See yourself as equal to most and superior to some. You have nothing to apologize for except your own negative attitudes. If you possess an inferiority complex, discover the cause of it and take haste to eliminate it. There can be no joy, no satisfaction, no rise to greatness for any individual possessing an inferiority complex. Deal in reality. Raise your sights. Co-operate with yourself. Get rid of false beliefs about your potential to become great. Treat yourself with dignity. Stand in awe of what you can become, can have and can enjoy. You set the standard of your own worth. Raise it. Feel good about yourself and you will develop through your million dollar mind, a million dollar personality.

HOW TO PRESENT YOURSELF TO BE REMEMBERED

One aspect of personal presentation which strikes others immediately is the level of your dress and grooming. An untidy manner of dress combined with poor grooming suggests a less than orderly mind. Poise and charm are enhanced by an attractive outward appearance. Select clothes which reflect quality and expertly fit your physique, coloring and personality. Simplistic design but elegant style, rather than conforming to fashion fads, reflects good fashion taste.

The late Cary Grant once told me that he made a point of having his clothes tailored in a middle-of-the-road style. 'When fashion changes, my suits are still in vogue. Sometimes they only require moderate alteration to bring them into current fashion. Some of my suits are 20 years old,' the screen star said.

Business dress should be conservative in style rather than flamboyant. This does not suggest that business men and women should not dress with a certain flair. High style usually comes from the better stores and is more expensive than run-of-the-mill style clothes, but is well worth the extra purchase price. If you desire to be remembered by those you meet, dress immaculately and be well groomed at *all* times.

HOW TO CREATE ATTENTION WITHOUT OVERSELL

Screen star Kirk Douglas has a dynamic personality on and off the movie screen. 'As a young actor, I displayed my anger far too often and far too much. I was angry with injustice and the poverty of my youth. My first wife said to me, "Kirk, you keep working like you're desperately trying to become a star. You are a star." Her words hit home and I stopped pushing so hard,' he said.

Make your mark, but don't oversell your personality. When you try *too* hard to impress people, they sense your operation overkill and back away. A pounding personality becomes an irritating factor. Adjust the dynamics of your image projection to the personality of the person you are socializing or doing business with. Some people love to associate with persons who are flamboyant. Others see flamboyance as insincerity and a cover-up for some personality weakness. Project a strong personality without being overbearing, demanding, self centered, arrogant and abrasive.

HOW TO MAKE YOUR MARK WITHOUT BECOMING A THREAT

Presenting a strong, dynamic personality can be a drawback if the person you are confronting feels intimidated by your manner and voice tone. Don't talk down to or in any sense attempt to put down a person you wish to court. Regulate your voice tone. Don't speak louder than is necessary. A harsh-sounding voice can make a person feel threatened which could bring an angry response.

HOW TO BE DIFFERENT WITHOUT IMITATING OTHERS

While watching a television interview with singer Tony Bennett, I was interested in his comments concerning personality as a tool for success. 'It pays to be different. When people see you as different, they are attracted to you. The best way to be different, is to be yourself. Don't try to be something you are not or attempt to be an imitator,' the artist said.

A young singer I knew in Hollywood some years back is related to Frank Sinatra. He told me that early in his singing career he tried to imitate the style of his famous relative but it got him nowhere. 'An agent told me to be myself, to present my own style. I realized that if people wanted to listen to Frank Sinatra they wouldn't be content with a carbon-copy. They'd go for the original. Now, I sell me,' the singer told me.

You are original. There's no person quite like you. Others can copy your personality and talents but they can't *be* you. Don't imitate others, no matter how much they may impress you. Be yourself. If you aren't dynamically impressive, make yourself so.

HOW TO COMBINE YOUR INNER AND OUTER IMAGE PACKAGE

The power of your personality appeal is derived from combining and exposing your inner and outer qualities once they have been examined and spruced-up. Take a close look at the Value Analysis Chart and complete the picture as *you* see yourself. Begin an immediate image restoration program. Go to work on improving yourself. Neither under-estimate nor overestimate what you think and feel you are. Make a real effort to discover the very best in you, improve on it and then make the world aware of it.

INNER QUALITIES: self assurance, self discipline, determination, self respect, personal integrity, self loyalty, generosity, compassionate, tolerant, loving.

OUTER QUALITIES: well dressed, well groomed, energetic posture, controlled movement, expressive manner of speaking, creative presentation of personal talents.

VALUE ANALYSIS CHART

Name _____ Date _____

PERSONAL LIFE

I CONSIDER MY LIFE	ADEQUATE	CHANGE
(a) Friends — Relatives		
(b) Spiritual Growth		
(c) Mental Growth		
(d) Education		
(e) Organizations		
(f) Recreation:		
Sports		
Hobbies		
Exercise		
(g) Health		
(h) Problems		
(i) Self Image Qualities		

COMMENTS:_____
_____
_____

BUSINESS LIFE

MY BUSINESS LIFE IS	ADEQUATE	CHANGE
(a) Job Position		
(b) Job Performance		
(c) Income Level		
(d) Administrative Capacity		
(e) Decision Making Ability		
(f) Problem Solving Ability		
(g) Human Relations		
(h) Client Relations		
(i) Use of Time		
(j) Creativity		
(k) Tension/Anxiety/Stress		
(l) Projected Image		

COMMENTS:_____
_____
_____

IMAGE PROFILE CHART

Name_____ Date_____

Average

SELF ASSERTIVE								SELF EFFACING	**INNER**
ANIMATED								LISTLESS	**QUALITIES**
GENUINE								ARTIFICIAL	
OUTGOING								RESERVED	
CHEERFUL								MOROSE	
UNAFFECTED								SELF CONSCIOUS	
TIMID								AGGRESSIVE	
LONG-WINDED								TERSE	
VAGUE								CONCISE	
INHIBITED								SPONTANEOUS	
WARM								COLD	
TENSE								RELAXED	
RASH								CAUTIOUS	
BRISK								PONDEROUS	

BODY ATTITUDE	ENERGETIC								SLUGGISH	**OUTER**
	ERECT								SLUMPING	**QUALITIES**
	GRACEFUL								AWKWARD	
FACIAL EXPRESSION	EXCESSIVE								NONE	
	APPROPRIATE								INCONGRUOUS	
GESTURES	EXCESSIVE								NONE	
	APPROPRIATE								INCONGRUOUS	
SPEECH Quality:	LOUD								QUIET	
	PLEASING								IRRITATING	
Enunciation:	PRECISE								UNCLEAR	
Interest:	MONOTONOUS								COLORFUL	

DISTRACTIONS TO IMPROVE

HEAD _____
FACE _____
    EYEBROWS _____
    EYES _____
    MOUTH _____
SHOULDERS, ARMS, HANDS _____
LEGS, FEET _____
GENERAL BODY _____

FORMULAS TO GROW RICH

- People you do business with must see you as a person of high status, an impressive, dynamic and likeable personality who can be trusted. The greater the impression you create, the more effective you are as an entrepreneur.

- Analyze the image qualities you are presently exposing. Tag your plus and minus personality factors and begin an immediate program to improve them where required.

- You are being judged via the way you think, look, talk, listen and react. Ascertain how you present yourself to others and it could reveal valuable information to help you improve your personal and business relationships.

- Expand your *information* base. Embark upon a solid reading program. Begin with editorials then progress to self-improvement books, biographical and historical works and good novels. Expand your vocabulary. Visit art galleries, museums, places of historical and architectural interest. Attend concerts, plays, movies. Study people, places and things.

- Via your personality you have an opportunity to show the world what you are and what you can achieve. Sincerity in what you project is essential. Place a high value on your intelligence and talents and sell them to the world enthusiastically.

- Learn to get along with yourself and you will have no difficulty getting along with others. Low self esteem destroys your enthusiasm for success.

- Your level of dress and grooming can have a marked effect on those who meet you. Dress-up your physical appearance. Dress with style and flair but do not be too flamboyant.

- Don't oversell your personality. Be yourself. Sell your plus factors by allowing others to *note* them rather than you hitting them on the head with them. When you try too hard to impress people, they sense your overkill and back away.

- Improve your speech patterns and voice tone. Don't talk down or put down another person. When speaking to others show them the respect you desire from them.

- Communicate positive voice and body language. Be conscious of what your posture and gestures are indicating. Complete the Value Analysis Chart and the Image Profile Chart and you will be in a better position to assess your self and projected image qualities.

HOW TO PREPARE GOALS–WINNING STRATEGIES AND TACTICS

HOW TO PROGRAM YOUR AMBITIONS

Your future success can be brought forward at an accelerated rate via a specific plan of action which pinpoints your desires and outlines a sensible proposal for their fulfillment. An action plan is very much like a road map. It is a guide to your destination offering the most *direct* route in the shortest possible time.

The reason many people do not participate in the riches of life is because they are vague about what they really want and have no definite plan to bring about success. Vagueness in achievement-building is to be avoided at all costs. Until you formulate clearly in your mind *what* you want, *when* you want it and *how* you plan to become successful, you will make little progress. The degree of your progress is tied to the degree of your strategic planning. The more detailed information-base you can assemble, the easier and faster your ambitions will be realized.

Establish that what you seek is available to you. Commit yourself to a workable plan of action and then pursue your dreams until you experience them, rejoice in them and benefit from them. This procedure reduces wasted energy, saves valuable time and stimulates you to grasp opportunity and take on bigger and better challenges.

HOW TO ELIMINATE CONFUSION AND FRUSTRATION FROM GOAL-STRIVING

Be precise when making a list of your aims. Write down exactly what it is you desire to be, what you want to have and what you want to do in life. Think goals through. Assess them in your mind. Visualize them. This process reduces confusion and frustration in goal-setting and goal-striving.

It is important to detail every aspect of a goal you desire to achieve. It is not enough to say, 'I want to be rich'. You must state an actual amount, *why* you want it and *when* you want to receive it. Wealth does not fall into your bank account because you think it should or dream that it will. Wealth-attractors know that a detailed plan of action must be prepared and then actively worked on. Surround each goal with information. Call for facts, opinions, ideas and intelligently use this information to arrive at workable strategies and tactics to accomplish your dreams.

HOW TO GO ABOUT EXPANDING YOUR BANK BALANCE

Bank-balance builders will need to specify in actual terms the size of each deposit they wish to make, when each deposit is to be made and the action that needs to be taken to accrue wealth. Name the bank you desire to do business with. Meet the manager. Open an account. Fill out deposit slips with the amounts you intend to bank and forward date them. Visualize your monthly statement showing the desired balance. Accept that you are entitled to be financially independent and will be through goal planning and positive goal-striving.

HOW TO PREPARE YOUR GOALS LIST

Follow the Goals Chart and list your aims and objectives clearly and concisely. Place your personal goals list where it can be read every day. Don't file it away where it is out-of-sight and out-of-mind. Use it as a stimulus to keep you on track. Audit your progress at regular intervals and revise your strategies and tactics if necessary. Be flexible in this regard. Don't stick to an unworkable strategy if there is an easier and better way to achieve a particular project. Learn from your setbacks and use the information to enhance your next move.

The two rules to follow when preparing your goals list are these:

1: IDENTIFY AIMS AND OBJECTIVES IN SPECIFIC TERMS.
2: PREPARE A DETAILED STRATEGIES AND TACTICS ACHIEVEMENT FORMULA.

ESTABLISH A PRIORITY GOALS LIST

Goal-striving can be a time-consuming and energy-draining exercise. Therefore, it is wise to give serious consideration as to whether a particular desire is really worth pursuing. If you aren't totally committed to a project, chances are you will run out of steam when approaching the first hurdle. Establish that what you presently *think* you want is in fact what you actually *need* and want before embarking upon a campaign which could result in wasted effort.

The foundation of your goals success rests on the *commitment* you make to your detailed plan of action. You must be prepared to persevere when problems confront you and not give in easily. If you aren't prepared to see a project through to a positive conclusion because it isn't especially important, then don't waste valuable time and energy chasing it. Your weak commitment will destroy your incentive to win. This in turn, targets your project for failure.

When your goals list is complete, analyze it. Give each goal a rating from one to ten. If goals with a low rating aren't of benefit to you, eliminate them. Spend your time wisely. Go after important, valuable and beneficial needs, wants and desires which greatly add to your enjoyment, growth, well-being and financial independence.

WHY YOU SHOULD ESTABLISH AN OBJECTIVES TIME-FRAME TO SUCCEED

Many people desire to be financially well-off long before retirement. Others wish to gradually accumulate a nest egg they can rely on after retiring from business or the work force. Decide *when* you need financial independence and when you should start to taper-off your activities. Calculate the age you will be when you expect to complete your goals. Allow plenty of time to *enjoy* the fruits of your labor. Having accumulated a sizeable bank balance, some people go to their final resting place without benefit or enjoyment of the riches they've earned. Winning the riches of life doesn't always come easy. Plan your empire-building activities judiciously. Leave yourself plenty of time to bask in the glory of dreams realized.

THREE BASIC TIME-FRAMES TO FOLLOW

Separate goals into three time-frames. Short-term desires are those that are easiest to accomplish, usually under one year. Medium-term aims may require up to five years to complete. Long-term goals are those of a complex variety which could take up to ten years or more to achieve. Give each goal a commencement and completion date. Within each time-frame, establish progress check-dates at three-monthly intervals to audit your goals direction.

It is best to remember that you do not have time to do everything. It is sensible to take on aspirations that can be won within a certain time-frame and have a worthwhile value. Some inconsequential aims may not be worth even a minimum expenditure of your time. Neither undertax nor overtax your time, energy and capability

HOW TO CONVERT YOUR DREAMS INTO REALITY

Some people at a very early age know exactly what they want to do, want to have and become. They begin dreaming early. Sadly, some of these same people allow their dreams to remain dormant like unlit charcoal lying in a barbecue pit. The dreams have the *potential* to manifest if ignited. Drifting through life dreaming about wealth and success is, for them, far easier than chasing opportunity, confronting challenges and facing up to responsibility.

It's axiomatic that you need a dream to make a dream come true. However, a dream doesn't come true until action is taken to make it come true. Support your dreams with a burning desire to accomplish them. Get them up-and-running. Be enthusiastic, joyful, energetic and courageous as you set about attracting a triumphant life. You have an awesome power which you can use to *make* your dreams come true. The realization of your dreams begins and ends with *you*. Make the first move. Take the first step on your journey into lavish living, ever-expanding personal growth, self actualization and financial independence.

HOW TO GET YOUR MIND INTO GOAL-WINNING MODE

Your mind, which functions like a computer, requires an efficient program fed into it on a regular basis. If you lose more times than you win, chances are your mind is not being programmed correctly. It is easy to detect poor programming. If you are a pessimistic thinker, a person of low self esteem, constantly stressed, anxious, fearful, avoid making decisions and taking action, your mental input is set for achievement-losing mode.

The opinions we humans form, the judgements we make and the actions we take are based on the indoctrinations we have received and mentally accepted. Babies know nothing of success or failure. They grow into winners or losers after a steady stream of indoctrination from parents, teachers, religionists, friends, relatives and sections of the media. Prepare a program for your mind which stimulates and strengthens your aspirations. Take over the responsibility for your destiny. Maintain your own self direction. Indoctrinate yourself with the right concepts and you will set in motion the right actions. Program your mind for goal achievement. Keep your thoughts focused on winning and you will become that which you are capable of becoming.

AIM FOR THE VERY BEST IN LIFE

A young businessman attended one of my seminars on entrepreneurship. He told me that he put off buying a new car until he could pay for a Rolls Royce. 'I was 22 years of age when I purchased my dream car. I could have bought an inexpensive Japanese car, but I would not have been content driving it, so I waited, dreamed and worked toward buying the very best car available. I work to be able to afford the very best pleasures of life,' he told me.

If you tell yourself that owning a luxury automobile is beyond your means, you will never push yourself hard enough to be able to own one. I often hear people say, 'I bought this item because it is all I could afford.' That statement is a subscription to mediocrity — accepting less than the best, being content with less than the best. Don't be content with a second-rate job, second-rate clothes, a second-rate house, car or second-rate possessions of any kind. Stimulate your imagination, visualize owning the best of everything. Subscribe to *excellence* in the way you look, present yourself and market your skills and talents. The best in life can be yours to enjoy and will flow to you ceaselessly and endlessly once you identify your objectives, apply the law of opulent thinking and vigorously go after what you desire.

HOW AN AUSTRALIAN BUSINESSMAN MADE IT TO THE TOP

John Elliott is reported to be worth in excess of $75 million. This hard-working entrepreneur maintains that his success is due to an attitude of *love* of what he does. 'For me, work every day is a holiday. Sometimes I put in 100-hours a week. I love what I do. I love to kick my goals along, to see them unfolding. Success in business is very much a matter of establishing a set of sensible goals and maintaining the right attitude to the accomplishment of them,' he told a newspaper reporter.

THE TIME TO START KICKING YOUR GOALS ALONG IS NOW

Job improvement, starting a new business, taking an overseas holiday, buying a house, extending education, selecting a new wardrobe, getting married, making an important financial decision are actions easily put aside by procrastinators. Important decisions often require commitments, the shouldering of responsibilities. For some, the effort is just too much. Whatever goals you desire to achieve must have a start date attached to them if you expect to achieve them. Nothing ventured, nothing gained. Kick your goals along, *now*. Give them wings. Let them take off, soar and land successfully. Don't just dream about your goals. Get up, get out and achieve them.

ALIBI STOPPED HIS DREAM FROM BECOMING A REALITY

While on vacation in the south of Spain, I met an elderly gentleman working as a waiter in a restaurant I visited. He said to me: 'I'm only a waiter at the moment. I'd like to own my own restaurant.' I asked him why he hadn't taken that step earlier in his career. 'I've been waiting for the appropriate time,' he told me. Excuses are easy to make and far easier than arriving at decisions which require an action commitment. The elderly waiter could have realized his dream much earlier in life had he been prepared to take action, commit himself to his goal and take on the responsibility of business ownership.

GO OUT ON A LIMB

Don't put off until tomorrow what you can begin today. You have no guarantee that you will be around tomorrow. Take advantage of *time*. In all things, it is of the essence. To win goals, you have to take a chance; not on others, but on yourself. Don't be afraid to *go out on a limb*. That's where the fruit is. Take a chance. Do it *now*! You might just surprise yourself with a big win.

BE ALERT TO SMALL OPPORTUNITIES THAT COULD MAKE YOU RICH

One of the important elements of empire-building is the skill to spot opportunities others miss — seeing something *big* in something small. Some businesspersons I know are myopic. They keep their eyes and ears fixed in the same direction as their competitors when they should be exploring other directions. It's called myopically following a trend. Following a trend is ok, providing you happen to get in early. If you are last in, you only pick up the scraps others before you have dropped.

When the mass are turning right, you head left. Do the *opposite* and you are likely to discover something worthwhile which could make you a fortune. Don't overlook what might appear to be small opportunties. From them could arise ideas for something big. A budding entrepreneur saw potential in developing a little valve to put in cans so they would release liquid. From the aerosol spray can he became a billionaire.

The statement I wish to make in this section is simply this: don't be content to stick with a conventional goals list. Keep your eyes and ears open for unusual wealth-making opportunities staring you in the face. The person who won't listen is far more disadvantaged than the person who can't hear. The person who can't be bothered looking is poorer than the person who can't see. Sharpen your awareness and perception of things around you. Come alive to opportunity. It's the way to grow rich.

AN EYE FOR OPPORTUNITY RAISED HELEN FROM TEA MAKER TO BANK CHIEF

Helen Lynch began her career making tea and coffee before climbing the corporate ladder to an appointment as general manager of Westpac Banking Corporation's South Australia and Northern Territory divisions. She is the first woman to hold this senior position. In 1989, she was named Businesswoman of the Year, an Aussie accolade she is justly proud of. 'One of the attributes that has helped me is an ability to identify an opportunity and then going for it. I've always demonstrated that I am flexible and adaptable and a person with lots of initiative,' she said.

Helen's other ingredients for success include: never letting people bluff her, facing up to challenge, being well organized and maintaining a smiling disposition. Her achievement ingredients aren't out of the ordinary. But her application of them has made Helen Lynch an extraordinary person.

HOW TO MAKE EACH GOAL AN OBJECT OF YOUR AFFECTION

Millions of people are imprisoned in a job rut. They work zombie-like in a trade, business or profession hating the work they do, living without hope of financial independence and personal satisfaction. Bored zombie-workers concentrate on filling-in time. They daydream about what might have been. They lead a Walter Mitty existence. This dissipation of time, energy and creativity, results in haphazard and un-co-ordinated career direction, attracting further boredom, anxiety and frustration.

If you wish employment fulfillment, you must enjoy the work you do. Working at what excites you, stimulates your creativity and engrosses your time and attention, eliminates boredom and attracts many wonderful experiences and rich blessings. Decide on the trade, business or profession you wish to enter. Get yourself trained to handle it. Move out of your job rut. You are not a victim of circumstances, conditions or

70

environment unless you allow yourself to be. You can attract and move into the work of your choice by deciding to make a new world for yourself, a world of job freedom and security.

HOW TO JUMP-OFF LIFE'S TREADMILL

People grow to greatness through facing up to challenges, taking calculated risks and grasping opportunities when they see them. People lose out in life through dissipation of their personal power, procrastination, physical laziness and a reluctance to give the very best that's in them. Mentally and physically-lazy people are on life's treadmill. They see no escape. They hold little hope of anything better than what they have.

Your fortune is not to be found in some far-off land. It is right where you are. Your opportunity to jump off life's treadmill presents itself *now*. You can rise above the misfortune and limitation of the world through a mental and emotional bond with the goals you set for yourself. The good life begins with you. It streams into your existence via your attitudes, beliefs and actions. The power to accomplish big things, to attract life's riches is locked in your subconscious mind. You hold the key. It is up to you to unlock the force that can dramatically alter your penny-a-day existence and turn it into a rich-person's paradise. It is within your power *today* to transform your life, to win goals, to be rich and to experience happiness.

HOW TO ORGANIZE YOURSELF FOR GOAL-SEEKING EFFICIENCY

Much of the effort you put forth can often be wasted if you aren't organized. Personal efficiency revolves around the best use of time and organized effort. A day-to-day diary is essential for the business person. This reminder of appointments and activities is also a time-organizer and a daily goals-scheduler. It keeps you on track. It helps you to avoid tension build-up due to disorganization. Proper organization of your time and energy-expenditure brings greater productivity, a happier disposition and less fatigue.

If you are always short of time, never seem to complete assignments, fatigued, tense and irritable, then take a close look at your daily routine. Are you spending too much time on routine matters that could be handled by others? How long does it take you to drive to and from work? Is there a shorter route? Are you taking long coffee and lunch breaks? Do you spend too much time on the phone? How much work do you actually get done during regular work periods?

Discover ways of doubling your effectiveness, of taking less time and expending less energy on each task you undertake. Conduct your own time and motion study of your daily work routine. Clock yourself. Check your actions. How efficiently do you operate within a given time span? Your daily goals achievement will improve greatly when you organize yourself, become *time* conscious and work to a written schedule.

GROUP ALLIANCE GIVES YOU A LEG-UP TO GOALS ACHIEVEMENT

The associates you select to do business with, socialize with or occasionaly meet, can form an important alliance with you which furthers your objectives and makes goals-striving easier. Ally yourself with as many people as you may require for the carrying out of your plans. Enlist the aid of those who have the knowledge, experience and skills that you lack. Be sure to join forces with people you can easily harmonize with. Their attitudes should not conflict with your own. Their concepts should inspire you, cement your determination to succeed and rouse your enthusiasm for achievement excellence.

Move into the circle of the successful. Taper-off relationships with those who are negative thinkers, unambitious, dishonest and physically lazy. Surround yourself with those who are sympathetic with your ideas and ideals. Co-operation with others of like-mind and the blending of various talents and ideas of others with your own, creates a powerful *action-alliance group.*

HOW AN INSURMOUNTABLE GOAL WAS ACCOMPLISHED

I read an article in a newspaper which supported my belief that the seemingly-impossible can be accomplished through determination. A group of seven blind Africans, all young, set as their goal a daring adventure — to climb Mt. Kilimanjaro and reach its 19,340 foot peak. It took the team just four days to achieve their goal. 'We wanted to prove that no handicap is beyond overcoming when one desires strongly enough to achieve a goal,' was the comment of one of the climbers. This amazing feat of courage and strength as well as determination, is an example of what can be accomplished through personal initiative and unshakable belief. *All things be ready, if the mind be so.*

SUPPORT YOUR GOALS WITH STRONG INCENTIVES

Your dreams will spring forth and be fulfilled when you take firm *controlled* action. They will carry greater value and reward if you give yourself specific and worthy incentives for their accomplishment. Your personal incentives should go beyond just wanting to make money or see your name in the hall of fame. Henry Ford's interest in success went beyond making money. His personal dream was to give all Americans an opportunity to buy one of his automobiles at a price they could afford. He did it through mass production. Accomplishing his dream made him outstandingly wealthy. The United States is one of the richest countries on earth. It doesn't produce miracles because it is capitalist, but because its basic philosophy is *free enterprise.* It encourages those who want to improve their lot in life to do so.

Your incentive for the attainment of a particular goal should possess an in-built benefit not only for yourself, but for others as well. If you want to be a wealthy person, make sure your wealth is used to spread good, not evil. Don't bury your money 'under a mattress' where it lies dormant, isn't beneficially used, enjoyed or multiplied. Use your wealth to build, develop, extend knowledge and open further doors to opportunity. Say to yourself: 'I am getting rich. In the process, I am making others rich.'

WHAT YOU ARE SEEKING IS SEEKING YOU

Many people fail to realize their ambitions because they follow the path of *least* resistance, the *wrong* path or continually look in the wrong direction. The driving force to rise higher in life, to develop skills, to gain knowledge is secreted within your desires. The answer to your problem, your worry, your setback, your fear, your challenge, is *within*, not without. The Guiding Principle of the universe is resident within you. It can inspire you, sustain you, protect you and guide you in wonderful ways if you attune to It. This Infinite Intelligence knows all, sees all. It gave you the idea and will reveal the plan to accomplish your idea. Open your mind. Join forces with the Intelligence of Life. *One with God is a majority.*

Frustration at your snail's-pace progress in life is the Life Force welling up within you, urging you to take positive action. When this occurs, muster your mind power and get moving. Call on your subconscious to reveal answers to your problems and challenges. What you seek in life is seeking you, but you must go out and *discover* the treasures which surround you and are available to you in limitless and inexhaustible supply.

> *Somebody said it couldn't be done, but he with a chuckle replied that "maybe it couldn't," but he would be one who wouldn't say so until he'd tried.*
> — EDGAR A. GUEST.

GOALS CHART

Name:

NO	SHORT TERM (1 YEAR)	START DATE	AUDIT DATE	COMPLETE DATE	PROGRESS REPORT	STRATEGIES (PLANNING)	TACTICS (ACTION)
1							
2							
3							
4							
5							
1							
2							
3							
4							
5							
1							
2							
3							
4							
5							

FORMULAS TO GROW RICH

- Your success can be achieved at an accelerated rate via a specific plan of action which pinpoints your desires and outlines a sensible proposal for their fulfillment.

- Be precise when listing your aims in life. Write down *exactly* what you want. This process reduces confusion and frustration and puts everything into proper perspective.

- Identify your aims and objectives, prepare a detailed strategies and tactics plan, then take action. Audit your progress. Be flexible and revise your plans if they do not enhance your position.

- Separate goals into three time frames. Establish a value on each goal and work on accomplishing what is important to you. Don't waste time and energy on worthless pursuits, valueless objectives. Life is precious. Make the best use of it.

- Don't be content with *second* best. Aim high. Start kicking goals now. Go after a new job, a better car, a new home, higher education, financial security. Commit yourself to achieving a prosperous and creatively-rewarding lifestyle.

- Keep your eyes and ears open to opportunity. Look for it everywhere. When you spot an opportunity, grab it. Don't be a procastinator.

- Support your goals with strong personal motives. Think of serving humanity as well as your own needs. Share your good fortune. When you establish noble motives for the things you desire, you will reap noble benefits and prosper beyond your dreams.

- The answer to all your problems, all your worries, all your needs, all your ambitions, is within your subconscious mind. What you are seeking is seeking you. Go *within*, not without to start empire-building. The power to succeed is within *you*.

- Don't be a zombie-worker. If you are in a job rut, get out of it. Get yourself trained in something worthwhile. You are not a victim of circumstance or environment unless you allow yourself to be. Jump off life's treadmill. Take on challenges.

- Get yourself organized. Be ever mindful of time. Use a day-to-day diary to log your appointments, activities and goals. Keep yourself on-track. Keep up the attack. Join the ranks of the successful. Join with like-minded achievers who stimulate your thinking and give you a leg-up the ladder of success.

HOW TO RISE FROM FOLLOWER TO LEADER

FORMULA 7

HOW TO GET OTHERS TO SEE YOU AS A LEADER

People who really count, those with their own power and influence, must see you as a person with strong leadership potential. If you desire to make it big in a corporate career or as a free-enterprise entrepreneur, you need to get people to sit up and take notice of you — to recognize you as a self power. Your personal presentation dynamics, therefore, must strike favorably and *instantly* important people meet you. You must quickly get yourself in the business of creating strong first impressions which set you apart from people in general.

Leaders are special people. They are seen to be *different*. To advance socially and professionally, you must get the right people to see *you* as different. As discussed in an earlier chapter, good impressions are created through voice and body language, dress and grooming excellence and a display of intelligence. Other impression-creating attributes include: strength of character, social popularity, achievement record, knowledge, speaking ability, etc. The more visible your individuality, the more dynamic the impression. The stronger the impression, the greater self power you command. The more self power you display, the more others see you as a natural leader.

Persons who hold leadership aspiration should not be content to let others do their thinking for them. While it might be less worrisome to take a back seat in life, the rewards are small. Leadership has many in-built advantages which, to my mind, far outweigh the responsibilities the role demands. Establish an unshakable desire for greatness. It will prove to be the turning point in your life.

LEADERSHIP BENEFITS COME AT A PRICE

Joining the leadership ranks is a matter of cheerfully paying the price. Membership calls on you to use all your courage to concentrate on the goals you set, to have high and sustained determination, to believe in your capability of greatness and to refuse to accept that there are circumstances, conditions or events sufficiently strong enough to defeat you.

If you want to be taken seriously as a leader, pay the price leadership demands. Strengthen your resolve to win. Utilize the latent powers within you to elevate your position in life. Visualize yourself in a leadership role. Lead yourself out of life's wilderness and into a new environment which challenges, inspires and motivates you to become a leader rather than a follower.

HOW TO LEAD YOURSELF TO SUCCESS IN BUSINESS

Whether you know it or not, you are in business for yourself even though you may work for someone else and be regarded as an 'employee'. You sell to your boss specific talents, skills and services. The boss then uses your efforts in a particular way to produce and sell a product or service. Both of you are in business with a common aim — to earn a living via the utilization and exploitation of what each has to market.

The smart business owner develops employees by using their abilities productively and places them where their knowledge and experience can best be used. As a broker of your own services, you should do the same thing. Take note of your general and special abilities and offer them where they can be utilized at a price which reflects their value. Manage yourself effectively. Don't undersell your talents and human potential. Bring to the attention of others your very special qualities.

The best path up the corporate ladder is the path you lead yourself through initiative. Do more than is asked of you. Show others that you aren't afraid to take on challenges, accept responsibility, spend extra hours on a project and work hard. Superiors will quickly become aware of your leadership potential. They will see you as management material and want to seal an alliance with you. Your climb to the top as a company person is determined by your display of dynamic action.

HOW TO GET PEOPLE TO RESPOND FAVORABLY TO YOU

In order to get others to see you as important and to respond favorably to you, it is essential that they feel that you regard *them* as important. If you treat people rudely, with an arrogant display of self importance, talk down to them, make them feel inferior in some way, your people relationships will quickly deteriorate. When meeting or doing business with others, bestow importance on them. This needs to be carried out with sincerity, not in an obsequious way.

Give each person you meet your full attention. Don't allow minor distractions to take your attention from the person you are speaking to. Hold eye contact, repeat his or her name frequently throughout the discussion and allow the other person to express viewpoints without constant interruption. In other words, give your partner the full high-status treatment. The importance you bestow on another, returns to you in the form of a better person-to-person social or business relationship.

OTHERS MUST SEE YOU AS PROBLEM FREE

Somehow, leaders aren't supposed to be affected by common everyday worries and problems. After all, that's why they are leaders, they are able to quickly dispense with such things. If people have marked you as a leader, you must stay within your ivory tower or your fans will be disappointed in you. You must refrain from negative conversation, gossip, criticism of your family, friends, business associates. Keep your worries and problems out of the public domain. There can be no place in your life for self pity, depression and gloom, particularly when you are in the presence of others.

Say nothing if you cannot express something uplifting, cheerful or constructive about a person, place or thing. This does not mean that you should refrain from commenting on important business or public matters which require critical comment. Express your viewpoint in a forceful way if necessary but rationally and intelligently. Don't whine, complain unnecessarily, display intolerance or prejudice. Remember, people listening to you and watching you are *judging* you. It is essential that they hold you in high esteem. Don't let them down. Show them that you are what they *hope* you are — a solid, sincere, straight-forward person of *real* importance.

> **You cannot be buried in obscurity: you are exposed upon a grand theater to the view of the world. If your actions are upright and benevolent, be assured they will augment your power and happiness.**
> —CYRUS

HOW TO SEPARATE YOURSELF FROM THE CONFORMISTS

If you desire to be a person others notice, admire, respect and accept as a leader, it will be necessary to separate yourself from the crowd — conformists, negative thinkers, average types. Don't worry about conforming. Don't feel ashamed, embarrassed or ever apologize for your non-conformist attitudes and actions — providing, of course, they are honestly based. Conformists are usually dull types, boring types, unimpressive types. They possess attitudes that conform, personalities that conform, careers that conform and the result is a less than satisfactory lifestyle.

It has been said that the ladder of success is crowded with conformists huddled on the bottom rung, all frightened and too embarrassed to leave the security of the crowd. As a self power, you cannot afford to mix in these circles. Conformists are followers, marked by the same uniformity of dullness, ignorance and fear. You must escape from the conformists' comfort zone. You must be anything other than 'average', anything other than frightened, ignorant, morose, unambitious and non-creative. You must stop being a nobody and start becoming a somebody with a clearly-visible individuality, a dynamic, unique and *different* person instantly recognized as a leader.

USE THE OPPOSITE TECHNIQUE TO DRAW ATTENTION TO YOURSELF

It is my opinion that the majority of people are negative by nature. Monitor the conversations of family, friends and business associates and you will discover that, more times than not, discussions are predominantly negative. Topics ranging from the weather to finances and lifestyle are nearly always downbeat. Many people love to complain. They readily run-off at the mouth, bore others with their problems and worries. Don't join their ranks. Whenever you become involved in a discussion and the conversation turns negative, immediately inject a positive statement. This draws attention away from the negative speaker and centers it on the positive speaker.

YOU DON'T NEED A UNIVERSITY DEGREE TO BECOME A LEADER

Your education, knowledge, skills, all contribute to your rise to leadership status. In addition, you must *see* yourself in the leadership role. You must *believe* that the qualities you possess are the qualities leadership demands. You don't require a university degree, a diploma hanging on your wall which spells out 'leader'. You need to be a free-thinker, a doer, a courageous, persistent person possessing worthy ideas and ideals with the will to win. Jump into a new, vital and exciting stream of consciousness. Lift yourself from the also-rans into the front ranks and run with the winners.

The measurement of your leadership and personality attraction lies in the impression you make on others — how well you show off your good points. Don't be nervous about displaying your honesty, creativity, self confidence, talents and skills. Develop and display a strong, non-apologetic front which stamps you as a person with backbone, a person with total self control, a liege of no one.

DON'T PLACE YOURSELF IN COMPETITION WITH OTHERS

You have no one to compete with and no one to fear except your imagination and the idea that you aren't as good as the next person. You are unique. There isn't another soul on the face of the earth who can *exactly* duplicate your thought, feeling and action. Therefore, stop putting up barriers to your progress by thinking you have to fight so-called competitors. All that really counts is, can you do the job you're being paid to do? If the answer is in the affirmative, go ahead and do it without looking over your shoulder in trepidation of someone taking something from you, exposing you or jumping ahead of you.

Your self assurance needs to be boosted if you are fearful of competition. The reality of life is that there are countless numbers of people who aspire to high achievement and success: accountants, actors, bankers, bakers, janitors, lawyers, mechanics, restaurateurs, tailors, waiters, etc. Even though others may be in the same business, trade or profession you are in and vying for the same position or business, you are *different* and will be seen to be different when you package and present yourself in a unique and dynamic way. This gives you an edge over so-called competitors.

Raise your self concept to high-value status. Show-off your skills and talents. Impress others with your confidence, straight-forward attitude and initiative. Cease wasting time competing with also-rans. The practice is self defeating and humiliating. You are supreme. You possess the potential to become whatever you desire to become. Your job is to arrest the attention of those in a position to use and reward you for your talents and uniqueness.

THE MAN AS LEADER

Leadership does not mean treating those who follow you in a poor way. Your self power and leadership status must not be used to browbeat, humiliate or treat others in a dishonest or unfair manner. Whatever you take from another, do to another, you take from and do to yourself. In dealing with followers, be courteous, friendly, helpful, but firm when the occasion demands it. Be a person of your word. Your personal integrity is an important leadership quality. Personal integrity breeds respect — even from your enemies. Be tolerant of those who haven't as yet reached your degree of success. Encourage them, praise them and lend a hand to them. Recognize the ingredients of leadership and follow them.

LEADERSHIP SECRETS REVEALED BY FAMOUS GENERAL

'Don't expect people to follow you if you aren't prepared to stand up for your beliefs,' said General Douglas MacArthur. The famous former leader believed in his ability to command, to take on challenging tasks with supreme confidence to win. 'If you haven't the strength to resist fear, you have no self confidence and small chance of success. Be unafraid of challenge. Wade into the tasks you set for yourself and keep at them until victory is experienced.' And, maintained the General, 'Your security is your ability to produce results.'

THE WOMAN AS LEADER

Women are carving a nice position for themselves as leaders, business managers and free-enterprise entrepreneurs. Business is no longer dominated by the male. Women have historically been denied business opportunities. Today, women are proving that they can succeed as competently as any male. They are prepared to take risks, work hard, put in long hours and rise to the top on their own initiative.

A fraction over half of today's millionaires in the United States are women. More than 30-percent of Australian businesses are owned or run by women and they are nearly twice as successful as men. It's also interesting to note, twice as many women as men are starting new enterprises in Canada and the USA.

Some women believe that it is important to compete with the male by being aggressive and emulating the male executive. This strategy is unwise and should be avoided. Retain femininity at all costs. It is a *plus* factor. Naturally, it is important to understand how men think and why they act as they do. This information is a clue as to how best to deal with them. But don't copy them or try to compete with them on their level. It's time and energy wasting. Use your talents and skills in a non-competitive way, in a pleasing, feminine way. You will quickly establish your own importance and be seen as a leader.

HOW TO AVOID ARROGANCE AND DESPAIR IN LEADERSHIP ROLE

The richest woman in Asia, Sally Aw Sian, also known as the Tiger Balm heiress of Singapore, has global enterprises covering publishing, real estate, tourist services, pharmaceutical manufacturing and sound recording. Miss Aw comes across as a straight-forward person. She is respected for her acute business acumen and control. She maintains: 'Life's challenges spur you on to greater efforts, train you to meet subsequent challenges and finally provide you with the moral and spiritual fibre to avoid arrogance in success and despair in failure.' Although she classifies herself as an 'ordinary' person, Miss Aw projects leadership qualities admired by those who have met and conducted business with her.

THE CHARACTER FACTOR SEPARATING FOLLOWERS FROM LEADERS

One of the special character traits separating followers from leaders is determination. Achievers need a high degree of stay-with-it-ness if they are to successfully overcome setbacks. Don't be thrown by unexpected adversity. Don't be afraid of a little opposition or fearful of temporary defeat. Failure isn't terminal until you decree it so. Keep on trying, even when the odds seem to be against you. Use adversity as a bridge to success.

When faced with temporary defeat, discover *why* your project has stalled and *how* it can be guided in the right direction. Don't sit waiting for a miracle to happen. Use *creative thought* to generate a solution to your problem. Be determined to see your project through to a satisfactory conclusion. Don't give in. Keep going. At the next turn in the road is your destination. Your *determination* to achieve, to succeed, to win, ranks you as a leader, a person of special status destined for outstanding accomplishment.

> The one I am sadly salutes the one I could have been
> — HEBBEL

HOW A NOBODY BECAME A SOMEBODY THROUGH DETERMINATION

He came from humble beginnings and was mostly self taught, but he was a man of drive, with an unusual degree of determination. One of his first ventures was to take up storekeeping. It failed. He then became an engineer, but this also failed when a hard-nosed sheriff sold his surveying instruments to pay debts. Undaunted, he tried again. He joined the army and fought in an American Indian war. He made the rank of captain only to be demoted to private and sent home because his 'performance was poor'.

The young man was determined to get ahead in life. He fell in love with a young girl and they were engaged to be married. Tragedy struck. The girl died. Lonely, depressed and heart-broken, the young man decided to fully occupy his mind with study for a law practice. Eventually, he opened an office. He couldn't make ends meet because he won very few cases. He decided he would enter the political arena but on his first try was defeated.

With so many failures behind him, the young man became even more determined to succeed. He stood for political office again and was elected. The nation came to know him as Honest Abe. Abraham Lincoln was a noble person, a man of overall vision with the determination to keep trying, to push aside adversity and succeed.

RETAIN LEADERSHIP CONFIDENCE ADVISES MARGARET THATCHER

Considered to be one of the toughest leaders in Britain's political history, former Prime Minister, Margaret Thatcher, had to constantly defend her imperious leadership style. 'A leader must lead firmly, have strong convictions and see that those convictions are reflected in every decision that is made. Leaders cannot afford to waiver or think of giving in when challenged,' is Mrs. Thatcher's view. Self confidence, determination and the ability to withstand criticism are exceptional Thatcher qualities admired by friend and foe of the former leader.

LEADERSHIP ROLE ISN'T FOR THE FAINT HEARTED

Leadership demands frighten some people — especially the weak-minded, life-shirkers and time-wasters. Running your own show demands that you accept responsibility for the decisions and actions you take. Offering yourself as a leader isn't going to work if you aren't prepared to stand up and fight for what you believe is right.

A lawyer I know was asked to lead a community group and he accepted the task without giving much thought to his responsibility as chairman. He saw a benefit to his law practice. After a month, he quit. 'They wanted me to assume responsibility for the decisions I made. Why should I stick my neck out for the benefit of others?' he asked. 'Because that's the price leadership demands,' I replied.

Some people do not want to become leaders because they are quite happy with their lives, do not want to feel pressured by a responsible role and fear ridicule if they do not perform as expected. These things are pretty much the reason 96-percent of the world's population are designated as followers and only 4-percent as leaders.

HOW TO DEVELOP A POSITIVE PROPAGANDA MACHINE FOR YOURSELF

Most of us have been brainwashed from birth with information which has influenced our way of thinking, feeling, believing and acting. Once attitudes form, we become a propaganda machine, repeating the concepts and beliefs we hold. Repeating false concepts and erroneous beliefs through ignorance of truth, leads eventually to personal downfall. It keeps us from creative achievement, limits our ability to accumulate riches and smothers our leadership potential.

Your personal propaganda machine is an effective publicity tool and should reflect your desires in a positive way. Therefore, it may be necessary to reprogram your personal publicity machine with affirmative concepts so that your cause is helped, not hindered. Feed it suggestions which inspire you, boost your confidence, broaden your projected image qualities and motivate you to tackle worthy challenges and opportunities. Positive brainwashing thrusts you into the success arena where you have an excellent chance of elevating yourself to greatness.

THE TWO KINDS OF LEADERS

There are two kinds of leaders: those who do the job through their own knowledge and skill and those who get the job done through the knowledge and skill of others. The delegation of tasks where numbers of persons are involved is an important function of the corporate leader. Delegation is more than allotting duties. It is giving authority and responsibility as well as encouragement and praise to those who become a sub-leader.

If you are able to function as decision-maker and action-taker then you have an advantage over those who must trust others to carry out important tasks. You have only *yourself* to rely on. For those who must work through others, a favorable working relationship needs to be established. Allow sub-leaders an opportunity to make decisions in routine matters. Show them that you trust them and have a high regard for their skills, talents and initiative.

MOTIVATING SUBORDINATES THROUGH LEADERSHIP SKILL

A leader must motivate followers to become loyal assistants and take on tasks willingly. Rule by force, intimidation or threat is unproductive. I once asked a construction worker on a building site how he felt when his foreman barked out the order: 'Get your backside off that seat, pick up that broom and clean up.' 'The job had to be done and I did commanded,' the man told me. 'Yes, but how did you feel about the command?' 'I wanted to break that broom over his head,' was the reply.

Create a friendly working relationship with subordinates in which it is easy to exchange ideas and express feelings. Because no two people are alike, we can make ourselves 'understood' and 'listened to' only by adjusting ourselves to each individual that we talk to, by 'sensing' the emotional response and not treading on the other person's self esteem.

Communicate your instructions firmly, fairly and clearly. Give the other person a chance to express grievances or present reasons why a task should be carried out differently to instructions. It may not change things but it reduces resentment and argument. Perhaps there is validity in what the other person expresses. At least, *listen*. As a leader, getting others to do what you want them to do will depend on your attitude toward them, your charm of manner, the incentives you offer them and your ability to enter into the interests, viewpoints and objectives they have.

DON'T HARD SELL PEOPLE

Some people go into a 'hard sell' mode when requesting others to carry out tasks. When you oversell your instructions you reduce your leadership power and effectiveness. Others become suspicious of your motives and if they do respond under pressure, it is usually with great reluctance.

Straight-forward requests should be that and no more. Don't embellish them, carry on about them or build-up their importance. Difficult requests or demands may need to be fully explained and a convincing argument put forth to get others to willingly carry them out. When you become a self power most people are going to have a reasonable if not high regard for you and in most instances will go along with your requests even though they may not always agree with you. Generally, all you need to do is state what you want in simple terms without trying to coerce anyone into action. When the thinking of others is undecided or opposed to yours, you may require a 'soft sell' approach to win them over.

When you need to make your thinking win, the best course of action is to state your position in a way which does not put others at a disadvantage or bring them under a stern threat of reprisal if they do not perform. What you seek is voluntary co-operation and the best way to achieve this is to convince others that what is good for you is also good for them in some way.

APPRECIATION AND COMPLIMENTS ARE STRATEGY MOTIVATORS

Compliment a subordinate who has carried out an assignment well. A few well-chosen words of praise sincerely expressed will be appreciated by the recipient and likely to motivate greater productivity on his or her part. Don't hesitate complimenting others on dress, grooming, attitude, loyalty, intelligence, honesty, willingness to work hard, etc. Appreciate those who work with you or for you when they go out of their way to assist your cause. A leader must motivate followers to become loyal,

...d productive assistants. A 'thank you' and a pat on the back ...nted will pay handsome dividends.

...) IMPROVE YOUR LEADERSHIP SKILL

...oping harmonious human relationships is essential if leadership is you... aim. To get along with people you need to *understand* people — the way they think and feel. Study your own attitudes and feelings. Are you thoughtful, helpful and flexible? Are you easily offended by the remarks of others? What motivates you to help others achieve their aims in life? Can you shake off feelings of envy, hate, jealousy, prejudice, anger? Do you resent being directed by others? Are you a team person or a loner? Discover your own behavior patterns and try to understand them. All of your emotions are consistent with them, so it is important to come to grips with them. The more readily you understand yourself, the easier it will be to establish beneficial social and business relationships. Even a very basic understanding of human psychology advantages you over those who are ignorant of it. When you know the truth about yourself, you will discover the truth about human personality generally.

REMOVE EXCESS BAGGAGE AND YOU WILL SUCCEED AS A LEADER

The axiom, *birds of a feather flock together*, should be noted by those lined up at the leadership counter. Timid, insecure, weak persons seek solace in the company of others of like personality. Forming any sort of association with weak-minded persons is a recipe for failure. No time-waster, procrastinator, negative thinker can be of positive service to any individual seeking power and wealth. No potential leader can afford to associate with wimps, whingers, vagabonds and layabouts.

When you associate with losers you *become* a loser. You carry excess baggage which is a severe burden to your progress. Disengage yourself from directionless, vacillating, immoral, dishonest life-wasters. Be hard-nosed about it. Dump them. Associate with those who have similar objectives to your own, who want to smash seemingly-impenetrable obstacles to control their destiny and prosper. Move immediately. Your time on this earth is limited. Account for every second of it. Discover with others a rich and rewarding lifestyle that is open to you — open to *all* who pursue it ambitiously and honestly.

HOW TO RISE FROM PRIVATE TO FIELD MARSHAL

Napoleon once said: 'Every soldier has a marshal's baton in his knapsack.' The army never tires of telling its soldiers the same thing. The potential to rise from loser to winner, employee to employer, servant to master, is within everyone. Sadly, some people are content to remain followers. They feel comfortable and secure in this role, preferring to let others make decisions for them, take actions on their behalf and, in general, do their day-to-day thinking for them.

TWO SOLDIERS WHO TOOK NOTE OF NAPOLEON'S DECREE

Viscount William Slim, rose from the ranks to become a field marshal and a great leader of men. He commanded the 14th Army in Burma, during the Second World War, turning defeat into victory. He served as Governor-General of Australia from 1953 to 1960. He was a man highly-respected for his leadership skill. He never hesitated to speak his mind and to stand behind the decisions he made. His rise from private to field marshal was due to his great inner strength, determination and exemplary character.

Viscount Bernard Law Montgomery, gained his marshal's baton via his leadership skill. A bishop's son, he dedicated himself to study high command. He took over the Eighth Army in the Egyptian desert in August 1942, when Rommel was almost at Cairo. His desert victories were a turning point for the British after many depressing defeats. His great quality, besides an intellectual mastery of his profession, was his self confidence which infected his troops. Some historians rank him as possibly the greatest British soldier since Wellington. As a leader, he combined simplicity with force and clarity. He was intensely thorough in the preparation and administration of all his battles.

A COMMENT ON A GREAT LEADERSHIP FEAT

The US-led effort in the Gulf War in 1991, is an example of sheer leadership-management skills which will surely be the object of analysis for decades. Generals Powell and Schwarzkopf and their staffs in tandem with leaders from 27 other countries had to co-ordinate an enormously complex, large-scale operation for the achievement of a specific task. The mobilization and movement of the allied forces was one of the greatest transport operations in history. The emphasis on *planned* priorities gave the operation cohesiveness and a real sense of purpose. The leaders knew what they were doing.

The indisputable achievements of the leaders of the Gulf War point to the following applied techniques which can be used in a variety of business situations:

1: Carefully-planned objectives.
2: Control over every aspect of the operation.
3: Harmonious, clear-cut chain of command.
4: Unwavering belief in the final outcome of aims.
5: Determination to stick to uncompromising priorities.

FIX THE THOUGHT PATTERN AND YOUR SUBCONSCIOUS WILL DO THE REST

Aspire to be a leader, a person of immutable character and incorruptible strength. Identify mentally, emotionally and spiritually with this idea and your subconscious will bring it to pass. A pure, noble mind is seldom affected by negative circumstances and events. It stands solid, hopeful and eager to take on challenges. It lifts you above mediocrity and rewards you with the life supreme.

> **One virtue stands out above all others: the constant striving upwards, wrestling with oneself, the unquenchable desire for greater purity, wisdom, goodness and love.**
>
> — GOETHE

FORMULAS TO GROW RICH

- People who really count must see you as a person of strong leadership potential. Therefore, it is essential to get people to sit up and take notice of you — to see you as important. Your personal presentation must strike others instantly and favorably. Strive to be 'different', confident and powerful.

- Others must see you as a problem-free individual, a person able to handle everyday pressures and challenges. Avoid self pity, fits of depression. Take control of your emotions.

- You have the potential to rise to whatever heights you set for yourself. Don't remain a follower when you could become a leader. The field marshal's baton is already in your knapsack.

- Lead yourself to great heights via personal initiative. Leadership comes at a price. Take on challenges. Don't be afraid to exploit your full potential, to go after big objectives. Inspire and motivate yourself to explore new horizons, develop the personality you want and achieve the degree of success you seek.

- Expose your special talents and skills. As a broker of your own services, place a value on them and sell them effectively. Show personal initiative. Let others of importance know that you aren't afraid of hard work, of making decisions and taking on responsibility.

- Don't be a dull conformist. Develop an individualist approach to life. Become anything other than 'average'. The day you seek to become a somebody you stop being a nobody. Your personal security in life is tied to your ability to produce results, to achieve and exploit your creative potential. Don't let yourself down.

- As a leader you will need to motivate others to help you, form a bond with you and carry out the tasks you assign them in a friendly and willing way. Do not try to rule others by force. Offer incentives. Be charming. Be fair. Listen to the other person's point-of-view. Express appreciation for help given. Be complimentary.

- To get along with people you need to *understand* people — how they think and feel. Study your own thoughts, feelings and actions. Know the truth about yourself. It will help you to understand people in general.

- Associate with persons who are great or with those aspiring to become great. You can't ride to success on the back of a loser, time-waster or negative thinker.

HOW TO STRENGTHEN
YOUR POWER-BASE
AS A DYNAMIC
COMMUNICATOR

FORMULA **8**

HOW TO BUILD A POWER-BASE AS YOU TALK

Entrepreneurship calls for superior communication skill — the technique of 'getting through' to people. To become a dynamic communicator, it is essential to think in a clear, logical way, to command a sizeable vocabulary and to confidently express viewpoints.

Empire-builders can build a strong personal power-base by developing the ability to enunciate ideas, needs, wants in an individualistic and appealing way. A lasting impression is made via *dynamic* self expression. When you make others take notice of what you say, you have a winning chance of motivating them to accept you and to accept your propositions, ideas and requests.

Poor verbal communication is detrimental to empire-building. If you aren't equipped to sell your ideas you have little chance getting them off the ground. Wealth accumulation rests on the development and growth of viable ventures and the compounding of assets. Nothing is more frustrating than being rejected every time a proposition is presented, no matter how good it may be. Therefore, before you are able to 'sell' a concept, you must be in a position to effectively *package* it and then impressively *present* it so that others respond positively to it. Your power, influence and control rise when you speak well, deliver your points-of-view rationally and clearly and present yourself in an eye-catching way.

HOW TO GET PEOPLE TO LISTEN TO YOU

You will be meeting people in business with the hope of influencing their decisions. Your aim will be to get them 'on side' to listen to your propositions and to respond to them favorably. The way you *express* yourself and *present* yourself will determine how successful you are as a communicator-motivator. Just talking *at* people is not suitable entice-ment to get them to really listen to you and act on your requests. You've got to talk *to* them, hold them under your spell and then impress them with a clear, well-spoken presentation.

Dynamic communication skill does not include shouting at people. You can be dynamic via the *energy* you use as you speak, in the body stance you effect and in the tone of voice you use to enunciate your dialogue. You must put others at ease as you address them. A nervous, fidgety speaker displays lack of confidence and often, lack of conviction which puts a strain on those who are listening. People will listen to you and sit up and take notice of you when you develop self assurance and project your personality in a likeable way.

POINTERS TO IMPROVE YOUR COMMUNICATION SKILL

The skill of effective communication can be developed. The first step is to discover your weaknesses of self expression. Audiotape a conver-sation with a friend or family member. Listen to how you project dia-logue in normal conversation. Do you mumble, slur words, speak too softly or loudly, use incorrect grammar? If your speech isn't impressive, a few lessons with a speech trainer would be well worth the expenditure. When you improve your manner of speaking, you individualism is enhanced and your self confidence is given a boost. The following point-ers will assist in this regard:

1: Gather your thoughts and speak them coherently.
2: Express your ideas in an orderly fashion.
3: Don't be a jargon speaker. Use simple terminology.
4: Be brief. Don't ramble, boringly repeat points.
5: Don't shout or speak too softly. Use a moderate tone.
6: Eliminate word whiskers: ums, ers and ahs.
7: Don't speak too rapidly or too slowly. Pace your dialogue.
8: Modulate your speech without being sing-song. Use rise and fall.
9: Use correct pronunciation. Don't use words you don't understand.
10: Eliminate stammering and stuttering.

HOW TO UPGRADE YOUR IMAGE VIA EFFECTIVE COMMUNICATION

Your personality lifts or drops every time you speak. Poor conversational ability, conventional greetings, mispronunciation of words, incorrect grammar, poor voice projection, are image busters. They are detrimental to those desiring major achievement. Entrepreneurs, lawyers, salespersons, seminar speakers, actors, religious practitioners, advertising and public relations persons are professional communicators who need to present a pleasing personality and an impressive manner of speaking,

When you tag your speech faults and take action to correct them, you automatically give your personality a boost. A pleasant-sounding voice plus an articulate delivery of your ideas draws attention to you and you are seen as someone special, someone worth listening to. When there is something about you that sets you apart from people in general, you are on your way to major achievement.

FURTHER COMMUNICATION POINTERS

Further points to improve your communication skill are these: spend 15 minutes each day reading *aloud* newspaper and magazine articles to improve your speech and reading ability. Read and speak slowly without stumbling over words. Place emphasis on *key* words without unduly pounding them. Gently underscore them by placing a slight pause prior to or after each word or by rising or lowering the pitch of the voice as you deliver each key word. Correct breath control is essential to fluid speech. Push out the abdomen as you take in air through the nose rather than sucking in air through the mouth. The more air taken in via the mouth, the dryer the throat becomes which weakens the thrust and strength of voice tone. Avoid shrill, rasping or nasal qualities. Drop the pitch of the voice if it is too high and weak-sounding. Cultivate resonance via chest tones rather than using head tones.

HOW TO STRENGTHEN YOUR PROJECTED IMAGE VIA BODY COMMUNICATION

Along with good speech, good body language helps to bring an instantly-apparent individuality. The way you walk, shake hands, position your body, gesture, look at others and respond to them, either impresses or repels them. It is necessary to be aware of what you express vocally *and* physically and to be conscious of the response of others, particularly during moments of stress, frustration and anger.

The moods you experience and try to hide often reveal themselves in physical ways which you may not realize as you speak. Your voice and body language tell others a great deal about you — they reveal your strengths as well as your weaknesses. Persons capable of reading voice and body language have an advantage when negotiating business deals and contracts. A weak-sounding voice coupled with poor posture, un-coordinated gestures, lack of suitable eye contact, hands fidgeting, shifting from one foot to the other, all convey to the viewer that you feel uneasy, lack confidence and therefore, lack control, not only of yourself, but of the situation you are in.

Take charge of the way you communicate and present yourself. If you feel uncomfortable about your speech and body appearance, enrol in a suitable training course where professional help is available. There will be much you can do to help yourself via recognition of problems and daily practice sessions to eradicate faults. In addition to recording your voice, you can also get a good look at yourself by standing in front of a full-length mirror to judge the image which confronts you.

BODY LANGUAGE POINTERS

The following suggestions should be assessed against your own projection of body language and, where necessary, used to improve your ability to communicate your specialness, your distinctive individuality.

- Stand tall. Keep posture erect without looking stiff. Keep the shoulders back. Don't slouch, which indicates laziness of posture or weariness.
- Keep the hands by the sides until you are ready to gesture in a co-ordinated and purposeful way. Don't fidget, scratch, rattle coins.
- Keep the arms close to the body when gesturing without masking the face.
- Keep the head at a level angle. Frequent jerking of the head indicates nervousness. The head tilted down, pressed against the chest, indicates shyness and lack of self assurance.
- Hold eye contact without rigidly staring at another person during conversation. Don't blink excessively or dart the eyes from side-to-side. Shifty eye movement suggests insecurity, something to hide, uneasiness.
- Use a firm handshake. This suggests a person who is strong, confident, ambitious. A weak handshake indicates timidity, a person not in control.
- When walking, don't drag the feet, take excessively-long strides which cause the arms to swing awkwardly about the body.
- Co-ordinate the entire body — head, trunk, arms, hands, legs — in an easy, natural and least obtrusive way.

HOW TO GET OTHERS TO WARM TO YOU

One of the most disarming practices one can use to get the attention of others is to smile when being introduced. A friendly smile breaks down a lot of barriers. It softens the attitudes of others, reduces their stiffness, coldness and aggressiveness. When you smile, hold the thought: 'I like this person. We're going to get along fine'.

ABOUT SMOKING WHEN COMMUNICATING

A great deal of emphasis is being placed on the bad habit of smoking. When meeting others you wish to impress, be conscious of their attitude toward smokers and smoking. Puffing smoke in an anti-smokers face isn't going to win that person to your corner. Refrain from lighting up in the presence of others or, better still, *quit* smoking.

THE MOST VALUABLE SUCCESS AID AWAITS YOUR COMMAND

One of the most precious possessions we humans have at our command is the ability to enter into a dual dialogue with others in which we are able to express and receive feelings. Seven out of every ten minutes of our lives we spend communicating. Via communication we are able to let others know our needs, wants, aspirations and feelings. Good human relations are based on adequate self expression. Prosperous business relationships are based on forthright, dynamically-impressive communication skill and performance.

THE REASON PEOPLE CREATE CONFLICT

Some business deals fail because one party implies something and the other party takes it to mean something else — a simple case of communication breakdown. A report read to a group of executives can often end up having several different interpretations attached to it. When that same report is taken by executives and relayed to others, distortions of the original are presented. The reason this occurs is because some people are poor listeners. They filter-out things that don't interest them or things they are opposed to. What is unimportant or misunderstood often gets lost in the retelling. Misinterpretation of a discussion or contract negotiation can create conflict.

Conflict can be avoided, to a large degree, by *clear* explanation of an idea or message imparted or relayed to another person. It may be difficult to eliminate all misunderstanding, but most of it can be eliminated via sensible, simply-expressed dialogue and, when listening, to really *hear* what the speaker is presenting.

HOW TO AVOID COMMUNICATION CONFLICT

When expressing a point-of-view, be certain that the listener fully understands what you mean. 'Is what I'm saying clear to you?', is a question you should ask if you have any doubt that your statement, request or instruction could be misunderstood. Get your message straight in the first telling and you will avoid problems which could create conflict in the future. Be specific as to times, dates, places, names, figures and conditions or demands. When on the listening end, write down important information and check it with the speaker. The reason contracts are entered into is to avoid misunderstanding. Conditions are specifically stated and agreed to by the parties concerned. Verbal agreements often suffer from one party forgetting or distorting the conditions discussed and agreed to.

Don't expect your listener to jump into your mind to decode a muddled, confusing set of instructions or expression of feelings. Speak your mind with clarity. It will not only help you to empire-build, it will bring you a string of appreciative listeners.

HOW TO WIN AN ARGUMENT

The more people argue the more vocal, irrational and uncontrollable the situation becomes. Arguments arise when people feel threatened. The hotter an argument gets, the more out-of-control those arguing become. The only *sure* way to win an argument is to avoid it. Arguments usually solve very little. When allowed to become violent conflicts, they do not solve anything. I am not aware of any war in history that has satisfactorily solved the reason it was entered into.

There are people of course who enjoy conflict. They argue at the drop of a hat. They love to 'bait' others, to stir them up. Persons engaging in this practice are immature. Be conscious of the motives of those who want to draw you into arguments. Using up valuable energy and time trying to win-over stubborn, illogical dopes, is purposeless. Steer clear of potentially-dangerous conversations which could lead into argument. Change the subject. Don't inflame the situation by making controversial statements. Don't respond to insults, name-calling, gossip and rumors in a heated way. Keep calm. If the other person blows-off-steam, starts shouting, don't raise your voice. Speak softly, slowly and confidently which shows that you are in control of the situation. Guide the conversation back to neutral territory, giving your opponent time to cool down or to save face. A word of sympathy or a compliment often works wonders. Other factors to help you win are:

- Never defend your position.
- Don't be critical of your opponent.
- Stifle anger.
- If you are wrong, admit it.
- Don't make your opponent feel inferior.
- Smile. Display understanding.
- Listen intently. Respond politely.

A COMMUNICATION SKILL WORTH ITS WEIGHT IN GOLD

Entrepreneurs need to talk a lot. They also need to *listen* a lot. It's something some people aren't very good at doing. Listening is a valuable tool when negotiating deals. Good listening puts you in touch with information you may need to better understand the person you are doing business with. Speaking well is only one half of good communication skill. Listening well is the other half.

Good listening centers on your ability to keep your mind on the subject under discussion. It takes mental discipline. Remove prejudices. Don't jump to conclusions. Refrain from interrupting others. Hear them out. When you are politely responsive via intent listening, others will see it as a mark of respect and respond accordingly.

HOW TO COMMUNICATE THROUGH WORD EXPRESSION

Power brokers communicate in a dynamic way through the skillful use of image-building words. Descriptive words create pictures in the mind of the listener and this brings about a better understanding of issues under discussion. The clearer a proposition is presented, the easier it is to promptly arrive at a decision.

Paint pictures with the words you use. Avoid double-speak, double-talk or jargon-expression. Carefully-chosen words showcase your ideas and help to win approval of your suggestions, requests and propositions. Image-creating words have a special *sales* power and their calculated use helps to stamp you as an articulate person.

HOW TO USE WORD POWER TO ATTRACT THE ATTENTION OF OTHERS

Words can be powerful communication tools when used wisely and colorfully. We use words to explain ideas, feelings, needs and wants.

Words expressed poorly or used incorrectly, are detrimental to objectives in business and to social relationships. Words spoken in anger, representing feelings of bitterness, return resentment to the speaker from those listening. They not only lower the speaker's image value, they close the door on rational discussion or negotiation. Choose words carefully and be in control of their presentation.

Word-power use involves a vocabulary stacked with positive-meaning words. Eliminate from use words which represent limitation, lack, discord. Statements carrying negative word meanings create negative feelings in the listener. If you say, 'I would like to start my own business but I don't have the brains or money,' then you are clearly indicating to the listener that you lack self confidence and your mental gloom is passed to the listener. If the person you talk to happens to be a bank manager in a position to approve a business loan on your behalf and you express yourself in a negative way, your loan has little chance of being granted. Use words which express positive feelings, which indicate that you are a positive-thinking person in firm control of your business, your emotions and actions.

SELECT WORDS WITH A RING OF AUTHORITY ABOUT THEM

The nature and quality of the words you use should not only enhance you as the speaker but, where appropriate, inspire the person listening to you. When addressing an assembled group, select words that are easy to understand but which have a positive and descriptive ring about them. Learn at least two new words every day. A dictionary and thesaurus are your best source of reference. The following list of words should be studied and injected into your vocabulary.

STRONG-SOUNDING WORDS LIST

ACTION	ENHANCE	IMPACT
ACTIVE	ETHICAL	IMPROVEMENT
APPRECIATIVE	EXCELLENT	INCUMBENT
AUTHORITY	ELOQUENT	INDIVIDUALITY
BELIEVE	FORBEARANCE	JOCUND
BENEFICIAL	FORTUNATE	JUSTIFIER
BEAUTIFUL	FUTURIST	KINDRED
CONQUEST	GAMUT	KINGLINESS
CONNOISSEUR	GALVANIZE	LACONIC
CONJUNCTION	GRACIOUS	LANCINATE
CONSISTENT	GRANDIOSE	LATENT
CONSTRUCT	HABITUALLY	LAUREATE
CONTRIBUTION	HEFT	LIBERATE
DEMONSTRATE	HEROIC	LUCRATIVE
DETERMINED	INSTANT	MAGNETIC
DÉTENTE	IDEALISM	MAGNIFICENT
DEVOLUTION	ILLUMINE	MASTERSHIP

METAPHYSICAL	REPUTABLE	SUAVITY
METEORIC	RESILE	SUBJECTIVITY
NOTABLE	RESOLUTE	SUBSTANTIAL
NECESSARY	RESOLVABILITY	SUCCESSFUL
OBJECTIVE	RESPECT	SUCCINCT
OBSESSION	RESPONSIBLE	SUPERIOR
OBSERVANT	RESTORATIVE	TACTICS
OPTIMUM	RESULTANT	TANGIBLE
ORATORY	RESURGENT	TASTEFUL
PALATIAL	RETENTIVE	TENACIOUS
PALLIATE	RHAPSODIZE	TENDENTIOUS
PARALLEL	RHETORIC	TENDER
PERFECTIBLE	ROMANTIC	THRIVE
PERSUADE	SACRED	TRANSCEND
POSITIVE	SAFE	TRANSFORM
PROFILE	SALTANT	TRIUMPH
PROFITABLE	SALUBRIOUS	TROJAN
PROSPERITY	SALUTATION	TRUSTFUL
QUALITY	SALVAGE	ULTIMATE
QUINTESSENTIAL	SANCTIFY	ULTRA
RADIANT	SANGUINE	UNITED
RALLY	SATISFIER	VENERABLE
RAPPORT	SCHOLASTIC	VENERATION
REDOUBTABLE	SCINTILLANT	VIBRANT
REGULATIVE	SCRUPULOUS	VITALISM
REJOICE	SECULAR	WEALTHINESS
RELEVANT	SECURE	WONDERMENT
REMARKABLE	STEADFAST	WONDROUS
REMEDIAL	STIMULATE	WORLDLY
REMUNERATIVE	STRATEGIST	ZEAL
RENOVATOR	STUNNING	ZENITH

HOW TO NEUTRALIZE ONE OF MOST FEARED WORDS IN THE ENGLISH LANGUAGE

One of the most feared words in the English language is *failure*. The word rears its ugly head more times than it should in social and business discussions. It appears with regularity in newspaper and magazine articles. It is a word entrepreneurs, as dynamic communicators, must avoid using whenever possible.

US boxing promoter Don King, an achiever, maintains that every person desiring to win as a boxer must eliminate the word from his vocabulary. 'Failure must be the last thing on the mind of a champion boxer or, for that matter, any person wanting to be number one,' Don says.

Replace the word failure with the word success. Don't say, 'I'm going to fail.' Change it to, 'I'm going to win.' Be conscious of the words you speak in everyday conversations. It will pay to speak in a positive way rather than in a negative way. Give your vocabulary a thorough going over. Toss out words which, through repeated use, encourage a pessimistic attitude and paint you as a doomsday prophet.

ALL PEOPLE REACT TO WORDS

People react to the words you speak. They are impressed, disappointed, encouraged, angry, loving, spiteful, happy, morose, gentle or violent according to their interpretation of what you say and how you say it. Your personality is given added appeal or diminished via the presentation of the words you use. If you are inarticulate, as many people are, this handicap will grossly affect your ability to command the attention of important people. Remember this point: people look for your talking to have an interesting, distinguished and intelligent ring about it. Make your presentation of words a tool for accomplishing your aims. Speak to people in a compelling way which shows them that you are what they expect you to be.

SUPPORT YOUR DELIVERY WITH ENERGY

Many people speak with little intensity. They sound tired and bored with life in general. The first thing people react to when they hear you is the energy level you display. A simple 'hello' can indicate your state of mind. *Feelings* pushed through words are a good barometer of whether you are down-in-the-dumps or on top-of-the-world. Your self-power base is diminished when you indicate to others that you are depressed, tired, unsure of yourself or unwell. It puts you on the defensive and thus vulnerable to the whims and motivations of others. When you retain your energy level you maintain the offensive, you carry the ball and your self power is upheld.

HOW TO ACHIEVE SOCIAL ACCEPTANCE VIA GOOD MANNERS

Correct behavior must be observed in business life as well as in one's social life. Those desiring social acceptance need to act with dignity and diplomacy. Following the rules of good social conduct reflects good breeding and a well-balanced mental attitude. Good manners add charm and elegance to even the most ordinary circumstances.

It is necessary to know instinctively which social errors to avoid. There are accepted rules of social conduct regardless of your age, place of living, financial standing or upbringing. The *first* rule is to always act in a courteous manner toward others regardless of their attitude to you. This marks you as a mature, *controlled* person.

THE RULES OF INTRODUCTION

FOR SOCIAL INTRODUCTIONS: the less important is introduced to the more important person. The man, regardless of rank or age, is introduced to the woman. This rule does not apply if the man is of considerable age and of eminence and the woman very young. The younger man is introduced to the elder man, the bachelor to the married man, the younger woman to the elder woman, the younger married woman to the much elder unmarried woman. The same applies to a young married man and a much elder bachelor. When introducing a man to a woman, use the following phrase: 'Mrs. Jones, may I introduce Mr. Black.' The woman may choose to extend her hand. The man does not extend his hand to greet a woman. Only Royalty or Vice Regal or persons of high eminence are not introduced to the woman. All other men, regardless of rank, are. Women without title are introduced to titled women. Men without title are introduced to men with title, regardless of age. Equals are acquainted with one another: 'Mr. Brown — Mr. Smith.'

FOR GROUP INTRODUCTIONS: (social or business) if a guest arrives at a reception, get the attention of the group and introduce the newcomer by saying: 'I would like to introduce Mr. Bentley.' It is not necessary to state the individual names of the other guests. It taxes the memory of the person making the introduction and may embarrass the newcomer. When introducing your wife or husband, do not refer to either as Mrs. or Mr. Use their Christian names: 'This is my wife, Jean.' — 'This is my husband, Bill.' When introducing a friend to your family, introduce the friend to your mother or wife first. Introductions in your business or social life should be made in a friendly manner. Smile and make both parties feel at ease.

FOR BUSINESS INTRODUCTIONS: it is generally accepted that the higher the person's position, the more consideration he or she is given. When introducing your employer to a new employee or client begin: 'Mr. Smith (the employer) this is Miss Brown.

FOR STREET GREETINGS: it is not advisable to introduce persons passing by unless for a special reason. If a woman passes two men one of whom she knows, it is correct for both to acknowledge her, but if she stops to converse with her friend, the other man walks slowly on. The same applies to a man meeting two men, one of whom he knows.

HOW TO CONDUCT YOURSELF AT INTERVIEWS AND BUSINESS MEETINGS

When a meeting with a superior is necessary or with a business associate, make an appointment through a secretary. Keep the meeting brief. Never sit until the person in whose office you find yourself *invites* you to sit. Rise when you get an indication that the interview or meeting is at an end. Do not smoke unless invited to do so. Use a firm handshake, maintain eye contact, be businesslike but friendly. Be on time for your meetings.

Under pressure, never use offensive language. It could be costly. Control your temper. When problems arise, discuss them with the party concerned. Do not go behind another person's back with complaints to a superior or associate. Don't gossip. Be straight-forward in your comments and stick to the facts. Speak clearly. Be concise and project your voice at a level others can hear, but don't shout, use crude expressions or try to sound like an intellectual snob. Be natural and you will be liked, listened to and well received.

If you are resigning your position, it is normal practice to give two weeks notice. If you are in a specialized position, this may need to be extended until a suitable replacement is found. A written letter of resignation with an explanation of *why* you are leaving should be given to the appropriate person *personally*.

HOW TO PLAY IT SAFE AT SOCIAL AND BUSINESS FUNCTIONS

At dinner functions do not discuss topics that could arouse the anger of the host or hostess or other guests. Religion and politics may be interesting, but they easily get others off-side if your views differ greatly to theirs. If the conversation drifts to controversial subjects, do not press your own strong points-of-view. Never enter into forceful discussions with your host or hostess or other guests. Do not flirt with others in attendance, complain about any 'state-of-affairs' or offer gossip. Do not be the last to leave. Stay sober. Show good manners. Thank the host or hostess. A note of thanks a day or so later is a polite way of showing your appreciation for being invited.

HOW TO WRITE A GOOD BUSINESS LETTER

Business letters should always be typed, *free* of spelling errors, incorrect grammar and obvious corrections. The length of a business letter should be kept to one page. The average length of a sentence should be 15 to 20 words and a paragraph about 6 lines. The letter should be as brief as possible and clearly state the subject in the first paragraph. Every good business letter is also a sales letter, presenting an idea, a product, service or a request. Letters requesting payment of a debt should be brief and firm without threatening the debtor. Acquire a natural style of writing, much as you would speak. Resist using flowery expressions. Make your letters interesting and a reflection of your personality. Never write any statement which could get you into legal difficulty. A letter of application should be respectful and on formal lines. The body of the letter should cover: the applicant's state of health, whether married or single, exact age, information about education and previous experience. It should also suggest references are available.

BUSINESS LETTER FORMS

The most commonly-followed form of setting out a business letter is the *block form*. Each paragraph begins at the left-hand margin of the page. The *semi-block form* uses a five-space indentation for the beginning of each paragraph. Both are proper for business and personal letters. Many business letter writers reduce punctuation marks in the address the letter is being sent to and following the salutation and sign off. The body of the letter still carries sufficient punctuation to make sense of the text. Business-letter stationery should reflect a quality (watermarked) bond paper either white or a very pale color with a matching envelope. Presentation of stationery and business cards should be simplistic and always in good taste.

ADDRESSING CORRESPONDENCE

Business letters should begin: 'Dear Sir,' 'Dear Madam,' 'Gentlemen,' if addressed to a company and if to a specific person: 'Dear Mr. Jones,' 'Dear Miss Shaw.' Suitable endings include: 'Yours sincerely,' 'Very truly yours.' The correct signature to a business letter is the writer's name usually *without* title.

Social letters can begin: 'Dear Jean,' if the recipient is a close friend, otherwise 'Dear Mrs. Smith.' For closing: 'Cordially yours,' or 'Warm personal wishes,' if the person is a long-time friend. Where the sender's address is used, no phone number is included. The receiver's address appears only on the envelope. The writer's name may be embossed in small type at the top of the letter.

Members of the clergy, politicians, eminent persons should be addressed correctly. An excellent reference source for the business and social letter writer is, *The World Book Encyclopedia*.

GET YOUR COMMUNICATION SKILL WORKING

Communication, whether by spoken word, body language or correspondence, is a vital tool in empire-building. Keep in mind that communication is a two-way exchange of understanding. Learn as much as you can about human relationships. Study people. Get a firm grasp of the language you use. Turn the way you speak into a highly-acceptable, crowd-pleasing, image-building presentation. Use it in a specialized, imaginative and emotion-stirring way to win the loyalty, respect and assistance of all those you come in contact with. The *power* of your personal communication ability should be exploited to help you to grow rich.

REACH FOR THE STARS

Whatever you can visualize you can achieve. Therefore, reach for the stars. Set your sights on worthwhile, meaningful and beneficial achievement. Become a vociferous reader, an eager course-taker, an information-seeker. Develop your mind and excite your emotions with the idea and ideal of personal lifestyle excellence, of becoming *somebody*. Focus on your *potential* to grow rich and *motivate* yourself to take whatever course of action is necessary to uplift your life into a new sphere of accomplishment.

FORMULAS TO GROW RICH

- Entrepreneurs must establish a colorful, impression-creating power-base. One way to do this is through superior communication skill, an ability to 'get through' to people. Self expression needs to be attention-getting. You may need to enhance your manner of speaking so that you can deliver your viewpoints effectively.

- Learn to get people 'on side' via not only *what* you say but *how* you say it. Sell your ideas along with your personality so that those listening to you *like* you.

- You can learn to be a good communicator. Gather your thoughts and know exactly what you want to say. Express yourself in an orderly fashion. Don't ramble, be a jargon-speaker or you will confuse your listeners. Speak clearly. Don't stammer or stutter.

- Tag your speech faults via a tape recorder. If you need assistance to speak well, take speech training. Really work on self improvement if you want to succeed.

- It is possible to strengthen your image through impressive body communication. Stand tall. Poor posture is a sign of laziness or tiredness. The way you walk, shake hands, position your body when seated or standing, gesture, look at others and respond to them, either impresses or repels them. Your emotions *reflect* in your body language.

- You must warm to people and they must warm to you if you want satisfactory relationships with them. Smile when it is appropriate. Hold the thought: 'I like this person'.

- Avoid getting into argument with others. Conflict puts you in a 'no win' situation. When confronted by hostility, remain calm. Don't raise your voice in anger. Refrain from exchanging personal insults.

- People are fond of talking but less fond of listening. Be a good listener and you are likely to learn a lot and consolidate friendships.

- Use image-building words to influence others. Paint word pictures for good understanding of your proposition, request or suggestion.

- Build a strong vocabulary of power-sounding words. Use words as effective communication helpers so that others mark you as an articulate person. Use the power of personal communication to exploit your achievement aims and to help you to grow rich.

HOW TO MULTIPLY
YOUR EFFECTIVENESS
AS AN ENTREPRENEUR

THE ROLE OF THE 21st CENTURY ENTREPRENEUR

Entrepreneurship has become somewhat of a buzz word to describe the clever business actions of get-up-and-go persons. Mistakenly, some people look upon entrepreneurs as high risk-takers. A successful entrepreneur is not an unthinking gambler, but an astute planner, a *calculated* risk-taker, a highly-motivated, action-oriented, hard-working achiever.

Entrepreneurs make things happen through disciplined self management. They are not content to fence-sit, wait on opportunity, dissipate time and energy or look to others to hand them success. They find challenge and excitement in going after new ideas and worthwhile ventures. They believe that life isn't about how you play the game, it's about *winning* the game, enthusiastically and honestly. They are persons prepared to assume risks in return for personal satisfaction and profit. Your role as an entrepreneur will need to reflect this commitment.

HOW TO SURVIVE AS A TRUE ENTREPRENEUR

The high-flying wheeler-dealer, the get-rich-quick corners-cutter is a person of the past. Today, an entrepreneur must be a professional manager, an individual capable of starting and building a business from scratch. The flash deal-doer, the circus entrepreneur trying to promote spurious ventures into instant personal gold mines has no chance of survival.

Wealth accumulation can be accomplished by a person who may start with little but through hard work, perseverance and commonsense, develops something worthwhile. Money people are becoming more conservative. In the present economic climate, investing in a financial paper-shuffle presented by a high-flier has little chance of succeeding — the smart money just won't be in it. A solidly-based proposition presented by a reliable, honest and hard-working entrepreneur stands a good chance of attracting investment and success.

STRONG ADVICE FROM A MAN WHO ADVISES MILLIONAIRES

Australian millionaire Geoffrey Hill, a businessperson who has made millions of dollars for the clients he has advised, says the days of the crash-hot deal-doer have passed and it's now back to hard work. He feels that the modern-day entrepreneur has got to be much more professional about putting deals together. 'You've got to have management behind you and you've got to build something out of something worthwhile, not try to get something out of nothing,' is his advice.

SHIFT THE FOCUS OF YOUR THINKING FROM OBSTACLES TO GOALS

Many wishful-thinking people focus their attention on the obstacles to success rather than on the goals they desire to achieve. Re-balance your thinking. Change your attitudes and get your mind firmly set on goal-seeking instead of obstacle-seeking. You have to *think* rich to be rich. You have to *think* achievement to become an achiever.

Give yourself practical advice. Talk commonsense. If millions of others can become wealthy and successful, then why can't you do the same thing? You can and you will if you give yourself the opportunity. Think-through your current position. What's the stumbling block? Are you scared to take calculated risks? Are you frightened to make mistakes in case you fail? Are you devoid of good money-making ideas? Are you waiting on something or someone to help you to succeed? Are you lazy? Do you have belief in your ability to succeed? What's the problem? Discover it and then give yourself this advice: *if I am to become financially independent and successful, I must take the first step. My own efforts are my guarantee of riches. I focus my attention on my goals. I visualize only achievement.*

HOW TO ENTREPRENEUR YOURSELF INTO THE FAST LANE

Bernard Benson made his first million dollars when he was in his early thirties. Since that age he has been adding at least a million a year to his income. The British-born Benson lives the good life in France. He became rich by combining his inventing ideas with a singular vision: to invent the best his mind allows. Benson patented a dartboard with an automatic scoring device. It was a good idea and it made money. He invented a navigational bomb sight, an acoustic homing torpedo. He has increased his wealth from chances he took in the computer business.

Offering some clues to those who are boxed into life's go-nowhere middle lane, Benson says: 'Personally, I can live destitute or loaded, but not in the middle lane. It's hell in that tunnel. To become rich, move into the fast lane. It's exciting. Discover what you need then chase it. Aim to live in paradise, not hell.'

Benson says he has always had a nose for 'sniffing-out opportunity'. He suggests looking at the long-range picture rather than the immediate. 'Plan ahead so there is something to aim at,' he suggests.

HOW NOT TO MISS LIFE'S GOLDEN OPPORTUNITIES

'Money-making opportunities are everywhere. People fall over them everyday without realizing it and some see them but fail to act on them,' a multi-millionaire property developer told me at a sales entrepreneurship seminar I spoke at in Los Angeles. I agree with his statement. Quite often I hear the remark, 'I could have been rich had I acted promptly.'

Opportunities come and opportunities pass — *quickly*. A keen and decisive mind is required to assess each opportunity as it arises. Procrastination defeats opportunity, especially where time is of the essence. My personal attitude on moving promptly when a worthwhile proposition comes up is simple: determine if the affirmatives outweigh the negatives. If they do, take immediate action.

> There is a tide in the affairs of men, which, taken at the flood, leads on to fortune; omitted, all the voyage of their life is bound in shallows and in miseries; and we must take the current when it serves, or lose our ventures.
> –SHAKESPEARE.

WAKE YOURSELF UP TO LIFE'S OPPORTUNITIES AND GET MOVING

Opportunities surround you, but do you recognize them? Some people are blind to the possibilities of personal accomplishment which face them each day. If you have been asleep to the potential of your own ideas and desires, wake up and get moving before it's too late. Beat your own path to the door of success. What can you lose — a little time, energy, perhaps some investment money? Surely these are small payments to make to achieve creative satisfaction, happiness and a more luxurious lifestyle.

Have faith in your desires. Your mind is the source of your real and influential power. Get yourself moving in life. Strengthen your resolve to generate worthwhile ventures and beneficial ideas. You've been allotted *one* life. Don't waste it. Wake up and succeed.

BECOME AN ENTREPRENEURAL VISUALIZER

Look into the future. Visualize your role as an entrepreneur. Visualization is a practical method of daydreaming. It directs your imagination along the path you need to tread to get your goals firmly established. With your inner eye, visualize your ideas and ideals. Place yourself in the center of your picture and feel the reality of future success. Through the universal law of attraction you will draw to you everything needed for the unfoldment of your dreams.

ATTACH TO YOURSELF ENTREPRENEURAL TRAITS

Personalize the following entrepreneural traits. The *Iam* is the *value* you place on yourself. Whatever you attach to the *Iam*, you become.

- *Iam* a disciplined thinker and visualizer.
- *Iam* an action-taker.
- *Iam* an absorber of useful information.
- *Iam* a seeker of excellence in all that I do.
- *Iam* analytical as a decider and problem-solver.
- *Iam* comfortable in my role as a leader.
- *Iam* the architect of my career and the instigator of my fortunes.
- *Iam* a loyalist to my personal ideas and ideals.
- *Iam* a successful entrepreneur.
- *Iam* capable of achieving my objectives.
- *Iam* a power source.
- *Iam* the recipient of life's riches.

A LESSON ALL ENTREPRENEURS NEED TO LEARN

A learning skill every entrepreneur must grasp quickly is the ability to turn every adversity into an advantage of some kind. We all make mistakes. Many of us learn by them. Others repeat their mistakes, thinking that the next time will be different. A business-person must learn to avoid falling into the same trench twice. You learn from each mistake and you don't do it again. Success cannot be attained via stupidity.

Look for the visible or *hidden* cause of your mistake and try to find a way to turn it into an advantage. See a problem as an opportunity to gain a clearer perception of the best course of action to take. This forces you to tackle it head on and with positive-mindedness to defeat it rather than it defeating you.

DON'T PANIC YOURSELF INTO A CORNER

Some people panic when a major decision has to be made quickly. They become highly emotional which voids the chance to think rationally. Making a good decision under pressure is essential to winning. Don't approach the task as a do-or-die situation. Steady your thinking. Be calm and get everything into perspective. Ask yourself: what is the worst scenario if things go wrong? Reduce the mountain into an anthill. Learn to make a crisis situation work for you by thinking about the rewards of a good decision. Change your attitude from panic-stricken to confident.

IF A DEAL CAN POTENTIALLY WIPE YOU OUT TREAD CAREFULLY

Making money entails risk-taking. Some ventures and opportunities require a high-degree of risk-taking and therefore, need to be approached cautiously. They need to be carefully thought-out. Where an opportunity is reasonably clear-cut and doesn't amount to a wipe-out situation if you don't win, then act quickly on it before someone else takes it from you. You aren't likely to win all battles you enter. But determine via sensible thinking, to win a majority of them.

AGE IS NO BARRIER TO ENTREPRENEURSHIP SUCCESS

Whether you are young or elderly, calendar age is no barrier to establishing yourself as an entrepreneur. Provided you are of sound mind and in good health, the winners' circle is open to you. Some super achievers are in their teens, others are past so-called retirement age. See yourself as young, energetic and highly-motivated. Feel the thrill of tackling challenging ventures, of empire-building. Your subconscious mind will accept your mental pictures and feelings and bring them to pass.

WHY A JUNIOR ENTREPRENEUR WILL MAKE IT BIG

At age 13, Daniel Guerin was named Australia's top junior entrepreneur. The young achiever used his time after school each day to sell chocolates and candies. His average weekly sales totalled $600. Daniel says he seeks the freedom to plan and work on his own ideas and to involve himself in bigger and better projects. 'I've learned to think for myself and to get out and earn. I enjoy it. I want to be my own boss and to make lots of money,' he said. A reader of motivational books, Daniel has established a constructive attitude to achieving what he wants and what he wishes to become.

WHY A SENIOR ENTREPRENEUR BECAME FAMOUS AND WEALTHY

When William Lear was a boy in Chicago, he made up his mind to take charge of his life. He resolved to make enough money so he'd never be stopped from finishing anything. 'I wanted to make money in a hurry, so I decided I'd have to invent something people wanted. I also knew that if I was ever to stand on my own two feet, I'd have to leave the security of my parent's home,' he told a media interviewer.

Lear joined the Navy, serving as a wireless operator. In his early 20s, he invented and developed the first practical automobile radio. Then he developed the first commercial airplane radio compass, then the first lightweight jet autopilot, the eight-track stereo cartridge and the Lear Jet executive jetliner. The discoveries made him wealthy and famous. Not content to sit back and rest on his fortunes, Lear, when he was 70, put in nearly 90-hours of work a week. 'For me, the joy is in the chase,' is a Learism worth quoting. In 1967, he sold his interest in the company for $28 million and retired. Becoming bored, he went back to developing a steam-powered bus which he said is, 'the greatest contribution I will have made.'

A SINGULAR VISION PROPELS YOU TO SUCCESS

If you desire to become one of the 'big guns' of business, develop a singular vision — *to be the very best at what you do*. Achieving outstanding business results is a commitment of time, energy and determination. It isn't something you tinker at during weekends. A part-time commitment is really no commitment at all. Jump in, boots-and-all. If your ideas are sound, your methods to produce your ideas practical, then press ahead and you will get results. Your first million dollars may not appear overnight, but with determination coupled to excellence at what you do, it won't be too long in coming.

ENTREPRENEURSHIP AND EDUCATION

The world is literally covered with institutions of learning. In universities, the campuses are crowded with thousands of students eager to learn and earn academic qualifications. Education has become the theme song of this progressive age. Millions of dollars are being spent on education and these study institutions should, it would seem, have an impact upon our society.

Taking knowledge and exploiting it to bring personal success should be taught in every school. Young people should be encouraged to be *self* managing in the exploitation of skills and talents. They should be instructed in the principles of self confidence, making decisions, planning goals and personal image value and presentation. A disappointing aspect of many of our learning centers is that little emphasis is placed on personal-enhancement training. Empire-building, wealth accumulation and creative accomplishment come out of dynamic personal initiative — a desire to be, to do and to have the very best in life. Educators have a responsibility not only to supply information but to see that persons receiving information are properly equipped to put it to maximum use.

While people should not be forced to strive for achievement excellence, they should be *encouraged* and given incentives to do so. Because our economy and society in general are struggling, the majority of people are seeking ways to improve their ability to earn more, experience more and accomplish more. Developing entrepreneural attitudes and skills in young people will have a dramatic impact in a positive way upon our society.

HOW TO BECOME A SUCCESSFUL ENTREPRENEUR

Broadly speaking, entrepreneurs are self-made persons. Some have impressive academic qualifications, others.a basic and general education supported by self-taught skills. Education alone is no guarantee of personal and business success. Empire-builders need to be dynamic personal presenters. They must have leadership ability, be self motivated, have strong determination, be lateral-thinking individuals with business acumen.

Becoming a successful entrepreneur will depend upon the degree of personal initiative shown after goals have been established and an action plan drawn. Achievement doesn't spring from being a good talker, but from being a good *action-taker.*

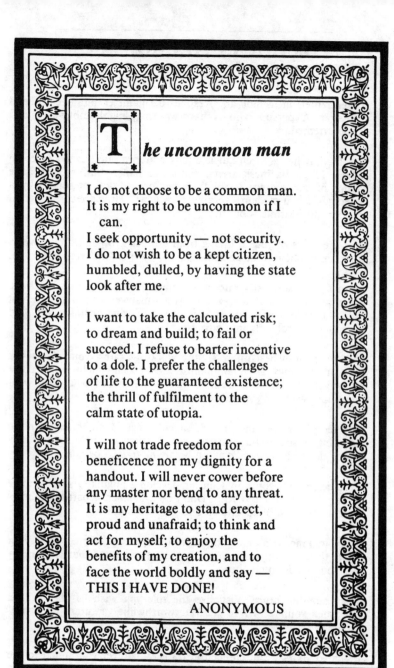

The uncommon man

I do not choose to be a common man.
It is my right to be uncommon if I
    can.
I seek opportunity — not security.
I do not wish to be a kept citizen,
humbled, dulled, by having the state
look after me.

I want to take the calculated risk;
to dream and build; to fail or
succeed. I refuse to barter incentive
to a dole. I prefer the challenges
of life to the guaranteed existence;
the thrill of fulfilment to the
calm state of utopia.

I will not trade freedom for
beneficence nor my dignity for a
handout. I will never cower before
any master nor bend to any threat.
It is my heritage to stand erect,
proud and unafraid; to think and
act for myself; to enjoy the
benefits of my creation, and to
face the world boldly and say —
THIS I HAVE DONE!

ANONYMOUS

FORMULAS TO GROW RICH

- An entrepreneur is not an irresponsible gambler but a calculated risk-taker. A person who is hard-working, highly-motivated and action-oriented.

- The high-flying, get-rich-quick circus entrepreneur has no place in today's tough business arena. Financial paper-shuffling has little chance of succeeding. A solidly-based proposition presented by a dependable, honest, hard-working person will always receive a good hearing and possible support.

- Shift the focus of your thinking from obstacles to goals. You have to *think* achievement to be an achiever. You have to *think* rich to be rich.

- Learn to turn adversity into opportunity. Everyone makes mistakes. The sensible thing is to *learn* by your mistakes and not to repeat them. Look for visible or *hidden* causes of your mistakes and find ways to turn problems into advantages.

- Act in your own best interest. Stop working against yourself. Define your interests and fast-track them to a beneficial conclusion. Become enthusiastic about your desires. Your belief about what you want determines whether you fail or succeed.

- Whether you are young or old, calendar age is no impediment to becoming a successful entrepreneur. Picture yourself as mentally *young*, physically *energetic* and a highly-motivated person.

- If you desire to become an achiever, develop a singular vision — to be the very best at what you do. Don't be a dabbler, a part-time entrepreneur. Jump in boots-and-all and get things moving.

- Money-making ideas and opportunities are everywhere. Open your eyes to them. Assess each opportunity as it arises and then act quickly once you decide to go ahead.

- Look into the future. Visualize the role you wish to play in life. Strengthen your resolve to generate worthwhile ventures and beneficial ideas.

- Attach to yourself entrepreneural traits. Whatever you attach to the *Iam*, you become. Decree that you are a successful entrepreneur. Believe it. Reach for the stars. Whatever you can visualize you can achieve.

HOW TO REMOVE STRESS FROM ENTREPRENEURIAL ACTIVITY

DOING THE IMPOSSIBLE REQUIRES A STRONG CONSTITUTION

Becoming a high-achieving entrepreneur — doing what others say can't be done — can be both mentally and physically taxing. Helping yourself to riches entails the output of an enormous amount of energy. Good health is therefore an essential part of becoming successful. Empire-building requires you to be on your feet and moving, not immobile in a sick bed.

One of the main problems associated with sickness today is stress. It is capable of producing heart attacks, cancer, ulcers, migraine headaches and an assortment of other debilitating illnesses. Stress can considerably be reduced if not eliminated totally by those capable of taking control of their thoughts and emotions. *Discipline* of thought patterns is the key to stress-free daily living.

SELF CONFIDENCE REDUCES STRESS

Goals striving requires a great deal of personal self confidence in your estimation of who you are and what you can do. Low self esteem is the breeding ground of stress. It casts doubts as to your worthiness as a skilled, talented and creative human being. Low personal appraisal destroys confidence and initiative. It drags you down mentally, emotionally and physically. Depression lowers your resistance to fight-off illness. Self doubt and confidence cannot live together. One or the other must reign. It is imperative to remove from your consciousness self doubt or conflicting opinion as to your human status. Put into your mind the affirmatives, the things you wish to experience and the person you desire to become. As you do this, your subconscious mind will form your world into your inner imagery and contemplation.

HOW TO ACT IN YOUR OWN SELF INTEREST TO REDUCE STRESS

Fear, anxiety, worry produce pain. Self confidence, mental stability and enthusiasm create inner peace and induce health and vitality. Organize your concepts and strengthen your beliefs which determine your behavior. Stop working against your self interest through mental poisoning. If you desire peace, harmony, happiness and good health, you must work to cast from your mind fear and false belief. Cease getting excited, upset, agitated and angry. Go within to your *center*. It is here you will discover the 'still waters', an inner peace and great calm. Draw into yourself and meditate. You will find a release from tension, worry, guilt, fear and anxiety.

HOW TO GET INTO A GOOD MOOD FOR WHAT'S AHEAD

Some people fear the future, worry unnecessarily about possible changes to their lifestyle and financial independence. Many of the worries we often lose sleep over have a habit of losing their sting or never coming to pass. The cure for worrying about the future is to rejoice in the thought of *forthcoming* success and prosperity. Get above worry. Wish for yourself bigger and better things. Should fear thoughts come, contemplate a happy, beneficial ending. Inject confidence into your thinking. Engage your mind to work out the solution to any challenge or problem confronting you. Place faith in the knowledge that the power of your subconscious mind can, when called upon, find a solution to *all* your worries. Don't be brain dead. Wake up. Come alive to the miracle power of your subconscious mind. Your life is what your thoughts make it. You experience nothing outside your own mentality.

HOW TO RELEASE YOURSELF FROM MENTAL AND EMOTIONAL INSECURITY

You will experience mental and emotional freedom and gain the inner security you desire when you come to the realization that personal power, inspiration and illumination are yours to command. Never allow a negative suggestion to linger long enough to penetrate the subconscious. No concept, constructive or destructive, can manifest except it comes via the deeper mind. Do not surrender your mind to fear. Request your subconscious to manifest serenity, poise and well-being. It will do so. You are putting into place the law of action and reaction. The action is your desire, the reaction is the response from your subconscious. This is the path to mental and emotional security.

DON'T RACE TO NOWHERE IS ADVICE OF DALAI LAMA

Some years ago, I had the pleasure to hear His Holiness the 14th Dalai Lama of Tibet, Tenzin Gyatso, speak on mind cultivation. He emphasized the importance of *logic* in developing mental powers and broadening the mind by a wide variety of *knowledge* which can be used to enhance personal living standards. 'Human beings should resist the urge to race to nowhere, for it creates great stress and impedes constructive use of mental powers. Meditation, concentration and discipline foster inner peace and harmony which, in turn, contribute significantly towards a healthier, happier and richer life,' the Dalai Lama said.

GAIN POWER OVER CONDITIONS AND CIRCUMSTANCES AND STRESS IS ELIMINATED

Freedom from fear, worry, anxiety and depression are sought by all humans. Release from inner torment is an escape from hell. Inner security and confidence come out of the wisdom you develop as your spiritual understanding of life expands. When you develop an 'inner knowing' of what life is about and your personal role in it, you will take on a strength and tranquility which the material world cannot steal from you. You will move through life *with* the Law, not against it. This puts *you* in charge, gives you power over conditions and circumstances and allows you to function as you were designed to function, happily and beneficially. The key is to seek truth. Establish a spiritual understanding of your *true* purpose in life. Read, enquire, study, observe every day of your life. Open your mind to new ideas, concepts, beliefs. Your life will take on new meaning, new vitality and attract to you inner and outer riches.

SOCRATES HAD THE ANSWER TO STRESS-FREE LIVING

Socrates, described by Plato as, 'the wisest and justest and best Athenian,' wrote over the old Greek Temple where he taught: *Know thyself.* Lack of *self* knowledge, suggested Socrates, is the cause of most of man's problems and ills. To understand your true nature in the scheme of things is to gain release from the limitations of the race mind. Stress-free living comes from understanding, not ignorance. The more you understand the modus operandi of your conscious and subconscious mind, the less you will struggle, fret and worry over your daily affairs. Get on top of your life. You were born to win, to succeed over problems and difficulties and to achieve great and glorious victories. To live any other way is to deny yourself life's riches.

Accept the fact that you have a personal power responsive to your thought and belief. Make this a strong conviction. Don't waiver in the knowledge that when you take control of your mind you set the measure of your success and you become master of conditions and circumstances. To accept this principle causes stress to disappear.

HOW NOT TO REACH YOUR STRESS BREAKING POINT

It is unwise to try to become a superperson by taking on too many tasks loaded with responsibility. It makes you a candidate for mental, emotional and physical burnout. Pace your workload. Organize your time. Don't coast for most of the day and then push yourself hard to complete work in remaining work hours. Undisciplined work habits create stress. Organize work commitments in order of priority. Make a list of daily tasks and allocate a time for their completion. The more organized you are, the less chance there will be of stress rising to a dangerous level.

THREE STEPS TO PRODUCTIVITY THE STRESS-FREE WAY

The simple and easy way to enhance personal productivity is to get into a work routine which allows you to work steadily throughout a designated period. Don't expect too much of yourself. You can only do what you are capable of doing. You have certain limitations as a human being and to push beyond them is a quick route to the grave. Success is hard work which may require you to put in long hours. But the question is, are you working harder than you need to and spending more hours than are necessary?

Three steps to follow to balance your work-time and effort are:

1: *ORGANIZE* TASKS AND TIME EFFICIENTLY
2: *DISCIPLINE* YOURSELF TO WORK STEADILY AND COMFORTABLY
3: *BREAK* YOUR ROUTINE WITH SHORT RELAXATION PERIODS

HOW TO KEEP PERSONAL PROBLEMS OUT OF BUSINESS AFFAIRS

Some busy executives, both male and female, allow themselves to become stressed by allowing an intrusion of personal commitments and problems into their business affairs. Personal commitments you may have with a spouse, family or friend should not overlap business commitments. You must decide which area of your life has priority and then set yourself *guidelines* to follow. If a situation arises where important work needs to be completed and a family member or friend demands attention, decide at the time which demand has priority.

Personal problems and family arguments should be left at home. Don't allow them to overlap work commitments. When you are at work, devote your full time and attention to work matters. When you are at home or with friends, close your mind to business problems. Make relaxation periods restful, comfortable and happy.

LEAVE YOUR WORK OVERLOAD AT THE OFFICE

It is not sound practice to continually take an overload of office work home to complete. If you are absolutely pressed for time then on occasion it may be ok to do so. However, those with a family may find that it creates a negative feeling among family members. Apart from using up valuable relaxation time, the home might not be a good work environment due to noise distractions. If you get your workday organized, it shouldn't be necessary to intrude on leisure time that could be spent walking, exercising, reading, gardening, enjoying a hobby, playing a sport or just relaxing with family and friends.

Grappling with a major problem during business hours is bad enough. Taking that same problem home to grapple with overnight or over a weekend often compounds the problem. Learn to isolate yourself from work-related thoughts during leisure periods when they could be more enjoyably spent fishing or playing 18 holes of golf.

HOW TO WITHSTAND THE PRESSURES OF A BUSY SCHEDULE

Being at your brightest when meeting new clients and during business meetings is essential to creating good impressions. Worry and work frustrations create stress. They make you short-tempered, vulnerable to poor decision-making and damage your image in the face of others. A *paced* work schedule and *emotion-control* bring order, making it easier to cope with business pressure.

Learn to conserve energy and to release it gradually throughout your work period. One of the reasons Winston Churchill was able to withstand the great pressures and stress of the war years was because he taught himself to conserve energy and to release it when *he* determined it was important to do so. Churchill took frequent catnaps. He said they were a great aid to recharging mental, emotional and physical energy levels. Often he would spend long hours working from his bedroom. This isolation allowed him time to think, read and plan without interruption.

Some executives I know burn themselves out early in the day by rushing about and wasting energy. By early afternoon they are flagged-out, irritable and in no position to make sensible judgements on important issues. The key to lasting a long business day out is to release energy *slowly* rather than using it up in dynamic bursts when it is unnecessary to do so.

HOW TO PUT YOUR FEET UP AND STILL BE PRODUCTIVE

A business friend spends 10 minutes in meditation prior to important meetings at his office. He told me: 'I close my eyes, put my feet up on the desk, loosen my tie and rest my mind and body. It prepares me for the meeting ahead. I enter the meeting totally relaxed and my mind is razor sharp. The meditation period is one of the best energy-builders I know.'

As busy as you may get, a daily meditation period could well enhance your personal productivity without taking up valuable work time. Entering an important meeting under an umbrella of anxiety and tension demotes your demeanor and certainly doesn't put you in the right frame of mind for positive decision-making.

HOW AN EX-PRESIDENT HANDLED IMPORTANT DECISION-MAKING WITHOUT STRESS

For Richard Nixon, making decisions while he was in the White House was a solitary process of reading and thinking. Mr Nixon made it a practice to think very carefully before making an important decision. He liked to read the conflicting views of his advisers rather than be briefed by them. In keeping talk to a minimum during meetings, precious time and energy were saved. The ex-president never agonized prior to or after making a decision. 'Worry destroys personal confidence, creates stress and clouds the mind which impedes the decision-making process,' he once said.

Mr. Nixon very often decided major issues while sitting alone beside a log fire in a rustic guest house at Camp David, the Presidential retreat in Maryland. This quiet setting was ideal to contemplate, visualize and come to a decision about difficult matters. It's an ideal way to relax and decide on personal and career objectives. The formula is simple: select a quiet spot where you can be objective about important issues requiring a decision. Do not be an 'agonizer' when faced with a difficult problem. Execution of your decisions will be enhanced if you are confident, serene of mind and physically relaxed.

BOREDOM AND INACTIVITY ARE STRESS RELATED

When life becomes a bore, depression sets in and energy is drained which creates fatigue of mind and body. Life will become boring if you deny yourself creative interests and achievement challenges. Inactivity due to laziness or sheer boredom is life-wasting. It can also be frustrating and stress inducing.

Take a keen interest in people, places and things. Get out and about. Visit friends and relatives. Get interested in and involved with community work. If you are in a boring job then leave it and find something which excites and challenges you. The more enthusiastic you are about life, the more involved you will become in career advancement and creative accomplishment and the less time you will spend feeling sorry for yourself.

FAMOUS COMEDIAN HAS NO TIME TO BECOME BORED

When comedian Bob Hope celebrated his 88th birthday in 1991, he was asked by a reporter the secret of his high energy level and formidable work timetable. The legendary entertainer replied: 'I keep active. I'm never bored. I love my work. I also take care of myself. I watch what I eat. Wherever I am I take a long walk after dinner and I don't smoke. Activity without worry and stress keeps me young.'

HOW TO DETECT IF YOU ARE A WORKAHOLIC

Addiction to work in some cases, is as much a problem as addiction to alcohol. Far too many businesspersons are affected. Stress, migraine headaches and heart attacks are standard presents workaholics receive. Ulcers are a badge of office for workaholics. The remedy is to shorten work hours and to learn to relax.

Workaholic danger signs are: persons who work more than 50 hours a week. Those who rarely take a vacation or relax over a weekend. Persons who cannot relax with family or friends, who prefer to be in the office working or discussing work problems. Persons who feel more secure at work rather than in a family or social environment.

The answer to restoring balance to your business and personal life is to allocate specific work times and when they are up, stop work and go home. The benefits will more than outweigh the work time you give up.

You will think better, be able to concentrate with less strain, feel more relaxed, more in control and at the end of the day you will find it easier to sleep.

EAT AT PROPER TIMES TO RESIST STRESS

It is surprising how many business persons miss eating breakfast. The common excuse is, 'lack of time'. A proper breakfast can help to resist stress buildup. Food is a fuel. It is the basic source of human energy. If you miss breakfast and wait until lunchtime to eat, about 16 hours will have passed since you last had an intake of food. Missing breakfast can cause tiredness and give you a headache. It ruins your ability to think well and to make good decisions. Your brain, muscles and nerves are crying out for fuel.

The body converts food to glucose which is then carried in the blood to feed the brain, muscles and nerves. When this fuel source is used up, the body raids its fat source which causes the hormone levels to fluctuate bringing on feelings of hunger, fatigue and often depression and lightheadedness. A hearty breakfast, high in cereals, is a wise investment.

CEASE PILL AND DRUG TAKING UNLESS YOU WANT TO KILL YOURSELF

At the first sign of tension, some individuals nervously swallow a pill, smoke a cigarette or resort to alcohol to quieten nerves. Drug and alcohol taking to boost confidence is as useless as it is purposeless. The rewards are shortlived and often create on-going problems which usually end in health disaster and sometimes death. Persons unable to cope with personal and career pressures should seek help when the danger signals appear.

MONITOR YOUR ENERGY LEVEL FOR BENEFICIAL STRESS MANAGEMENT

The important law of stress management is to keep a check on your energy level, particularly during busy work periods. At regular intervals monitor how you feel — buoyant, happy or tired, depressed. When stress gets to you, your energy level drops rapidly. Try to slow down. Make a conscious effort to relax tense muscles, loosen stiff limbs and quieten the mind. Get up, take a walk around the block. Center your thoughts on pleasant things. Take deep breaths and exhale slowly. These simple techniques will relax your tension and insulate you against stress attacks.

LEARN TO ROLL WITH THE PUNCHES AND YOU WILL LIVE LONGER

A business friend in Vancouver, Canada, said to me: 'People I work with make me so mad. They waste time, are incompetent and contribute very little to our company. Many of their actions literally make me ill. I put in extra hours and do my job properly. Somehow, persons under me are being promoted and management seems to overlook my efforts.'

The frustration, anxiety and wrath of this executive created for him severe headaches, bouts of depression and a peptic ulcer. Over a pleasant dinner at the Hotel Vancouver, I explained to him that the seeming injustice had created in his mind a poison pocket resulting in physical illness and emotional torture. His negative attitude, making him resentful, angry and jealous, was the reason management chose others for promotion. Thinking over my remarks, he said to me: 'Yes, I can see your point. My anger has caused me to be irritable and highly-stressed. I need to remove this deep-seated resentment.'

When problems arise and personal or business troubles get to you, look upon each situation rationally. Allowing yourself to be pulled down by adversity nullifies your personal power, energy, self esteem and ability to think and act beneficially. Whenever anger, resentment, ill-will or spiteful thoughts enter your mind, cast them out. Your body is subject to your thoughts. It demonstrates what you think, feel and believe. A relaxed mind, free of enmity, fear and hate, helps you to rise above gloom and discouragement. It is a barrier to stress and physical discomfort. Learn to roll with the punches and you will not only live longer but you will live far happier.

TECHNIQUES TO STAY CALM AND RELAXED

When you feel tense, relax by directing your attention to your muscles. Command them to release tightness. Roll the head clockwise then anticlockwise until you feel tension releasing from the neck. Lift the shoulders and let them drop. Stand and stretch each leg. Shake each foot. Shake each arm and wrist. Repeat these exercises until you feel comfortably relaxed.

HOW TO DETECT AND STEM A STRESS ATTACK

It is a fact of modern-day living that stress is a killer. Nearly three-quarters of present-day illnesses are in some way related to stress. Knowing when a stress attack is imminent is important so that changes can be made to blunt its effects. Uncontrolled stress does the body great harm. Catching it early by heeding the danger signals saves the body from unnecessary punishment. Signals of a stress attack include:

- Heart beat quickens.
- Body heat increases.
- Excess sweating.
- Trembling hands.
- Muscles tighten, especially in the hands and neck.
- Shortness of breath.
- Recurring ulcers in the mouth.
- Rapid speech, slurring of speech.
- Loss of eye focus. Blurring of vision.
- Memory loss momentarily. The mind goes blank.
- Loss of self confidence. Feelings of inadequacy.
- Inability to think rationally and to make decisions.
- Stomach pains, nausea, flatulence.
- Irritability. Frequent mood swings.
- Lightheadedness.
- Loss of sense of humor.

- Fatigue. Unable to sleep.
- Frequent trips to the toilet.
- Loss of sexual drive.
- Frequent headaches.
- Drooping posture.
- Nervousness and an inability to relax.

ACHIEVERS CAN HAVE THEIR CAKE AND EAT IT TOO

The possibility of a heart attack caused by stress is a fear that overshadows many high-powered entrepreneurs. A hefty pay packet and acclaim are worth little if you fall victim to a serious illness. The late Larry Adler, an Australian insurance tycoon, once said that if a heart attack was the price he had to pay to maintain his furious pace he would 'pay it gladly'. Unfortunately, he paid the price. Pressure, stress and an enormous workload took their toll.

APPLY MORE BRAIN THAN BRAWN

Many executives thrive on hard work. Some spend up to 15 hours a day in a quest for big money and success. A sensible executive watches for the danger signs, avoids worrying over problems, relieves tension through exercise and through efficiency, makes the most of each work hour. The aim is to work *smarter*, not harder, by using more brain and less brawn.

POOR EATING HABITS AND DIET DEFICIENCY AFFECT YOUR LIFESPAN

Eating like a horse *or* starving yourself detrimentally influences the state of your health. Overweight people are unhealthy people. People who cheat themselves of a sufficient intake of good food are often subject to bouts of nervous tension, loss of vitality and mental alertness. Either extreme is dangerous. Eat according to what your body sensibly requires, not according to what you crave or because you want to become super slim.

Reduce your intake of starches, sugars, chemicalized and highly-processed foods. Fruit, vegetables, cereals, fish and poultry are sources of necessary protein, vitamins and minerals. Refrain from eating fried foods, fatty meat, rich pastries. Use honey as a sweetener. By developing good habits of daily exercise, adequate sleep periods and eating nourishing foods, you will improve your appearance, stay younger longer and attain physical well-being to carry you through a busy work schedule and energetic lifestyle.

ESTABLISH A WORKABLE LIFESTYLE PLAN

Establish a plan, a philosophy, a habit pattern which produces for you a *balanced* lifestyle filled with vitality, confidence and creative fulfillment. As an entrepreneur, a success-seeker, a person desiring to grow rich, you must manage your life efficiently, responsibly and effectively. Sort out your priorities. Take command of your mental and physical activities. Avoid a chaotic, stressful existence and you will fill your niche in life and be ready to confidently meet all challenges and obstacles.

STRESS
DANGER ZONES

When tired

When hungry

When lonely

When feeling ill

When fired from a job

When finances are low

When challenged on opinions

When involved in an accident

When rebuffed by another person

When a business enterprise has failed

When wrong decisions have been made

When under business tension and worry

When rejected by friends or a loved one

When placed in an embarrassing situation

When suffering from the loss of a loved one

When promises have been made by others and broken

When commencing a new business enterprise or project

FORMULAS TO GROW RICH

- Entrepreneurship can be both mentally and physically taxing. Good health is essential. The main problem facing high-powered executives is stress. Discipline of thoughts and emotions is required so that actions do not create tension and illness.

- Low self esteem is a breeding ground for anxiety, frustration and stress. Uplift your human status. Gain rock-solid confidence in your potential to become successful.

- Worry produces stress. Many problems we fuss over often do not come to pass. Spend time contemplating the success you desire and what you can *do* to bring it about. Cease fretting, fuming and fearing the challenges of life. Do not surrender your mind to fear. Place faith in your greatness, your skills and talents.

- Socrates said: *Know thyself.* Understand your true nature in the big scheme of things. Get an understanding of your true purpose. You were born to win. Open your mind to new ideas and beliefs. Don't be ignorant about life. When you gain knowledge and immerse yourself in the truths of life, problems and stress are overcome.

- Swallowing a pill, puffing on a cigarette, gulping down alcohol never has and never will cure anxiety, emotional problems and physical tension. Learn to cope without pill-popping. *Pace* your workload. Organize your time. Break work routines with short relaxation periods. Keep personal problems out of business affairs. Don't take business problems home. Make sure relaxation times are spent restfully, comfortably and happily.

- Learn to conserve energy. Don't burn yourself out early in the day. Release energy *slowly* rather than in dynamic spurts. Churchill took catnaps to conserve energy.

- Spend short periods throughout your workday in meditation. This is the quickest and simplest way to reduce tension.

- When life becomes a bore, depression sets in. Get enthusiastic about your life. Involve yourself in things that interest, excite and motivate you to get ahead.

- Don't allow others to depress you. Don't try to change others. Concentrate on your aims and objectives. Remove jealousy and resentment of others from your consciousness. Learn to roll with the punches.

- Monitor your mode of living. Eat the right foods. Get plenty of exercise. Make sure you have adequate amounts of sleep. Balance your lifestyle. Remain stress-free and you will live longer.

HOW TO GENERATE MILLIONAIRESHIP VIA YOUR OWN BUSINESS

FORMULA **11**

GOING IT ALONE CAN BE TOUGH BUT THE REWARDS ARE HIGH

It is the dream of many people to set themselves up in business, be their own boss and become successful and wealthy. There is a particular satisfaction derived in seeing something worthwhile develop from an idea, desire or achievement aim. Going it alone often requires tough decisions to be made along with long hours of hard work. It does not mean automatic success.

One of the most attractive aspects of self employment is an opportunity to 'do your own thing' without having to justify your actions to others. The downside of this is that the 'buck' stops with you if decisions and actions taken turn out to be wrong. Getting your act together then carefully proceeding with well-laid business plans safeguards your investment of time, energy and money. When you do it right, the rewards more than outweigh the risks which need to be taken.

THE REASONS SOME BUSINESS PERSONS DON'T MAKE IT

Surveys indicate that 90-percent of small business enterprises fail in the first 8 years of operation. Some 25-percent fail to reach an income of $200,000 per annum. Seven out of 10 business operators blame high interest rates, hefty taxes, economic downturns and incompetent employees as the cause of failure. While these factors play a role, the basic reason is management incompetence. Astute business practices must be adhered to, including keeping a watchful eye on income versus expenditure. Untrained and disinterested employees can easily ruin a business. Lack of finance and a hazy sense of sales and marketing direction are further reasons for business crashes. At the heart of it all, the person at the top is the *key* to long-term success.

THE EXPERTISE NEEDED TO WIN IN BUSINESS

The bottom line of any business is the *income* it can produce. Business longevity is tied to the *profits* received at the end of a financial period. Spending more money than taking in may be necessary in the beginning stages of a business. However, operating at a loss must be reversed as quickly as possible. Mounting debts can spell disaster.

Your business safety net is strengthened when you have strict control over expenditures, seize genuine opportunities, undertake well-calculated risks and have an overall strategy to generate ongoing income. Also, you will need to finance opportunities and gather the necessary marketing resources to exploit them. A lot of small businesses fail because of limited resources. If you lack the necessary capital to develop an idea, you will need to call on others for help. Make sure that your product, service or idea is innovative, has a ready market and is within your expertise to develop.

The essential ingredients to win in business revolve around personal presentation skill, decision-making and problem-solving ability and the determination to achieve carefully-planned goals. Strong belief is required in your organizing ability and effectiveness as a business person. Your objective is to minimize the chance of failure while maximizing the chance of success. Developing the aforementioned skills will help you to reach that objective.

WHEN YOU GO INTO BUSINESS GO IN TO WIN

The heyday of boxing was during the 1920s. In America, the colorful gambler Tex Rickard, became famous for his million-dollar boxing promotions. Prizefighting during this period became the most fashionable of all professional sports. Rickard promoted several world title fights with million-dollar gates including two heavyweight title fights between Gene Tunney and Jack Dempsey.

Jack Dempsey was known as the mauler. Once the bell sounded, he leapt into the fray like a wounded bull and habitually devoured his opponent round-after-round. Dempsey possessed an extraordinary dedication to winning at all costs. 'Whenever I step into the ring, I go in to win. I psyche myself into believing that I am the toughest man in the world,' Dempsey once told a sports writer. After his boxing days, Dempsey opened a restaurant in New York. 'It's the same principle in business. Go in to win,' was the champ's advice.

COMMITMENT TO WIN TURNED HOBBY INTO MULTI-MILLION-DOLLAR BUSINESS

Bill and Helen Parker are action-takers. Helen decided to sell beauty products as a hobby. Her selling skill and personality pushed the part-time venture into a full-time viable enterprise. 'Within two years I was grossing $2 million. I was earning more money than my husband. I needed a partner, so I convinced Bill to quit his job and join me. After 18 years managing someone else's business, Bill feels it's the smartest thing he's ever done,' Helen told me.

The couple employ a team of salespersons and yearly income now exceeds $7 million, just five years after commencing the operation. Bill didn't think the business would expand as quickly as it has and taking the decision to quit his secure job was a tough one. 'I've discovered that success in business has to be based on the premise that to win, it is necessary to commit oneself to making prompt decisions and taking fast action. If there is no commitment there is no action and therefore, no chance to win,' Bill advises.

HOW TO CONDITION YOURSELF TO WIN IN BUSINESS

Like the Parker formula, winning in business rests with your personal commitment to fully support your ideas — your personal causes — and take action on the possibilities and opportunities available to you. Where there is no commitment to your cause, there will be no action taken, no incentive to get up, get out and succeed. Condition yourself to win by firing your imagination with visions of the rich rewards success can bring. Open up new possibilities in your life via attitude expansion — *flexible thinking* — fixing your sights on a definite goal and then inciting an internal revolution which forces you to take the necessary action to accomplish your goal.

A loser is only a misguided winner. Picture yourself as a winner. Remove any conflicting opinions about yourself. Build yourself up. Believe in your cause. Belief determines your behavior, your path to winning or losing. Get your attitude set on getting into your own profitable business or expanding the business you are already in. When you *condition* your mind to win, there is no limit to how successful you can become.

IGNORE THE DOOMSDAY-SPRUIKERS

When you announce to relatives, friends and associates that you plan to go into business, you may be confronted by tear-down merchants, idea-spoilers, knockers and doomsday-spruikers who will attempt to dissuade you from taking such action. Following their advice, opinions and criticisms could be the undoing of an otherwise useful and potentially-profitable idea, career move or business venture. Always consider the source of the advice. Does it come from a successful business person, one you respect and is qualified to offer advice and guidance? If not, don't allow your shining idea to be dulled, your enthusiasm to be smothered and your actions to be dragged to a stop by an incompetent who can offer no more than negative suggestions.

CLASSIC CASES OF DOOMSDAY-SPRUIKING

There are hundreds of stories making the rounds of prominently-successful persons being advised early in their careers to stop wasting time on unworkable ideas or career moves. I outline some of the classic cases where, in some instances, the opinions and advice came from highly-intelligent business professionals. Condemning another person's idea is a common human pastime. Consider the following stories.

WON'T GET RICH BAKING COOKIES

Debbie Fields had a dream. She wanted to bake cookies and sell them. 'You won't get rich turning out cookies,' she was advised. Undaunted, Debbie started her business from her home kitchen in 1977. Debbie's edible idea now turns a neat profit of some $160 million a year. Mrs. Fields Cookies is a highly-successful American enterprise.

TALKING PICTURES HAVE NO FUTURE

D.W. Griffith was a respected silent picture director. He predicted that talking pictures 'won't stand a chance' because voices couldn't be synchronized with the images. How wrong he was. Lateral-thinking movie people pressed ahead with their claim that 'talkies' would revolutionize the motion picture industry.

TV HAS NO POTENTIAL—PEOPLE WON'T WATCH IT

Farsighted as they were about talking pictures, some in the film industry thought television would die quickly because the screen image was too small and it would be a strain on viewers' eyes. Even the *New York Times* felt people wouldn't sit with their eyes glued to a TV set because the average American family was 'too busy' to be bothered with it. I'm sure that every person reading this book has at least one TV set and spends several hours each week watching it.

FLYING IS AN IMPOSSIBILITY FOR MAN

In 1901, astronomer Simon Newcomb, said that 'flying for man is impossible'. Not long after this statement, the Wright brothers took to the air. Today, supersonic aircraft reach great heights and speeds, proving once again, how *possible* is the seemingly impossible.

BEETLE WON'T SELL IN GREAT NUMBERS SAID AUTO EXPERT

Sir William Rootes, who had a successful run making Britain's Hillman, Humber and Sunbeam Talbot cars, predicted that the VW Beetle 'won't sell in any great numbers' because it didn't meet the requirements of a motor car as perceived by the car-buying public. The Beetle became the biggest-selling car in the world.

FAILURE TOLD DETRACTORS TO SHUT UP AND BECAME A SUCCESS

Barry attended one of my success seminars. He was 29 and a self-admitted failure. 'My friends call me a loser and my family tag me a no-hoper. I'm in a dead-end job and I detest it. I've had a strong desire to open a retail store but everyone says I'll fail,' Barry told the group.

I asked him if he had enough money to rent premises and buy sufficient stock to get his business idea up-and-running. He said that he had saved five-thousand dollars and his bank manager had promised another five-thousand if he decided to set up in business. 'Do it,' I advised him. Find a suitable location, go see your bank manager and get started as soon as you can. I also advised him to listen to and respond to his *own* desires and aspirations and to turn a deaf ear to his detractors.

Three years have passed since Barry attended the seminar. He now owns five stores retailing ladies shoes and his income exceeds $4 million a year. 'I told my detractors to "shut up" and let me get on with making my life a success. It was the best move I've ever made,' Barry told me.

GENIUS TOLD HE WOULD NEVER AMOUNT TO ANYTHING

Albert Einstein as a schoolboy spent hours in the classroom working out equations on scraps of notepaper. One day an irate teacher snatched one of his notepads and angrily told him that for a boy of 14 he was 'incredibly stupid' and suggested he would never amount to anything.

A year later, the Einstein family moved to Milan. Albert studied physics and mathematics in nearby Switzerland. His parents thought him to be retarded as he wasn't making much progress at school. Fortunately, an uncle encouraged young Albert to pursue his interest in mathematics. In 1900, at age 21, Albert graduated and began developing his ideas in physics, setting himself the seemingly impossible task of linking time, space, matter and energy. Eventually, he published his theory of relativity and it brought him fame. This genius of science was told he would be a 'failure' in life. Einstein became the world's greatest thinker and one of the greatest physicists the world has ever known.

FAMOUS WRITER TOLD HIS WORK HAD NO POTENTIAL

Rudyard Kipling was sacked from the San Francisco *Examiner* in 1869 because the editor felt he wasn't talented at writing. 'I'm sorry that I'm the one who has to tell you, but you do not know how to use the English language, Mr. Kipling,' the editor told him. Fortunately, Kipling took no notice of the editor's opinion and continued writing.

COMIC STRIP (NOT WORTH MUCH) MADE MILLIONS

In 1938, Joe Shuster and Jerry Siegel were told that they had created a 'nine-day-wonder' when they tried to sell their Superman comic strip. Convinced the detractors were right, they sold the strip to Action Comics for a mere $130. Superman captured an enormous audience through comic books, newspaper comic pages, a TV series and blockbuster movies which grossed hundreds of millions of dollars. 'We listened to the wrong advice and it was poor judgement on our part to sell Superman,' Jerry Siegel lamented some years after Superman became a world-wide success.

ADVISOR TO CZAR TOLD HIM TO SELL ALASKA

In 1867, Czar Alexander II sold Alaska to the Americans for the paltry sum of $7,200,000. An advisor urged the Czar to 'get what you can' for the frozen wasteland. Twenty years later, one man alone, Alec McDonald, mined $20 million worth of gold out of his Alaskan claim. Today, hundreds of millions of dollars worth of oil flows from what was once described as a worthless, frozen wasteland.

NO BIG MONEY IN SELLING HAMBURGERS

When Ray Kroc told some business friends that he was going to buy a hamburger stand from two brothers named McDonald, they laughed and told him to find a business that would make 'big bucks'. Kroc ignored their advice. He ended up making almost a billion dollars selling McDonald's hamburgers. Ray Kroc was a man of vision, a natural winner with energy and good merchandising ideas.

DREAMS OF POTENTIALLY-SUCCESSFUL CAN BE RUINED BY DETRACTORS

The lives of many potentially-successful persons have been impaired through the cruel, stupid, ill-timed and unwarranted opinions and criticisms offered by well-meaning family, friends and business associates. Stand up and fight for what you believe in, what you want to accomplish and have. Your good fortune doesn't rest with the opinions of others. It rests with you, the energy you exert, the calculated risks you take and the confidence you establish in your ideas and ideals. Look to the future. See yourself happy, successful, wealthy and creatively-productive.

Tell the knockers to be quiet. You have the potential to succeed but you've got to get up off the seat of your pants and with gumption get yourself moving. By taking action, you will make things happen. You will expand your creative horizon and become the person you wish to become.

ESTABLISH THE RIGHT INCENTIVE BEFORE GOING IT ALONE

Examine the reasons for establishing your own business. The thought of reaping millions of dollars is a good incentive but it might not be realistic. Do you possess the necessary business skills, temperament, financial resources and entrepreneural attributes to succeed on your own? As mentioned in an earlier chapter, don't be a silly risk-taker, an unthinking action-taker. Give careful consideration to what you want to do and how you propose to raise the capital to set your business up. Give yourself a rational *incentive* to win. Money may be part of it, but consider the following incentives: creative satisfaction, respect from others for your achievements, an opportunity to employ and assist others, financial independence.

RATE YOUR CHANCES FOR SUCCESS

Study the following list of business-success attributes and score one point for each attribute you possess. A score of 8 or more and you can be reasonably confident that you are a good candidate for starting and succeeding in your own business.

—STRONG-WILLED SURVIVOR	☐	—OPPORTUNITY SEEKER	☐
—FLUENT COMMUNICATOR	☐	—INFORMATION GATHERER	☐
—METHODICAL PLANNER	☐	—ASTUTE MONEY-HANDLER	☐
—DISCIPLINED ACTION-TAKER	☐	—SELF-MOTIVATOR	☐
—PERSONABLE PEOPLE-MOVER	☐	—PRECISE TIME MANAGER	☐

SEEK THE RIGHT ASSISTANCE

There are efficient and practical ways of operating a business which should be discovered and followed. A business operator should have a working knowledge of how to keep acceptable records of income and expenditure. The taxation office no longer tolerates haphazard bookkeeping methods. Therefore, your corporate records need to be kept up-to-date either by yourself or a person qualified to do so. Seek a good accountant. When you find a person you can establish a rapport with, stick with him or her. An accountant needs to know how you operate your business and what its strengths and weaknesses are.

Get to know a good lawyer. There will be times when you will need legal advice — contracts read and written, negotiations conducted. Being your own lawyer may cost you little in the short term but could cost you plenty should you run into problems. Never sign a lease agreement or contract without *first* having it vetted by a lawyer.

Training is a solid investment for every person wanting business success. There are numerous courses covering public speaking, motivation, goals planning, sales and marketing, small business management, negotiating, letter writing, bookkeeping, operating a computer, etc. Seek them out and improve your business acumen and personal presentation.

ESTABLISHING YOUR OWN BUSINESS

Once the decision has been made to operate your own business, you will need to explore the market you wish to sell to and arrange the necessary capital to establish your enterprise. Location of your premises is important. A retail business must have a steady volume of passing trade with ample parking for customers. A manufacturing industry doesn't need to be in a high-rent area but should be near public transport for the convenience of employees. Those in a service industry or profession may require an up-market image. Therefore, premises in a good area, easily accessible and impressively decorated, should be considered. Whatever type of business you establish, it is recommended that you join your local Chamber of Commerce and any organization specifically related to your enterprise. Membership in a Lions or Rotary Club is also beneficial. It gives an opportunity to participate in community functions and events which help others in some way.

SELECT AN APPROPRIATE BUSINESS NAME

A good business name should reflect the product or service you offer. Avoid a non-descript name: *Abbot Services.* It offers no clue as to *what* service is offered. A name which specifically spells-out what you offer is good advertising: *Success Training Company, Jane Bell Beauty Products, Thrifty Cleaning Supplies, Business Computer Services, Golf Imports.*

It is a requirement that every business name be registered with an appropriate government authority. This law applies even if you intend to use your *own* name but with an attachment to it: *John Brown Electrical Contracting*. Banks, suppliers and consumers need to have confidence in a business they deal with. A legally-registered business helps to establish this basic trust.

SELECTING THE RIGHT BUSINESS STRUCTURE

There are several forms of business structure, each having its own legal and accounting requirements that should be considered. You may begin with one form and convert to another as your business expands. The four basic structures are: sole trader, partnership, limited liability (private) company, public corporation.

SOLE TRADER: if you intend to go solo or hire employees, you can trade under a business name with any appropriate government licences that are required. All the profits are yours, but so are the liabilities and responsibilities if the business doesn't succeed. You are master of your own fate as a sole trader.

PARTNERSHIP: Any two or more people may form a partnership, joining together to share expenses, profits, effort and expertise. If no formal partnership agreement exists, it is deemed by law that they are *equal* partners. Be cautious in this regard. Liability is unlimited and may fall on any of the remaining partners if one absconds or dies.

LIMITED LIABILITY COMPANY: for a small to medium-size business, the appropriate structure is a proprietary limited company. If you form a company you become an employee *and* a director. Your responsibilities are set out by a government Companies Code. A company is a separate legal entity and can sue or *be* sued, but the liability of company members (in most instances) is limited. Generally, directors are required to give personal guarantees when the company borrows funds, takes out a lease or orders substantial amounts of stock. Company accounts must be filed annually. There are certain tax advantages to a company formation and these should be explored.

PUBLIC CORPORATION: if you intend to trade nationally or internationally and the size of the operation is big in terms of producing a product or service with a large number of employees and capital requirement, then floating a public (shareholding) corporation may be a necessity. Rigid rules apply and where shares are traded, the company must be an open book and follow strict guidelines as set forth by the appropriate government authority.

Whatever structure you decide (in consultation with a lawyer and accountant) is right for you, be sure that you fully understand your obligations and responsibilities, both legally and professionally. The rule: *iron-out difficulties before taking on responsibilities.*

TAKING ON A FRANCHISE

Franchising is very popular. It is a type of business ownership whereby an individual, partnership or company can operate an independent business under the cover of an already established enterprise. Franchising offers easier access to finance, direct benefit from group advertising and marketing, better group buying power, management and industry support.

A franchise agreement outlines the rights and obligations of both the franchisor and the franchisee. It is a legal contract and binds both parties to certain rules and regulations from which income will result. An operations manual sets out how the business is to be run which circumvents 'doing your own thing'. You join a team and every team member must adhere to the business formula set out in the franchise manual. In addition to an up-front fee, royalties, or percentage of turnover are charged.

HOW TO SPOT THE TRAPS

Franchising or buying an already established business can have traps for the unwary investor. An unreliable franchisor, one minus a strategic business plan, industry knowledge and back-up, could well spell disaster, resulting in the franchise system collapsing. Have a franchise agreement vetted by a lawyer. Scrutinize the operations manual. Talk to existing franchise holders. Establish the motives for franchising when you check the track record of the franchisor. Clarify any vague claims made by the franchisor. When buying an existing business, satisfy yourself that what you are being told and shown leave no room for misunderstanding or misrepresentation of the offering.

ARRANGING FINANCE

You may find it necessary to take out a loan or establish a bank overdraft to get your business up-and-running. A friendly, generous bank manager is a necessity. This person is sometimes hard to find. Some bank managers are not readily accessible. If the manager of your present account branch isn't known to you, call him or her and make an appointment. A bank manager can help or hinder according to 'whim' or to his or her assessment of you. Therefore, you must present yourself as a reliable, responsible, forthright person. Your bank manager must establish confidence in you and see you as a good bank customer rather than a high-risk client.

On your first meeting, give your bank manager a business proposal. Present the full facts: what you desire to achieve, how you plan to market your product or service, its market potential, an estimate of running expenses and income, a list of assets and liabilities, the loan or overdraft amount you require and for what period of time you will need financial assistance. Remember, a bank manager is not there to tell you how to run your business or how and where to spend the money the bank may advance. It's the manager's job to build up a portrait of your character and examine your capabilities in order to judge whether you are a 'risk' or someone the bank regards as a 'viable' client. Banks make their money by making loans. If you present well, you shouldn't have any difficulty persuading a bank to help you get your business up-and-running.

ESTABLISH SUITABLE RECORDS

Basic records should be kept to keep your business affairs orderly. You will need to produce up-to-date information on the state of your business so you know *how* you are going and *where* you are going. A computer is a worthwhile investment in this regard. Such aspects as stock, finance, inventory control, wages, insurance, expenses, customer information, marketing trends, costing, production scheduling, profit projections, sales planning, mailing list, etc. can be programmed into a computer and retrieved as required.

Survival in business is largely dependent on having accurate and timely information on the financial state of your business and whether or not it is running according to plan. The general business climate needs to be assessed from time-to-time in order to change strategies and tactics if necessary. Good record keeping greatly assists in spotting potential problems so that quick action can be taken to circumvent them.

Separate your personal records from business records. Keep your business bank account separate from your personal account. If you do not draw a salary from your business, you will need to show where your living expenses are drawn from. When your enterprise becomes viable, it is best to pay yourself a salary in keeping with what the business can afford. Otherwise, draw one cheque for all your personal needs each week or month but do not take any other money from the business account for personal use.

INSURANCE PROTECTION IS VITAL

Establish a rapport with a helpful insurance broker. You will need insurance protection in business and a knowledgeable insurance agent is the best way to establish your needs and find your way through the insurance traps. You will need to ascertain what type of cover is best, how much you should buy, what types of risk each policy covers. Some insurance companies sell a special business pack which covers several risk areas under the one policy: fire and theft, stock loss, public liability, tenant's liability, employee dishonesty cover, revenue loss, products liability, etc. Know exactly what your premiums are buying and be sure to adequately cover yourself against possible loss.

ESTABLISH A WORKABLE BUDGET

Basic budgeting techniques should be applied to six areas essential to business success. Your business will face a range of costs and these are affected differently by changes in business activity. It is necessary to know what monies you must pay out each month, what your break-even point is and what costs are fixed or variable. By working to a budget you have a chance to plot a steady course of action and to make changes to your marketing strategy should it be necessary to do so. The six budget areas are:

1: SALES
2: INVENTORY
3: PURCHASES
4: EXPENSES
5: PROFITS
6: CASH FLOW

ADVERTISING AND MARKETING

The lifeblood of many businesses is the income generated through marketing and clever advertising. Marketing helps to establish whether there is a *need* for your product or service and how to *meet* that need profitably. If you do not understand the principles of basic marketing, there are many books and short courses available for the business-person wishing to establish an overview of the subject.

Your budget may or may not stretch to hiring the services of an advertising agency to promote your goods or services. Advertising must reach your target audience and be clear in composition to motivate them to buy from you. Advertising in newspapers, on the radio and TV can be costly. Therefore, it must be determined which areas of advertising will be cost effective. Mail order items require a good mailing list, clever brochures or catalogues which may need the support of newspaper advertisements. A unique mail order item may achieve high sales via television commercials. It would pay to discuss your needs with experts in this field. If your budget allows for it, discuss your requirements with advertising experts who will quickly assess your needs and offer advice on getting your product or service before consumers.

SALES AND ADMINISTRATION EXPERTISE

The two major areas related to business success are sales and administration. In any business, nothing happens until someone *sells* something. Selling ability — communication and motivation — is a skill that can quickly be learned through training. If you feel that you lack sales ability, then enrol in a sales course. Good administration calls for a practical, sensible and orderly way of conducting your business. Planning, budgeting, record keeping, invoicing, bill paying, employee and customer complaint handling, all come under the banner of *administration*. It is often time-consuming work, but necessary, if you desire your business to run smoothly and profitably.

HOW TO AVOID MANAGEMENT PITFALLS

Management experts identify ten errors often made by inexperienced business persons. Study the list and if applicable, quickly move to upgrade your position and thus minimize the risk of business failure.

1: LACK OF SKILLS TRAINING
2: POOR ADMINISTRATIVE ABILITY
3: INADEQUATE RECORD KEEPING—BUDGET CONTROL
4: NO BUSINESS PLANS (MARKETING STRATEGY)
5: INSUFFICIENT CAPITAL—POOR CASHFLOW
6: MISUSE OF TIME—DISSIPATION OF ENERGY
7: PERSONNEL AND CLIENT MISHANDLING
8: FAILURE TO ASSUME MANAGEMENT–LEADERSHIP ROLE
9: FAILURE TO DETECT AND ADAPT TO CHANGING MARKET CONDITIONS
10: LACK OF SALES ABILITY AND POOR PERSONAL PRESENTATION

TAKE POSITIVE ACTION EVEN IF IT HURTS

Failure to act quickly when problems arise can often lead to business collapse. Some decisions may give cause for concern, particularly where they adversely affect others. Weigh the pros-and-cons of tough decisions to be made and go with what is fair, honest and in the best interests of your business. The rule is to take positive action *quickly* — even if it hurts.

EMPIRE-BUILDER TOOK POSITIVE ACTION WHEN CONFRONTED WITH LOSSES

Dr. An Wang passed away at age 70. He will be remembered for his advances in computer technology. Setting up Wang Laboratories in 1951, he worked from the back room and first floor of his electrical hardware store in Boston. By 1964, the company had made huge inroads into the business computer market which catapulted it into the billion-dollar bracket when it introduced the desktop calculator.

Dr. Wang was a brilliant, decisive and caring man who built his empire by applying sound business principles and taking tough decisions when required. During the 1980s, the company magic declined and it reported losses. Dr. Wang had to make a very difficult decision regarding his eldest son Frederick, who was Wang's chief operating officer. Frederick was removed from the position of company president and placed into another position. 'The reality of business is that there can be no sentiment expressed when it comes to hard decisions which have to be made,' Dr. Wang said at the time.

SURVIVING TOUGH TIMES

With interest rates high and likely to stay that way, with consumers purchase-selective and ultra careful in the way they spend their hard-earned money and with taxation grabbing hugh chunks of business profit, survival in business is difficult — but not impossible. The secret to survival in tough economic times is to be financially strong. Highly-geared businesses, those in debt and tied to banks, are the first to fall when a business slump arrives. Traders who can minimize debt and maximize cash flow are in a position to ride-out tough times and experience better days.

The key to business survival is to take remedial action promptly. But don't panic. Adopt a workable strategy and stick to it. Try to get as much cash on hand as possible. Look to reduce expenditure. Assess what you don't require, how you can cut costs without affecting your cash flow. Concentrate on areas which bring major profits. Don't order stock which requires up-front money to purchase but returns a small profit. Keep in mind that profit is not realized until the debt is paid and you have sold the item or service. Good stock control means cutting back on stock you need least.

Fixed overheads such as rent, electricity and telephone are hard to reduce. However, look at office or shop expenditures which can be cut down. Items such as stationery, staff amenities, equipment which can be repaired rather than replaced, vehicle costs, etc. Look to reduce staff levels. Non-productive people — those who do not produce income — can be carried when times are good, but not when times are tough.

CHASE DEBTORS WITH A FIRM HAND

Your suppliers will expect prompt payment for the goods and services you order. You also must see to it that those owing your business money, pay promptly. Don't be afraid to get on the phone every day and ring debtors. It's a business fact that arm-twisters and nuisances get paid first. If your accounts are on 7, 14 or 30 days credit, then make sure debtors pay on time. An inducement of some small percentage for paying within the stated time often works well because it adds to the purchaser's profit margin. Keep a watch on all clients for signs that they are going bad. Smaller than usual orders, late payments for goods or services received, retrenchment of employees, are indicators which should not be ignored. Read the finance pages of newspapers and magazines. These are a good source of information on how well or poorly a company is operating. Trying to collect money owed to you once a company has declared bankruptcy is fruitless. You are placed on the debtors' list and may or may not receive a penny.

EXPAND YOUR CIRCLE OF CONTACTS

Business networking is essential to business expansion. Cultivate support contacts. Everyone you meet may be capable of assisting you in some way at some time in the future. Always have a business card ready to hand out whether you are mixing with people in business or social circles. The phrase, 'Perhaps I can help you at some time,' is a useful one to use when giving out your card. Mixing with people is a good way to gain access to previously unknown information which could lead to an opportunity, an increase in business or ideas that could be incorporated in your business. Talk, listen, become involved and through networking, many opportunity-doors will open to you.

HIRING SUITABLE BACKSTOPS

Every person you employ must contribute in some way to the income you wish to produce. Employee selection is critical. Every person working for you must contribute in a positive way to the image you desire to create, the customer/client list you must build and the company loyalty you expect. Employees should be capable of working honestly and with total dedication to the goals you set. Look for a suitable backstop, a person capable of taking over your duties should you fall ill, travel overseas or need to be away from your business for any period of time.

EMPLOYER-EMPLOYEE RELATIONSHIPS

The golden rules of employer-employee relationships are these: keep your distance. Don't become overly friendly with those you employ. Should problems arise, it is difficult to take firm action. Give clear instructions so that there can be no breakdown in communication of your wishes. Set a dress, performance and time rule at the outset. Otherwise, you may lose control of the running of your business. Expose your company policy to your employees so that they fully understand it and are able to express it to those you do business with. Surround yourself with a leadership-managerial aura. If your employees think of you as a dope, they will treat you accordingly. Employees must see you as important, smart, knowledgeable and successful — a person they look up to, wish to emulate and associate with. Treat all employees firmly but fairly.

AND FINALLY ...

Going into any enterprise has as its principal aim *profit*. Without it, your dream will be shortlived. Accumulating losses is easy. Accumulating profits takes skilled management on your part. Building a strong business future will be dependent on how soundly your business is structured. Remember, under-capitalization is one of the reasons a business fails. Make sure you do not rush into a no-win situation through an insufficient capital base.

Make sure that there is a demand for the type of business you contemplate in a particular area. Be satisfied that this demand will grow, taking your business with it. The location you select must suit the needs of your business in terms of passing trade, parking facilities for deliveries, clients and employees. The area you select should reflect the image you wish to create for your business.

Check your lease agreement for restrictions: can you sub-lease, have 24 hour access, carry on your specific line of business, is there an option to renew? Owning your own premises is the ideal way to go. It allows you to add improvements to your premises which add to your corporate image as well as to your real estate investment.

Determine your immediate, short-term, medium-term and long-term requirements for stock, plant or equipment. Ascertain with those who supply your stock whether you have the right to return unsold or unsatisfactory stock. Check on the nature of warranties covering plant and equipment.

Analyze the best structure for your business: sole trader, partnership, limited company or public corporation. Careful legal planning will help to protect you and a knowledgeable accountant will indicate how to maximize after-tax profits. There will be a need for complete record keeping of income and outgoings. And you will need insurance to cover and protect your business interests. Also, information on employee salary awards and entitlements and the relevant terms and conditions of employment.

Millionaires are emerging every hour of every day in all countries of the world. The opportunity to succeed in your own enterprise is alive and awaiting your call. You too, can become a self-employed millionaire through workable ideas, taking on challenges and having the intestinal fortitude to stick with your aspirations and dreams through to fulfillment.

FORMULAS TO GROW RICH

- If your dream is to set yourself up in business, be your own boss and become successful and wealthy, *now* is the time to begin assembling your ideas, making plans and getting your act together. Remember, the buck stops with you. Your decisions and actions will decide whether you stay at the bottom or reach the top. Being in business for yourself does not guarantee success. Statistics indicate a hefty failure rate. Plan carefully.

- The bottom line is how much *profit* your business can generate. Strict control must be exercised over expenditure. You must be capable of generating on-going income.

- Go into business to *win*. Fight like a champ — fairly — to achieve your aims. It will take strong commitment to your ideas and ideals. Don't be a misguided loser. Picture yourself as a winner. Believe in your cause. Be a *flexible* thinker and incite an internal revolution which drives you to take on challenges, see them through and win.

- Ignore doomsday-spruikers — friends, family and business associates who want to tear down your success-seeking aims.

- Establish a suitable *incentive* before starting out. Give yourself a really good reason to empire-build. Be realistic, not a silly risk-taker. Your motive must be rational, realistic and attainable.

- Always seek advice from professionals who have experience in matters that you do not: accountant, lawyer, finance advisor, etc. Be cautious. Even experts can be wrong.

- Explore the market you wish to cater to. Know that your product or service offering has potential so that your business grows along with the *need* for your offering. Market research is the key to discovering the viability of a product or service.

- Select an appropriate business name and the correct business structure. If you take on a franchise business, make sure you know what you are committing yourself to and have contract and lease agreement vetted by a lawyer.

- Get on friendly terms with your bank manager. Be sure to establish suitable records for accounting and tax purposes. Select carefully the amount of insurance cover your business is likely to need. Set out a workable budget. Plan your promotional and advertising requirements with the help of professionals.

- Sensible management principles must be applied if you are to survive in business. Get training in skills you need. Here's your chance to make it big.

HOW TO NEGOTIATE YOUR WAY TO POWER AND RICHES

FORMULA 12

LIKE IT OR NOT YOU ARE A NEGOTIATOR

Everyone is in the business of negotiating — communicating and motivating. All persons in business, commerce and the professions must, on a day-to-day basis, negotiate to improve their position, status and income. Whether selling a product or service, entering into a contract, settling a dispute or establishing a favorable purchase price for a desired item, negotiating skill is the key factor which gives one person an edge over another. Like it or not, good at it or not, you are a negotiator. The more skilled you are at negotiation, the more expedient will be your rise to power and riches.

COMMUNICATION CONFIDENCE IS ESSENTIAL TO POCKET PEOPLE

Any person lacking communication confidence is destined for an unexciting existence. If you feel uncomfortable when confronted by others and cannot confidently put across your ideas and opinions, you are going to be stepped on and easily intimidated by others. A nervous, weak-minded person is the first to fall whenever problems, difficult situations and tough circumstances arise. A strong-minded, self-assured person, good at *self* expression, is a front-runner, a power-broker who ends up a winner whenever challenging situations come up. Your desire to become a successful entrepreneur demands that you raise your level of importance via the ability to sway (through emotional appeal), convince and change the opinions, ideas and actions of those who oppose you. When you acquire negotiating skill, it makes people consciously take notice of you and it raises their estimation of you. When you do that, you will win them over, gain their trust and pocket them effortlessly.

IDEA ENUNCIATION IS ESSENTIAL TO BUSINESS SUCCESS

Every day in the course of your business dealings, you will be meeting people and influencing their lives in some way. Therefore, you must enunciate your ideas and business philosophy in a lucid and dynamically-appealing way. The art of communication calls for an ability to express clearly *exactly* what you think and feel. If the person listening to you cannot grasp what you are saying or is confused by your statements and requests, then you are a poor communicator and therefore, a hopeless negotiator. Your aim in this regard is to enhance your speaking skill, enabling you to communicate easily, naturally, confidently and persuasively.

HOW TO IMPROVE YOUR NEGOTIATING ABILITY

Entrepreneurs, business managers and leaders are called upon to balance numerous conflicting situations and business dealings. Where a negotiator has little experience in this regard, results can be costly, time consuming and frustrating. Negotiating skill is an essential attribute for the leader and business manager. If you are a poor communicator and motivator, you must quickly take steps to improve your position or you will be at the mercy of those who sense your weakness. Reading books and listening to tapes on the subject are most helpful. Combine this with a formal training course or workshop which gives you an opportunity to try out newly-discovered techniques on others in the course.

When you are in a position to quickly resolve problems, disputes and negotiation issues, the more time and energy there is to spend on transforming goals into a reality. You will experience fewer stressful and frustrating periods and more productive and creative times as the effective empire-builder you desire to be.

THE CORRECT INTERPRETATION OF NEGOTIATION

The meaning of the word *negotiation* is simply this: to confer, bargain, discuss with a view to reaching agreement. The goal to set in order to reach an agreement is to achieve a fair, mutually-acceptable and amicable settlement. While one party may not be (totally) happy, it should feel that the matter has been handled justly and without bias.

ESTABLISH A FAIR-MINDED ATTITUDE

There are people who are of the opinion that negotiating personal or business contracts and disputes is a matter of getting the best of an opposing party, taking a person down or through unfair means winning without conscience. This attitude is a fast-track to losing rather than winning. Never replace fair and honest negotiation strategies and tactics with verbal assault, intimidation or ruthless aggression. Long-term personal and business relationships are established when you earn the respect and trust of others. Strike an attitude of understanding, friendliness and fellowship. It quickly disarms those who may harbor antagonism and resentment toward you.

THE FIVE FACTORS TO NEUTRALIZE OPPOSING FORCES

Courting others, fawning over them, giving in easily to them are not the suggested ways of good negotiation. The important factors in harmonious human relationships are five in number. When you apply them, antagonistic barriers are removed.

1: Extend common courtesy to others.
2: Show respect for the opponent.
3: Acknowledge the other person's point-of-view.
4: Display impeccable manners.
5: Be willing to give a little.

ALWAYS FOLLOW THIS PRINCIPLE

A simple rule to follow in all business dealings is: never leave your opponent the total loser. When you *win* all, leaving your opponent to *lose* all, you create an enemy. Not all persons you do business with will love you, but you should never go out of your way to cause them to hate you. Treading others into the dust rules them out for assistance in the future. Don't burn bridges you may need to cross at a later time. Be satisfied with a winning *edge* over an adversary. Leave enough spoils for that person to rise and meet another day. Remember, a favor given is often a favor returned.

DEFINE THE PROBLEM BEFORE SETTING THE GOAL

Preparing a negotiation strategy is fruitless until you take as a first step *definition* of the dispute, claim against you, objection *to* or rejection *of* your proposition. Set out in written form and in simple, concise terms the differences which exist between you and your opponent. What is the *reason* for the dispute? What are the facts surrounding it? Is there validity to the claim, argument, proposal being presented by the other party? What are the possible consequences of a *for* or *against* decision once it's been made?

Call for the facts. Don't be swayed by emotive outbursts or exaggerated claims. Get to the *core* of the matter. Call for research material which will support claims made, dates given or figures stated. Study any contractual or legal provisions which could affect the negotiations. The more information you have, the easier it will be to mount an effective proposal, counter argument or satisfactory settlement offer.

ESTABLISHING A WINNING STRATEGY

When you have defined the issues at hand, plot a course of action — the *basis* of the argument you intend to put forth to achieve your goal. In order to do this successfully, you must evaluate the position of your opponent(s) if there is a disputation to resolve. Where you are negotiating a contract, you need to get a 'feel' for what the other party will accept, whether he or she is likely to compromise on certain points and the bottom line or cut-off point. Try to figure out the position your opponent is likely to take. Will you be confronted by one or more hostile persons? What questions might be asked of you? Do you have all necessary information at hand to competently answer them? Do you fully understand the issues? What are the interests, motives and concerns of each party?

Your strategy should aim for simplicity in defining your wants, presenting your points-of-view, pressing your claims and presenting an offer of settlement. It should confine itself to the issues and specifically the major points. It should steer clear of personality bashing. Other points to consider when plotting your course of action are:

- Be specific about what you want.
- Support your arguments and claims with facts.
- Establish what your first offer will be.
- Decide on the concessions you are prepared to make.
- Arrive at your bottom line.
- Decide who should attend meetings.
- What questions need to be asked of the other party?
- Should the negotiations be conducted in stages?
- Summarize the proposal in a list of key points.

DETERMINE WHERE NEGOTIATIONS SHOULD TAKE PLACE

Negotiating simple deals such as purchases, refund amounts, standardized agreements, should be conducted in the most convenient location for those involved. Formal contract negotiations should be held in a quiet, comfortable meeting room or office and be free of distractions and interruptions. When trying to interest a client in a product or service, make sure the meeting area is noise free and not in a busy customer or employee atmosphere. Attempting to convince a prospective client to purchase a product, sign a contract or enter into negotiations in an unfavorable atmosphere will prove to be, more often than not, unproductive. Where conflict is likely to arise due to controversial issues to be negotiated, it is best to conduct the meeting privately in your own premises which gives you a psychological advantage. People are less likely to engage in shouting matches when they are guests and in unfamiliar territory.

Sitting behind a large desk in your private office or at the head of a board table are other advantages which may work in your favor. Where a group is involved in negotiations, a round table is the accepted seating arrangement giving both sides equal presentation status.

SET APPROPRIATE TIMES FOR IMPORTANT MEETINGS

The late Howard Hughes conducted some of his important meetings in hotel toilets during the early hours of the morning. This supposedly gave him a psychological advantage over his adversaries. A hotel toilet after midnight might be a suitable venue to intimidate another person but I suggest it is not conducive to on-going harmonious business relationships. A hotel dining room over a pleasant meal is a more appropriate place, offering a chance of a better result in *your* favor, particularly if you are picking up the tab.

DETERMINE WHO SHOULD ATTEND

Group meetings to iron-out problems, resolve contractual obligations or make a product presentation require several people in attendance: lawyers, accountants, bankers, union officials, sales persons, management personnel, etc. Keep the number as small as possible. Invite only the principals concerned with decision-making. Where there is a disputation, there is a chance that too many persons involved could side-track issues, engage in heated exchanges and bruise egos, thus lengthening the debate, upsetting your strategy and destroying an opportunity to negotiate an agreement.

I have witnessed good product demonstrations crippled by the careless, inane remarks of a minor employee, a secretary and a wife of a company director — all imagined themselves qualified to comment and sway the decisions of the decision-makers. Too many cooks in the kitchen can be a problem. If you have a group presentation coming up, make sure you are the only cook serving to a group of buyers anxiously awaiting your offering.

GROUP PRESENTATIONS SHOULD CONCENTRATE ON BENEFITS

When dealing with a group of buyers, concentrate on the *benefits* your product or service offers. Answer questions about the various features, the marketability and success already experienced. Steer clear of critical issues such as price and contractual terms and conditions. Even one negative response can destroy your chance of signing prospects. Presentations should be kept simple and to a time schedule. Where necessary, use charts, product models, video, slides to emphasize your main points. The secret to group sales and negotiation success is to be as brief, informative and entertaining as possible. Price and trading terms should be discussed with individuals at the *conclusion* of the presentation rather than to the group during the presentation.

Instead of calling for questions ask the group what further information you can provide. It sounds more inviting, less threatening than, 'do you have questions?' The thrust of your message should be: 'I'm here to help all of us win.'

SEEING IS BELIEVING

When putting a proposition to a group, it is better to show, where possible, the benefits which are likely to accrue rather than just talk about them. *Seeing is believing.* Use visual aids which clearly display the main thrust of your point-of-view and support your proposition as being worthy of their serious consideration. When your audience can actually *see* the benefits with their own eyes, there can be little argument or suspicion of your proposal and statements of claim. The *show* rather than *talk* technique is a persuasive communication tool for the professional negotiator.

PREPARE ANSWERS TO LIKELY QUESTIONS BEFORE MAKING A PRESENTATION

Professional public speakers know that *preparation* is the key to successful presentation. This rule also applies to those desiring to become successful negotiators. If you find yourself embroiled in argument with a group you are attempting to win over, then you have let yourself down by not preparing your presentation in a well thought-out way. Anticipate likely questions and prepare suitable answers. There's always a 'smart person' waiting to cut a presenter down to size. If this should occur, directly confront the stirrer. Hold eye contact and give your answer in a steady, strong and measured tone of voice. It may be appropriate to begin: 'That's a very good question and the answer is this . . . ' Don't let yourself become rattled or moved to nervousness displaying nervous gestures. The stronger you confront the 'wise-guy' the more your audience will side with you. Stand firm against intimidation. Be ready for it. Prepare a strategy to handle it.

HOW TO HANDLE THE INTERJECTOR

When negotiating a proposition to a group, you may be confronted by one or more interjectors desiring to test their own power and influence over you. Don't be unnerved by these thoughtless individuals. Regardless of what might be said, maintain your composure. Where appropriate, smile and ask: 'Do you have a legitimate question to ask or are you making a personal observation based on your limited knowledge of my proposal?'

A person deliberately rude should be handled politely but firmly by saying: 'I'm quite sure it is not your intention to be rude, so I will continue.' It is unwise to enter into a verbal sparring match with interjectors. There is a possibility you could come off second best, lose your composure and the sympathy of the audience. At all costs, remain in control of your presentation and your audience. Confidence, charm and politeness will keep an audience on *your* side.

HOW TO IMMEDIATELY WIN AN AUDIENCE

Negotiating with a group of people can be tricky. It is easy for them to remember your name, but not always easy for you to remember the names of all those present. Name tags solve the problem. The sweetest sound to a person's ear is the sound of his/her name. Pinning name tags on your audience helps you to personalize your presentation by addressing each by name. If at all possible, gather as much background information as you can on each person attending. People are easily flattered when you build them up in front of their peers. For example: 'As Jean West, manager of accounts for the Brody company is well aware, the cost savings of a proposition such as this, are enormous.' Speaking to members of your audience and using their names, puts the group at ease and removes the chance of them being overly-formal and unresponsive. Your objective when dealing with a group is to establish a friendly, relaxed atmosphere.

HOW TO PSYCHOLOGICALLY CONTROL A GROUP

Negotiators and speakers too often communicate their points-of-view at about kindergarten level. They talk down or worse, talk above the heads of their listeners. Either way, it is insulting. Neither underestimate nor overestimate the knowledge and intelligence of those you address, attempt to persuade or want to successfully negotiate with. Don't directly lay the blame for the problems faced to any *one* person within the group. It is the quickest way to build an enemy. Put your message across in a deliberate, rational and well-planned way. Offer *solutions* to problems which require resolving. Support your arguments with evidence, not hearsay or vague opinion. Extend gratitude and praise to those who warrant it. Stern criticism may be warranted, but it is better to avoid it. The more people you get off-side, the harder it is to win your argument. Avoid touching on the negatives. Keep hitting the positives: ideas, concepts, suggestions, facts and practical solutions. Capture the attention of your group and build an interest in your proposition. Try to move them *emotionally* rather than intellectually but without talking down to them.

WHETHER ADDRESSING ONE OR A THOUSAND PERSONS USE THIS TECHNIQUE

The mental communion technique is a practical method of getting others to subconsciously open their hearts and minds to you. It is tough going trying to penetrate the consciousness of a person with a closed mind. Unless you can pocket others, you will find that you cannot successfully get through to them. You've got to get others to *listen* to you, be *moved* by you and *act* on your suggestions and instructions. It is possible to do this when you engage in mental and emotional communion with them.

Apply this technique. Each time you speak to another person, hold the thought: 'I will assist this person to greater good. His/her good is my good. Together we benefit from our meeting, association and dealings.'

HOW TO HANDLE AN OBSTINATE PERSON

When a person you are negotiating with is adamant about his or her point-of-view and refuses to compromise in any way, it is prudent to concede that there is merit in what has been presented and bypass the stand taken. Move on to other areas and *give* a little. This brings your opponent or business prospect into a more favorable position because he/she will have won something. This one step backwards often results in several moves forward. It costs little and in the long run gains you goodwill and a softening of attitude on the part of the other person. Bypassing objections allows you to continue with your presentation minus hostility building up in the opponent's mind. It helps to avoid ego-bruising and thus gives you a psychological advantage to win-over your opponent. *The key*: side-step argument by agreeing that there is some merit in what your opponent is putting forth: 'Yes, I agree, you have a valid point.'

HOW TO JUSTIFY YOUR POINTS-OF-VIEW

Never be trapped into making rash statements which can be refuted by an opponent. When planning a negotiation strategy, make sure you have *all* the facts at hand. Base your proposition, personal viewpoints and figures on easily-proven facts, never guesswork. When called upon to justify your statements, you can relate the facts and this immediately enhances your position and strengthens your credibility. Adequate research is the key to establishing the information you may need to present a foolproof proposition and impressive presentation.

STEP-OFF ON THE RIGHT FOOT WHEN BEGINNING A NEGOTIATION SESSION

Tread warily when opening a negotiation session. Don't jump in boots-and-all in an attempt to slap your opponent down. Express appreciation for the time given by your opponent or prospect to discuss the problem and add: 'I believe it is in our mutual interest to resolve this situation as quickly, as beneficially and as amicably as possible. I trust you endorse this position.' This places both parties on an equal footing, dampens hostility and clears the way for a rational and anger-free discussion.

Your attitude should be one of right *thought*, right *feeling*, right *expression* and right *action*. It will pay handsome dividends to entice your opponent or prospect into the same frame of mind. Try to keep your opponent in a pleasant mood. An angry, bitter, jealous person will seldom respond in a rational way and will be unmoved by sound argument on your part. Harmony must reign between the parties if a quick and satisfactory settlement is to be negotiated.

PREPARE AN ALTERNATIVE SOLUTION AS A FALLBACK POSITION

Should you find yourself in a stalemate situation, break off negotiations for a short period and prepare an *alternative* proposal to the ones put forth by you and your opponent. Include an *incentive* which clearly favors your opponent without damaging your own position. Call another meeting and suggest that, in the spirit of compromise, you wish to put forth an alternative which does not disadvantage either party. An alternative solution often brings speedy settlement to what otherwise might have turned into a lengthy and costly court battle.

THINK TWICE BEFORE HEADING TO COURT

Moving from a stalemate situation to court should only be considered as a last-ditch-stand. Even then, think twice before seeking your day in court. Legal proceedings are extremely costly. Sometimes a winner ends up a financial loser. Take the case of John, a manufacturer of office furniture who took a customer to court for non-payment of goods the customer received amounting to ten-thousand dollars. The customer said some of the goods were damaged and had to be sold at a discount. He offered to settle the account for eight-thousand dollars. John refused. The judge awarded John the full amount plus partial court costs of two-thousand dollars. Legal fees charged by John's lawyer amounted to six-thousand dollars. Thus, John won the case but only received six-thousand dollars after deducting his lawyer's fees. Had he settled out of court he would have received a better return without the trauma and expenditure of time and money.

SIZE-UP YOUR OPPONENT BEFORE SELECTING THE MODUS OPERANDI

Clever negotiating skill requires an understanding of the way humans think. Generally, people are self-centered thinkers. They seek *self* benefits when purchasing, selling, negotiating and competing with others. Hard-nosed persons are not prone to generosity. Compassionate persons can often be softies who give in to others without much complaint and often make decisions through emotional appeal rather than reason appeal. *Personal* motive is a power which operates on the will of humans, causing them to act. When a personal motive is satisfied, influencing and convincing others is a relatively easy task.

Size-up your opponent before deciding how you will present your proposal, argument or offer of settlement. Are you dealing with a hard-nose, a softie, a highly-emotional or calm and rational person? Does this person make decisions based on *instinct* appeal, *reason* appeal or *emotional* appeal? In your discussions with your opponent, observe how he or she reacts to your statements and questions. Decide which category your opponent matches and then formulate your modus operandi.

HOW TO PERSUADE OTHERS TO ACCEPT YOUR PROPOSALS

When you require to rid yourself of a nuisance situation or need to get quick acceptance of a proposition, present your opponent or client with an offer that is so attractive it is hard to resist. The greater the incentive, the greater the response. Be sure to place a time limit on your offer. This puts pressure on the other party to decide promptly. What you give away is often more than compensated for by a saving in time, energy and stress.

WHEN YOU HAVE DONE THE DEAL LEAVE IT ALONE

After making a settlement offer or accepting one, stick by your commitment. Don't go weak in the knees and try to squirm out of it. Changing your mind after agreeing to a deal reflects poorly on your character. A contract or verbal agreement entered into by two or more persons should be honored without any attempt to abrogate the terms by those who are party to it. Be sure to make your word your bond, even if it causes a loss. Better to suffer some loss than sell-out your integrity. Keep in mind the proverb: *Don't pull the tail of the sleeping tiger.* When a deal is done, leave it done.

CALM THE RAGING BULL

Far too often, quick-tempered persons damage their position by angrily confronting others. This approach only hardens the enemy. Give yourself breathing space, time to cool off before rushing into a meeting like a raging bull. Check your *thinking*. Check your *emotions*. Check your *reactions*. And be sure to check your *facts* before making accusations which could permanently damage personal or business relationships. Standing your ground doesn't mean that you should raise your voice or for that matter your fists, which could bring far greater problems including court action against you.

DON'T FIGHT YOUR BATTLE ON QUICKSAND

Anger, aggression and loss of reason through frustration and sheer stupidity, are part of human error. When engaged in argument, most of us refuse to give an inch and stand our ground which often ends in a bloodied nose. The Gulf War is an example. All-out-war creates *loss* for both sides. In order to establish a power-base and benefit from an unpleasant situation, it is necessary to be in total control of what you say and do. Losing your temper greatly diminishes your chance to control the direction of any confrontation. Soften your stance. Sit on anger. Maintain control of your thinking and you will produce a truce which allows your opponent an opportunity to re-think his or her position in an unemotional way. If you decide that you must stand your ground, be sure that you have a firm footing and are not going into battle on quicksand.

HOW TO WIN YOUR CASE

A noted judge once told me that he found it necessary to discount some of the arguments put forth by opposing lawyers. 'I keep a score card. A higher score goes to the lawyer who sticks to the facts, speaks the truth, as far as I can determine, then presents arguments which do not insult the intelligence of the court. When a lawyer debates facts and the truth rather than lies and distortion of the facts, he or she establishes very strong credentials in my court,' he said.

This is a sound technique to follow when debating with others and hopeful of a successful outcome. It is vital that your opponent sees you as an honest person and a rational thinker. When you establish impeccable credentials, your arguments, points-of-view, opinions and proposals become credible and acceptable.

HOW TO TURN A DISADVANTAGE INTO AN ADVANTAGE

Telling the truth may at times seem to be an impediment to winning an argument or negotiating an important deal. A businessman I was negotiating with in Los Angeles, said to me: 'Look, the truth is, I'm not really doing you a favor. It may seem that way, but I must in all honesty tell you that this proposition works more in my favor than yours. Perhaps my telling you this will stop the deal, but it's a fact.' We did not proceed. Two months later I had a call from a prospective client of the man, who wanted a reference on him. I was high in praise and said I would not hesitate doing business with him should the opportunity arise. I learned that the businessman received a contract for work which amounted to more than $3 million. Honesty is certainly the best policy.

WHEN IT IS TIME TO TAKE ACTION MOVE SWIFTLY

Negotiation strategy should always include a *time* factor. Allowing negotiations to go on too long can spell disaster, especially where the other party desires to end matters quickly. A prospect eager to enter into a contract, make a purchase or settle an account should be accommodated as speedily as practical. Circumstances and situations can change overnight bringing a change of heart and a reverse decision. Some people are easily swayed by others and change their decisions after listening to the opinions of friends or relatives. Some people are nervous decision-makers and back away from a commitment, believing they have done the wrong thing. In some cases, it is best that they be let go, because their nervousness can cause inconvenience and perhaps greater loss at a future time.

Arriving at a decision should not be done with undue haste, but after careful consideration of the proposal being put to you or after careful assembly of the proposal you wish to put to others. Once you decide on a matter, move to finalize It. If your normal course of action is to write a letter, *fax* it or give notice by telephone and then confirmation via fax or mail.

USE THE TANGO METHOD TO REACH SETTLEMENT

A difficult opponent must quickly be told that the greater the conflict the further apart each party will grow with little chance of fair settlement. Explain that this situation could land both in court with one party likely to suffer a major loss. It takes 'two to tango'. Impress upon your opponent that *both* sides must *share* the responsibility of arriving at a sensible and fair settlement. If the entire responsibility is placed on one person then that person will, by necessity, favor his or her position. This is likely to prolong the argument and further strain relations between the parties. Remember, it takes two to start an argument and two to settle it. Both sides must co-operate — tango together — if negotiation progress is to be made and satisfactory settlement achieved.

EVERYTHING IS SOLVABLE

There is no problem, no argument, no situation that has to be faced that hasn't been solved previously. Some people feel that a particular problem is unique to them and is unsolvable. Be positive. Whatever situation you create or has been created by others can be overcome through proper thinking and acting. Don't allow fear to grip your thinking. Turn the problem into a challenge. Rise to the challenge. Solve it via proper use of your million dollar mind. Think-through each challenging situation. Be your own source of inspiration and generate ideas which create the results you seek.

FOLLOW THIS ADVICE

The late Edmond Samuels, a theatrical personal manager who achieved negotiation success for his clients, often used to say to me: 'Charm of manner is the most persuasive negotiation tool at our command.' Charm has won many a faint heart. With charm of manner, it is possible to disarm an opponent, thereby favoring your bargaining position.

NEITHER INTIMIDATE NOR BE INTIMIDATED

Never use intimidation when you want to win over the opponent. And don't allow an opponent to intimidate you. Stop the proceedings. Quietly and calmly suggest that matters appear to be getting out of control and it is best that another meeting be scheduled. Where an opponent becomes emotional and resorts to threats, it usually results in a stalemate and this pushes settlement further away. Irrational behavior stems from irrational thinking. Fair-minded settlement requires fair-minded and sensible thinking.

DON'T BECOME A CAPTAIN QUEEG

In the stage play *The Caine Mutiny*, Captain Queeg becomes psychotic over missing strawberries. His thinking and behavior are irrational. He loses his nerve and his command. Some business people are like Captain Queeg, refusing to apply commonsense. They shun compromise, seeing it as a sign of weakness. They intimidate their opponents in order to triumph over them. For a person with a powerful mind using bullying tactics, it is relatively easy to box in, demoralize and denigrate weak-minded persons in order to win. Some victory. Don't be brutal and unconscionable. Be understanding and compassionate.

THE TRADE-OFF FACTOR

One of the techniques of negotiation skill is to know *when* to offer a concession. Don't be in a hurry to give-in too early or to make the first concession. When the first concession is given to you, immediately respond with one. This makes the other person easier to get along with and more prone to making further concessions. Where no concessions are being offered by either party, suggest a trade-off: 'Miss Jones, I'm happy to refund your money provided you purchase another item and if you are willing to do that, I will deduct a further 20-percent from the price of the item you select.' A trade-off is often a satisfactory way of bringing both parties to a quick settlement.

THE BOTTOM-LINE FACTOR

The bottom-line or end-of-the-road factor can become a crisis point in winning or losing a deal. Determine what your own bottom-line is, the point where you can go no further. Never begin negotiations by making a bottom-line offer because it leaves you no bargaining power. Begin high and work your way down to the bottom-line. Sense when you have hit the bottom-line offer made by your opponent. Don't be greedy. Settle at this point. Continued negotiations could upset your opponent and cause a stalemate.

When your opponent has suggested what you conceive to be a reasonable offer and can't reduce the price further, counter with: 'Good, Mr. Williams. I accept your position and it's a fair price, but what's the bottom-line for cash or if I pay within one week?' This signals the other party that you have accepted the deal based on a further small concession which is usually given.

THE LISTENING FACTOR

Listening is a vital tool in communication as I've pointed out in an earlier chapter. It is important to *hear* what your opponent is on about, what is expected of you, what problems need rectifying. Ask questions of your opponent and listen carefully to the answers given. This is where you will pick up important information and clues on how to deal with the situation. Withhold evaluation until you have the facts and the other party has fully stated his or her case.

THE PEN-TO-PAPER FACTOR

Henry Kissinger when in government was recognized as a pretty good negotiator. He made a point of asking an adversary to state in writing what was wanted, what the adversary was prepared to accept as a bottom-line and what would be offered in return in order to reach a fair settlement. Kissinger wanted to satisfy himself that he fully understood the demands before discussing concessions. He would test an opponent's reactions by floating suggestions which presented an opportunity to offer a little more or a little less. His strategy was to go in easy, run up flags to test the wind, negotiate from strength and not give in to irrational demands. He believed that a good negotiator should never succumb to giving in too readily. 'If it's too easy, an opponent will go in for the kill and press for more and more. If I feel an opponent is giving in too easily, I'm wary. There's probably not much value in what is being given away,' Mr. Kissinger told a TV interviewer.

CHAMBERLAIN WAS TOO QUICK TO GIVE IN

Hitler saw Chamberlain as a weak person and took advantage of him. The 1938 Munich Conference was a pushover for Hitler. Chamberlain accepted second best, put trust in the word of an untruthful opponent and caved-in to Hitler's outrageous demands. As Prime Minister, Neville Chamberlain was an appeaser, quick to settle differences at disastrous cost. Chamberlain's deal with Hitler was *no* deal. It didn't bring 'peace in our time' but war in our time. It was a war that possibly could have been averted if Hitler had faced strong opposition and competent negotiators early in his leadership days.

KENNEDY STOOD FIRM AND WAR WAS AVERTED

The late John F. Kennedy faced a bullying Nikita Khruschev in October of 1962. The Russian leader had sent missiles to Cuba which threatened the safety of the US. Kennedy stood up to Khrushchev, pointing out the consequences of his actions if they weren't reversed. The Russian backed away and the missiles were removed. While Kennedy did make concessions which some feel shouldn't have been made, Khrushchev knew that he was dealing with a strong adversary and settlement was achieved.

THATCHER TOOK NO NONSENSE

Margaret Thatcher stood up to Argentina when it grabbed the Falklands. She grabbed them back. Unfortunately, negotiations didn't last long enough to stop what turned out to be a costly exercise for both countries. The loss of life was appalling. I do not wish to debate the rights and wrongs of this short-lived war except to say that I believe it could have been averted had commonsense prevailed. It proved that it takes two to start an argument and requires two to settle it. When one side stops talking and starts fighting, there is little chance of an amicable, fair and lasting solution to the problem. In this instance, both parties raised their fists and the fight was on until one side had its nose bloodied. I'm sure there are some lessons to be learned here about negotiation and, hopefully, put to good use, not only by world leaders, but by people in general.

PAMPER A HUMAN BEHAVORIAL TRAIT

Human beings are a sensitive lot. Egos are easily bruised. Command that an action be taken, demand rather than request a service be given and chances are, you will receive a hostile response. Ego punishment seldom returns a positive result. It generates resentment which in turn makes a person stubborn and un-co-operative. A request made in a pleasant way with an incentive thrown in, is usually all that is needed to make a person go to work with a will.

HOW TO SPOT DIFFICULT PERSONALITY TYPES

You will soon discover that there are a number of difficult personality types you must deal with as you enter the entrepreneurial ranks. They give certain signs which you must spot early in your negotiations and dealings with them. They will attempt to shake your confidence in order to increase their power and influence over you. In order to retain your personal power, never allow others to step above you or ruffle you. The main personality types to become aware of are:

1: THE EGO TRIPPER. This person's attitude is: 'I must win, always.' Usually, this person is a smarty, intent upon locking horns in a power duel. Never become defensive with this type. Stand your ground. Bounce-off the jibes and rudeness this type uses. Keep your cool and you will retain control of the situation.

2: THE FRED C. DOBBS. Greed is the motive of this character. This selfish individual wants it all. Don't get into argument. Point out that you are not prepared to lose all and will happily agree to a *just* proposition. Stick to that line of reasoning.

3: THE BULLY. Likes to issue an ultimatum, a threat. Handle the bully with friendliness. Don't respond in anger. The bully wants you to cave-in quickly. Don't relent to fear. Hold your ground. Avoid a shouting match at all costs.

4: THE LIAR. Lots of them around. The means justifies the end. But don't rely on what is said. Sift-through the falsehoods and protect yourself against possible future problems by getting every promise in writing.

5: THE STALLER. Offers every excuse available to avoid making a decision. A sheer frustration when negotiations need to be hurried along. Keep pressing, 'delay means loss'. Present a clear-cut proposal without alternatives so that a 'yes' or 'no' can be given. Too many alternatives confuse the staller encouraging procrastination. Go for a quick close.

6: THE IMPULSIVE. Be cautious. Giving away too much too soon could present problems at a later date. Perhaps what you are getting has little value and is a ploy to get you to make far greater concessions than are being offered. Keep pace with the action but know what you are receiving and weigh it against what you are being asked to give in return.

7: THE CONCEITED. A know-all. But it will be hard to separate fact from fiction. Flattery is the best antidote. Keep patting the ego and you will win.

8: THE SUSPICIOUS. Have all the answers. Hold eye contact. Greet with a firm handshake. You will be tested through direct questions and sized-up to determine your character. Play straight-down-the-line without deviation or you won't be taken seriously.

9: THE TALKER. Doesn't want to listen to your point-of-view. Keeps telling you it's 'the principle' of the thing. The talker wears blinkers and doesn't hear or see anything other than his/her position. Listen until this character has no more to say. Acknowledge that what has been said has merit then present your own proposition commencing with: 'I believe this is in your favor. I'm sure you will find it interesting and beneficial.'

10: THE SILENT TYPE. Very hard to find out what goes on in the head of this person. Grunts a lot, says very little. Throw a series of easy-to-answer questions to motivate a response. Keep eye contact. Stand close. This is unnerving and usually works to challenge this person to talk.

DEALING WITH MEN Vs WOMEN

Because of differences in psychological make-up, negotiating with a male sometimes requires a different approach to negotiating with a female. A male tends to approach matters *objectively*. A female generally views matters from a *subjective* point-of-view. The male likes to toss around facts and figures but at the same time can be a gambler running on 'hunches'. The female tends to be more conservative in decision-making. Her emotions play an essential part of what she agrees to accept, give and do. It is important that she likes and trusts you.

HOW TO RETAIN SELF POWER

Your personal power and influence are established and retained while others see you as in *control* of every situation in which you participate. You must graciously sell people on yourself, get them to respect you and they will respond favorably to you. As a self power, avoid offending and antagonizing others. Your charm and confidence are the basis of your influence. Your strength of mind doesn't require you to take cheap pot-shots at others or insult them. Rise above such behavior. Your personal power has a governing effect only on those who see you as extraordinary and in command of your position in life. You must never reduce your thinking and acting to the level of the common person. Be a person of strong will. Let others note it through your actions. A display of honesty, integrity and inner strength are the personal assets you need to negotiate your way to power and riches.

FORMULAS TO GROW RICH

- Like it or not, you are in the business of negotiating every day of your life. The more skilled you are at communicating and motivating, the more expedient will be your rise to power and riches.

- Your aim is to get your ideas across in an appealing and persuasive way. Your influence over others will be determined by the level of your confidence and your ability to present yourself as a person of importance and of good character. Good negotiators never attempt to take others down or to win by unjust means.

- Never set out to make an opponent a total loser. It is the fastest way to create an enemy. Be satisfied with a winning edge and try to keep a friendship going. The favor you give today could enhance your future. Be willing to *give* a little.

- Prepare a negotiation strategy. Call for the facts. Get to the core of the matter so that you can deal with it rationally and argue from strength. Be specific about what you want. Decide on the concessions you will make. Decide who should be at meetings. Set an appropriate time and place for your meetings.

- One-on-one meetings are easier to handle than group presentations. If your meeting is disrupted by an interjector keep your cool. Stay out of verbal slinging matches.

- Get into a mental and emotional communion with others. Hold the thought: 'I will assist this person to greater good.' Side-step arguments. Don't bruise the ego of an opponent. Your attitude is important. Harmony must reign if you want to win friends and influence people.

- Understand the way humans think. People seek *self* benefits. Satisfy their desires and you will pocket them. Quick settlements require some measure of compromise or incentives too good to refuse.

- Every problem is solvable. Sensible thinking will find an answer to any difficulty. Don't become a Captain Queeg, a person unable to compromise, to see things from another perspective. Withhold evaluation and judgement until you have *all* the facts at hand.

- Never negotiate a final agreement or settlement until you are satisfied that you are receiving a *fair* and *just* proposition. Once you agree to a deal, stick to it.

- Learn to spot the various personality types who could make your business dealings and negotiations difficult. Handle them carefully. Retain your personal power over them without bullying them.

HOW TO DUPLICATE
THE WEALTH-GATHERING
IDEAS OF MILLIONAIRES

FORMULA **13**

HOW TO DEVELOP THE SKILL OF WEALTH ACCUMULATION

The skill to enrich your bank account can be learned. Good fortune in money-matters has nothing to do with so-called 'luck'. Usually, when a wealthy person attributes luck as the source of acquired riches, that person is using the term to describe strong personal *initiative*.

The best method of acquiring wealth is to follow the principles used by the wealthy. What the rich have learned to do, you also can learn to do. Read books and magazine articles about successful entrepreneurs. Take note of success-making ideas and where appropriate put them to work. Develop an intense personal *desire* to turn your ambitions into reality and so reap the riches you seek.

OPEN YOURSELF UP TO THE WEALTH AVAILABLE TO YOU

It is often said that there is nothing new under the sun, but there is unlimited opportunity to improve and refine what already exists.

Humans have desires they want to fulfill and problems they seek to overcome. Fortunes have been made, are being made and will continue to be made by enterprising persons, those capable of satisfying human demands and finding the answers to human problems.

Open yourself to the opportunities which surround you. Develop a constant awareness by keeping your eyes, ears and mind alert at all times and taking note of what is happening around you. At some place at some time an idea will light up the screen of your mind and challenge you to take action. The cause of good fortune is often an idea which offers a better way of doing things, of saving time, energy and money in the course of manufacturing goods or supplying services. When you discover an idea which provides an answer to a universal problem, you are on your way to wealth accumulation.

TAKE THE LONG VIEW TO ATTAINING MILLIONAIRE STATUS

Wealth assembly seldom occurs overnight. For most people, it is a long, slow road to travel, prompted by a desire to ease job tedium and financial restriction. Your road to success may be longer than some or shorter than most. The important factor to keep in mind is that you possess an innate ability to improve your life but you must give yourself the opportunity to succeed. You must support your aspirations through persistence, allowing yourself sufficient *time* to achieve your goals.

Warren Buffett, the investment genius, urges the 'long view' to wealth accrual. He said: 'I never felt I had to get rich this year or next year. Becoming a millionaire does take time. Take the long view.' Sensible advice from a top thinker who is worth more than $3000 million.

AIM FOR THE IMPOSSIBLE IS ADVICE OF OILMAN

Flamboyant archaeologist, author, oil concessionaire and centimillionaire Wendell Phillips, encourages budding entrepreneurs to 'aim for the impossible and get stuck into making money using brains, brashness, ideas and skills'. The secret of his personal success is to put together a proposition, go to the *top* person and personally handle negotiations. 'Don't waste precious time talking to the wrong person. Get to the person who can make a decision. Time is too important to spend courting the wrong people. It can be frustrating and demoralizing,' the entrepreneur maintains.

BECOME A TRIER, A DOER AND A PERSEVERER SAYS REAL ESTATE GURU

One of Australia's top real estate deal-makers is long-time friend John Walsh. His professional approach to selling and his business ethics have rewarded him with success and industry respect. 'Today, young entrepreneurs need to dream the big dream then get moving. Dreams are the starting point. They should inspire action and encourage determination to achieve. Become a trier, a doer and a perseverer. It's the way to become number one, to reach the top,' John says.

John has been a professional sales entrepreneur for many years, concentrating his time, energy and skill on land sales. His reputation is enhanced by the fact that he has not received a serious complaint from any client during the 30 years he has been selling. This enviable record stems from John's sales philosophy: *I base every transaction on the Golden Rule, selling to others only what I would be pleased to buy.*

IDEAS FROM FORMER NEWSBOY WHO MADE MILLIONS

Leslie J. Hooker, known as the czar of Australian real estate, began his climb to millionaireship as a Sydney newsboy. At age 12, he decided land and home sales would be the business most likely to return big money. When he retired from active business at age 65, Leslie Hooker's penny earnings as a newsboy had grown to assets worth $55 million. He attributed his success to three essential habits: *determination, persistence* and *hard work.*

Through the application of these actions, Mr. Hooker acquired widespread interests in real estate, land development, home and commercial buildings, hotels and pastoral holdings. His name is carried on franchise outlets in several countries. The first L.J. Hooker office was opened in a Sydney suburb in 1928. Few persons have had such a profound influence on Australian commercial development in postwar years as the determined, persistent and hard-working Leslie Hooker.

NETWORK YOUR IDEAS ADVISES YOUNG TYCOON

I've known Jason for many years. He made his first million dollars at the age of 26, after devising a unique computer program for small business operators. His idea didn't bring overnight success. Jason told me he placed numerous advertisements in local papers for his program but very few orders were received. Then he canvassed his program door-to-door but only sold a limited number which didn't cover his expenses. 'I became discouraged. One day, I met a man who owned a computer shop and he became interested in my program. He advised me to call on all computer outlets in our area and offer a worthwhile commission for them to sell my product. I signed up 20 stores and sold more than 200 units over a few weeks. My success came from promoting a good idea to the right outlets — networking. My business has grown from a one-man operation to 15 people over a three year period. Network, network, network,' Jason advises.

NETWORKING IS MORE THAN DISPENSING BUSINESS CARDS

Some sales people I know hand a business card to each new person they meet and hope for the best. True networking requires follow-through after cards have been dispensed. Don't wait for prospects to call you. The more face-to-face meetings you can arrange, the more chances you have to sell your concepts.

Sharing ideas and clients is often a profitable and pragmatic way to help yourself and others up the success ladder. It isn't an exercise in handholding, but a means whereby valuable advice can be obtained, useful information collected, creative ideas exploited and business opportunities advanced. Good *networking* helps to make things happen.

GET ON THE WINNING SIDE ADVISES FAMOUS ACTOR

Michael Caine is a successful actor whose wealth allows him to live in a grand way. It wasn't always so. Born Maurice Micklewhite into a poor, struggling family, it didn't take the young Cockney boy long to discover that there were two types of people — rich and not so rich. He knew he wanted to get on the winners' side and experience a luxury lifestyle he'd observed others enjoying.

'I determined to become a winner, to dream the impossible dream, to fight the concept of defeat. Being poor has nothing going for it. I've been poor. I know what it's like. It's better to have money than not, to live in luxury than not. When I was an unknown, broke actor, living on sandwiches and coffee, I got angry and made up my mind to get on the winning side of life, to go after what I wanted and to stop listening to the knockers. I promised myself that if fame and fortune could be won through determination and hard work, I'd become famous and wealthy.' Caine's attitude may seem to some as being coldly materialistic. But it's brought him a lifestyle easily envied. He's able to live where he wants to live, dress as he desires to dress and enjoy the riches life offers.

ELIMINATE FEAR IF YOU WANT TO BECOME GREAT ADVISES FRANK SINATRA

Frank Sinatra was once so broke he couldn't afford to buy his wife a Christmas present, so he borrowed the money. Now, a millionaire many times over, the singer-actor said in an interview that people wanting success should eliminate the fear of losing. 'If you think you can't make it, it will stop you from trying. Some people fear spending money because they think they can't make it back. I've made a lot of money and spent a lot of it. Money doesn't interest me. It was meant to be spent, to be moved around. It's best to view life as a terrific opportunity to lead the sort of life that appeals to you. Fear is a killjoy. If you want to make it big, don't be frightened to try, to grab hold of a challenge and ride with it.' Mr. Sinatra's advice is worth thinking about and applying.

SHOUT LOUD AND LONG ADVISES MILLIONAIRE

William Bestner stuttered badly during his youth. 'I wanted to become a salesperson after leaving school but was advised against it unless I could overcome my speech defect. I was told by a drama teacher to practice shouting poetry loud and long. After three months of driving my neighbors crazy, I lost my nervous stutter and could speak as well as anyone. I became a salesperson and have used the advice to persist with my aims and objectives until I achieve them. Too many people too often give in when things go wrong. My sales income has not dropped below half-a-million dollars a year for the past four years. I sell business machines and the competition is rough. But I believe in the products I sell and I go after business no matter what the economic climate is or how bad others say business is. I shout loud and long and it pays,' William told me.

FOLLOW ADVICE OF GREAT POET

Longfellow wrote some wonderfully-inspiring poetry, particularly the following suggestion applicable to those who tend to give in too quickly: *If you only knock long enough and loud enough at the gate, you are sure to* wake up somebody. Perseverance — hanging on until what you want is accomplished — is one of the major factors entrepreneurs use to accumulate wealth.

LEAVE BUSINESS PROSPECTS WITH SOMETHING TO REMEMBER YOU BY

Janet Harders attended one of my seminars. She had just set up a new business advisory service and it was booming. I asked her the secret of her success. She told me that she had a management consultant put together an impressive resume and brochure on her activities. 'I leave each prospect with something to remember me by. The professionally-produced package is my business persona put into words. It is who I am, what I do and what I can accomplish for a client. My resume indicates a person who is reliable, hard-working, persistent and achievement-oriented. It is designed to be an impressive sales presentation on paper. Each client who has received it has told me it was the deciding factor in hiring my services,' Janet said.

The writing of a good resume and sales message to promote yourself and your ideas is surely the most fundamental business skill needed if you want to succeed. Whether seeking a job or new clients, investors or business partners, a professionally-written resume is essential. A resume is about *you* and your earnest desire to prove to the reader that you are the *right* person to fill the job vacancy or satisfy a product-service need. Like Janet Harders, you too can leave those in a position to increase your income with something to remember you by — a high-powered sales resume. As a footnote, Janet became a millionaire after just eleven months in business.

GARAGE SALE WAS ROAD TO WEALTH ACCUMULATION

John and Sylvia Angwin were finding it hard to make ends meet so they decided to hold a garage sale and sell-off unwanted possessions. The weekend event brought them two-thousand dollars. 'I was simply amazed at the result,' Sylvia told me. 'We discovered that money can be made from used and unwanted household items. The following weekend we had another sale which, to our amazement, brought in more than the first one. We decided to try selling goods (bought at garage sales) at flea markets. This too was successful. Now, two years after our initial venture into selling used items, we operate 10 market stalls each weekend using young people to sell for us on a commission basis. We also operate a bargain store and small warehouse to store purchased stock. Our overheads are low and our profits high. We've made a lot of money and the work is fun,' Sylvia said. A smart money-making idea from a couple of ambitious entrepreneurs.

KNOWLEDGE IS KEY TO SHAREMARKET SUCCESS

When sharemarket investor Charles Viertel reached the age of 83, he had a personal fortune of some $50 million to help him celebrate his birthday. After leaving school, he studied accountancy, took a job with a bank and began making modest investments during the 1920s in real estate. During the depression years, he worked as a trouble-shooter for ailing companies which gained him an intimate knowledge of company structure and successful business operation. With this information, he spent the next 40 years investing in the sharemarket.

Viertel offered the following investment strategy to those desiring to accumulate wealth via share dealings: 'Buy good, solid shares for the long-term rather than engage in short-term trading. Study the market intensively. It's a life-long study. It can't be learned in a week or month. Keep accurate records of sharemarket transactions. Read company reports and stockbrokers' circulars. Build a network of reliable contacts. Study business trends. Correct information and sound knowledge bring sharemarket success, not stupid gambling. A novice sharemarket investor stands to lose, not win on get-rich-quick dealings.'

FROM SHOESTRING OPERATION TO MILLIONS OF DOLLARS THROUGH TRAVEL IDEA

Back in 1976, Goromwy Price was a student with little money. He got together a group of 10 people and charged them a few extra dollars on top of costs for a trip to Nepal. The extra dollars paid for his own ticket. After financing several trips in this manner, he decided to work full-time as a travel agent. He joined forces with another travel agent Christine Gee and together they promoted an adventure travel company offering holiday tours in far-flung places such as Peru, Nepal and China. Within 10 years, the annual income of Australian Himalayan Expeditions had reached $11 million and become the largest adventure travel group in the world. 'The key to our success was having the right product at the right time and faith in our ability to market it,' Price said.

DEVOTION TO WORK ROUTINE IS NOVELIST'S SUCCESS KEY

Barbara Taylor Bradford is one of the richest, most successful novelists in the world today and she attributes her astonishing achievement to a rigid work routine. She hit the jackpot with her fifth novel, *A Woman of Substance*, which sold 12 million copies, prompting her publisher to pay an advance of $10 million on her next novel.

'Novel writing is a rigid routine. I sit at a typewriter and look at the roll of film in my head, which is my imagination. I am at my desk by 6.30 in the morning and put in 12 hours a day, sometimes every day of the week. It is hard work putting a lot of emotion on paper,' the author said.

GET IN SHAPE AND LOOK GOOD IS ADVICE OF ENTREPRENEUR

Joe Thomson reached millionaire status when he changed his image. 'I was a fat, poorly-dressed, arrogant slob. I was fired from my job because of my obesity and rudeness to customers. I went into business for myself and did poorly until a friend told me why so many people disliked me and wouldn't do business with me. I took a look into a mirror and saw the reflection of a very stupid person,' Joe told me.

Joe enrolled in a personal development course, joined Weight Watchers and committed himself to a dramatic image change. He shed excess weight and purchased a new wardrobe of clothes. His arrogance and rudeness were converted to charm and politeness which brought immediate, positive results. 'My business improved the moment I took on a new look. The fat jowls, pot belly and ill-fitting suits were as unacceptable as my attitude. Fortunately, I woke up before losing my business. Today, my company pays me a salary of $500,000 a year as its top gun. My advice to young people seeking a successful career is to explore the elements of personal presentation: physical fitness, dress and grooming excellence and charm of manner. Learn to look good and sound good and you will find it easier to do what you want to to,' Joe told me.

LEND AN EAR TO IMPORTANT GOSSIP ADVISED BILLIONAIRE

Aristotle Socrates Onassis, at the age of 16, emigrated to the Argentine with a bankroll of $60. Six years later he was a millionaire tobacco importer. In 1926, he snapped up six Canadian ships worth $12 million for $120,000 and began a career of wealth-gathering estimated at his death to have reached more than a billion dollars. He had a special ability to make money. Asked about his success formula, he replied: 'Take calculated risks. Take action on ideas and don't be put off by criticism and envy of others. Work 20 hours a day and most important of all, lend an ear to important gossip. Listen and sift-through information. Often it can lead to a successful deal or purchase of valuable property at a bargain price. Personally, I've made money by taking action on important gossip.'

READING HOW-TO BOOKS PAVED WAY TO FORTUNE

John H. Johnson founded *Ebony* magazine in 1945. He conceived the magazine as a picture-format publication for returning World War II black GI's, playing up the positive said of Negro life. Johnson, as a high school student in Chicago, decided to improve his position in life through 'thinking' his way out of poverty. He read dozens of how-to books on personal development, borrowed $500 on his mother's furniture and launched his first magazine, *Negro Digest. Ebony* followed. Its press run was 25,000 copies which expanded to more than a million copies after a few years with an advertising revenue of more than $12 million a year. With this success, Johnson added other publications, a radio station and a cosmetics line to his rapidly-expanding empire. This self-motivated entrepreneur claims his success is due to the inspiration he got from reading books on success and developing strong belief in his own capacity to succeed.

HOW THE DREAM MERCHANTS BECAME MILLIONAIRES

They came from Poland, Germany, Russia, Hungary and other European countries in the 1920s and earlier, to found a new industry in America. It was moving pictures which dealt in dreams and brought in millions of dollars at the box office. Many of these immigrant Jews to whom Hollywood owes its success, were former furriers, junk dealers and clothing salesmen. Names which quickly became world-famous included: Zukor, Loew, Cohn, Laemmle, Fox, Schenck and Selznick. Louis B. Mayer and Samuel Goldwyn were tough showmen who became fabulously wealthy. All of these Hollywood moguls were skilled in deal-making — entrepreneurs with driving ambition, creative flair, enthusiasm, high energy and supreme confidence in their ability to win.

Some were tough, ruthless and unethical in their race for fame and fortune. Some were loved, some were despised, but all had their sights set on success and succeed they did.

MADE MILLIONS OF DOLLARS SELLING ICE CREAM

Howard D. Johnson passed away at age 75. He was a millionaire, the founder of the Howard Johnson restaurant-and-motel chain in the US which gained a solid reputation from its famous 28 flavors of ice cream, quality food and accommodation.

In 1925, Johnson bought a newspaper store with a soda fountain in his hometown of Wollaston, Massachusetts. He experimented with ice cream flavors, doubled the butterfat content and came up with a scrumptious taste which was an immediate hit. 'If you want to succeed, find out what the public wants and supply it. People love ice cream, so I figure, sell them the most delicious-tasting ice cream there is and it will bring a fortune,' Mr. Johnson told a staff member. Each year, the company sells more than 6 million gallons of ice cream, supporting its founder's success theory.

PERSISTENCE BROUGHT GREAT IDEA TO MARKETPLACE

Rolene Markson invented a disposable baby's bib because she couldn't stand cleaning stained bibs — they took so much washing. She took some housekeeping money and made the rounds of 54 manufacturers before anyone would produce her idea. Knowing her idea was a good one, Rolene persisted. 'When I discovered that no manufacturer made disposable bibs I decided to do it myself. Finally, I convinced a manufacturer to support me,' Rolene said. Determination to succeed has paid off. After a year in business, domestic and overseas orders have topped the $2 million mark. It's another example of the power and value of persistence as an entrepreneural trait.

SELF DISCIPLINE AND ENTHUSIASM ARE REQUIREMENTS FOR FORTUNE SEEKERS

Self-made millionaire, electronics wizard, adventurer and publisher Dick Smith, is out to make another fortune as publisher of Australian Geographic. After selling his successful electronics empire, Dick Smith piloted a helicopter alone around the world. The knockers said it couldn't be done, but Smith succeeded, just as he is determined to succeed as a publisher.

The keys to success are self discipline and enthusiasm, Dick says. 'You must have incredible discipline to run your own business, whether it be small or large. You can't be slack. You have to work hard and with lots of enthusiasm go after your goals. Having the right idea is important but putting all your energy into accomplishing it is absolutely vital,' is the Dick Smith success philosophy.

PARKING LOT KING SAYS DELEGATE BUSINESS AUTHORITY WISELY

Jim King is an entrepreneur who feeds on ideas. He pays the best people top money to operate his parking lots while he searches for new ideas. 'I made my money from a great idea. While driving around the city I couldn't find a parking spot. That was 1956. I decided there was money to be made in providing parking space for people driving into major cities, so I took a short-term lease on a lot and opened my first car park. Business boomed and I opened 50 more lots. As city buildings came down, I rented the vacant land,' Jim said.

Mr. King believes in delegating business authority to key employees. He selects employees carefully and then pays them well but he expects them to perform successfully. Jim claims that delegation of work load has been a major factor in making him a millionaire. 'Get the best people you can find then let them go to work for you so that you have only the major decisions to contend with. If your day is taken up doing tasks others could be doing for you, there's no time left to expand your business,' is Jim's belief.

HOW TO BECOME A MILLIONAIRE WASHING CARS

Sid Chambers was a miner and then a boundary rider in Australia's outback region before seeking fame and fortune in Sydney. He arrived in the big city with a desire to find himself a business in which he could achieve success. He purchased an American magazine and read a story about the expanding car wash business on the West Coast of the USA. 'I felt a similar service would do well in Australia so I flew to America to learn all I could about the car wash business. Returning to Australia I opened the first Whale Car Wash system in Sydney. Business boomed and it wasn't too long before the numerous wash centers I opened were taking in more than $8 million a year,' Mr. Chambers said.

Sid Chambers attributes his success to finding a workable business idea, learning how to operate it, then taking the plunge. 'I discovered a service people need and I backed myself to win. Anyone can do it. Personal success demands action. It's necessary to move quickly and confidently when the opportunity presents itself,' is Sid's advice.

HOW AN OLD SEWING MACHINE AND A DREAM BROUGHT WEALTH AND SUCCESS

Clair Jennifer, another enterprising Australian, was given an old sewing machine for her seventh birthday. She used it to make dolls' clothes and at age 11, made a wedding gown. By age 21, Clair had made her first million dollars from the clothing business. With $2,000 in her purse and no formal business training, Clair opened a boutique when she was 19. Within a couple of years she established a small chain of fashion stores. Her goal is to own 100 stores around Australia.

'I made a few mistakes but sought out professional advice to point me in the right direction. Determination is one of the most important qualities that a business person needs. Also, it's essential to keep your finger on the pulse and know everything about your business. Give service. Be optimistic and keep ahead of trends if possible,' advises this successful entrepreneur.

HOW A LEBANESE BOY BECAME A MILLIONAIRE CUTTING HAIR

Stefan Ackerie arrived in Australia from Lebanon at the age of 17. He couldn't speak English, but he quickly learned and got to work studying hairdressing. He made a deal with a man who owned a hairdressing salon but had no hairdresser to operate it. Eventually, Stefan bought the shop. He bought a second salon. Business was lean so he offered free haircuts. If clients liked the cut, they came back. Borrowing $16,000, he opened a salon in Brisbane, got himself a regular spot on a TV show discussing haircare and within a few years owned 30 salons.

Today, Stefan Ackerie owns close to 80 salons and his personal wealth is estimated at around $15 million. He owns lavish homes, drives exotic cars, mingles with important people and encourages his 800 employees with incentives such as sports cars, overseas trips and expensive gifts.

'My grandfather advised me to get into business and to learn to negotiate. I've coupled that idea to studying new hairdressing techniques, ways to promote and make my business more successful. I don't think about money. I think about serving people and taking care of the people who work for me.' Good advice from the enterprising owner of Stefan Hair Fashions, the largest privately-owned hairdressing empire in the world.

MULTI-MILLIONAIRE SAW OPPORTUNITY WHERE OTHERS SAW PROBLEMS

Harry Weinberg died in 1990 at the age of 82. He was the consummate self-made man. Born in Austria, he grew up in a poor section at Baltimore. He dropped out of school in the sixth-grade to sell newspapers and work in his father's auto repair shop. Later, he and his brother William bought houses at tax sales with money they had saved. They fixed them up and resold them at a profit. The first lesson he learned in business was to detect opportunity where others saw only problems. He used this principle to expand his property-focused investment portfolio.

In the early 1960s Harry moved to Hawaii, where he further expanded his business interests. In the year he died, Forbes listed him number 70 in the 400 wealthiest individuals in the USA, with a net worth of $950 million.

'Don't flaunt wealth. Don't be a duck in a shooting gallery. If you put your head up too often, some envious person is likely to want to shoot it off. I've found it prudent to be a lone wolf in business, not to brag about success. The quickest way to wealth is through property. Buy land, develop houses, factories, office buildings. Look for opportunities wherever you travel. Many people miss out because they do not use their imagination. They look at things in a pessimistic way,' was the advice given by this clever wealth-accumulator.

ESTABLISH A GROWTH MENTALITY ADVISES CANADIAN MILLIONAIRE

William Brannigan migrated to Canada from Ireland when he was 10 years of age. He finished school at the age of 19 and went to work for a small supermarket. The manager asked him to find a way of disposing of the store's empty cartons. 'I was offered extra money to remove their waste and it wasn't long before I discovered that just about every store in town had the same problem with large packing cartons. I decided to get into the business of waste removal, so I spent a lot of time at the library reading books on ways to dispose waste. Pretty soon I had a flourishing business. I applied two formulas. One, to keep up with the latest technology related to the business I was in and two, sock away in an interest-bearing account business profits. It's surprising how quickly money will accumulate when you save on a regular basis, particularly where it is earning a high-rate of interest. Given that a person is of sound mind, is healthy and can work and establishes a plan of action, making money isn't really that hard. I believe that the people who lack wealth are those who are too frightened to take a gamble on their own worth. It may sound silly, but I've made a lot of money removing garbage. As a business, it may not be everyone's cup-of-tea, but it's made me rich,' William told me.

BUY REAL ESTATE IS ADVICE OF MAN WHO BOUGHT EMPIRE STATE BLDG.

Harry Helmsley as a small boy dreamed of being a real estate tycoon and of one day owning the Empire State Building in New York City. His dream came true and he became known as 'the man who owns more of New York than anyone else'. 'I began my career as a $12 a week office boy in a realty broker's office. It didn't take me long to see that big money could be made buying and selling good property. I bought all I could. My advice to young entrepreneurs is to buy real estate, rent it out or do it up and resell it. After I bought the Empire State Building for nearly $80 million, I had offers of $200 million to sell it,' Harry told a TV interviewer.

AN IDEA AND PERSISTENCE KEY TO WEALTH

Danny Kishon was an unemployed Londoner travelling around the United States on a restricted budget and sleeping on Greyhound buses. Today, he is a millionaire, all due to the board game he named *September*, which became Britain's best-selling game.

'I bought a bus pass for $99 but I could never travel directly to where I wanted to go. I was allowed to travel on B routes, not on A routes. The B routes were always the indirect ones. The pass gave me the idea for a blocking game that involves forming a line of plastic pieces across a board by blocking your opponent's path. I knew I had a winner but 30 toy companies I called on turned me down. I believed in my idea and persisted. One night I met a businessman at a party and he gave me financial backing. In the first month of the game's release we sold 110,000 units. The game is now sold around the world and my persistence has paid-off,' Danny said.

Danny Kishon maintains that success and wealth allude many people because they give in too quickly. He suggests that any worthwhile idea can be made to succeed by giving it support and promising yourself that you will not quit in the face of adversity or because others knock your idea.

ACCEPT THAT YOU ARE A WINNER AND A WEALTH-ACCUMULATOR

The convictions you carry in your subconscious mind can make or break you, keep you poor or make you rich. Your deeper mind does not reason the whys-or-wherefores. It accepts. It takes a command and delivers it. Stop short-selling yourself. Keep reminding your subconscious of your right to be rich and successful. Use your conscious mind — through your minute-to-minute thoughts — to impress upon the subconscious your desire to experience life's riches. Prosperity-oriented desires develop *into* prosperity when you believe in them and take action to achieve them. When your subconscious mind accepts that you are worthy of a greater income than the one you now receive and that you are capable of high achievement, your fortunes will change dramatically. Your mind moves from the concept to the real. Constantly contemplate the life you want, the job or business you desire to have and the wealth you wish to accumulate. Keep your mind focused on success and you will be drawn toward it.

KEEP GOING FOR AS LONG AS YOUR STRENGTH ALLOWS

When you elevate yourself into a better, higher-paying job or begin your own business, adversity will at some time confront you. This is the moment to stand up for your right to win. Anchor your mind on the power within you. Get rid of fear. Know that you can be king or queen of your domain by taking charge of your thoughts and controlling your reactions. When doubt crosses your mind, annihilate it before it creates mental conflict. Throw onto the screen of your mind the perfect solution to your problem or challenge. Imagine the victory. Fill your mind with confidence, calmness, harmony and faith. Don't give in. Keep trying and you will overcome, *win* and be rewarded in many substantial ways.

> *When firmness is sufficient,*
> *rashness is unnecessary.*
> – Napoleon.

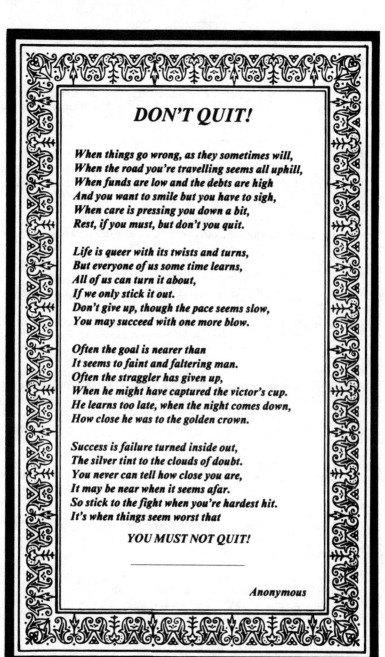

DON'T QUIT!

When things go wrong, as they sometimes will,
When the road you're travelling seems all uphill,
When funds are low and the debts are high
And you want to smile but you have to sigh,
When care is pressing you down a bit,
Rest, if you must, but don't you quit.

Life is queer with its twists and turns,
But everyone of us some time learns,
All of us can turn it about,
If we only stick it out.
Don't give up, though the pace seems slow,
You may succeed with one more blow.

Often the goal is nearer than
It seems to faint and faltering man.
Often the straggler has given up,
When he might have captured the victor's cup.
He learns too late, when the night comes down,
How close he was to the golden crown.

Success is failure turned inside out,
The silver tint to the clouds of doubt.
You never can tell how close you are,
It may be near when it seems afar.
So stick to the fight when you're hardest hit.
It's when things seem worst that

YOU MUST NOT QUIT!

Anonymous

FORMULAS TO GROW RICH

- The skill needed to enrich your bank account can be learned. Forget about luck. Develop strong personal initiative, an intense *desire* to reap the riches of life.

- There may not be anything *new* under the sun but there are lots of opportunities to *refine* what already exists. Find some way to satisfy a human demand and you can become wealthy. Ideas are money-in-the-bank if you develop them.

- Wealth doesn't always appear overnight. Take the long view and be patient. But don't cease your efforts to improve your life, your health, your bank account. Become a trier, a doer and a perseverer.

- Discover the keys to success by reading about the rich and famous. Whatever others have accomplished you too can accomplish. Maybe not in exactly the same way, but in a similar way. If you are of sound mind, healthy and willing to work hard, you can be successful and wealthy.

- Eliminate the fear of losing. Don't be frightened to give success a try. Grab onto a challenge and ride with it all the way. Follow the poet Longfellow's advice: *If you only knock long enough and loud enough at the gate, you are sure to wake up somebody.*

- Present yourself and your business in a professional manner. Prepare a resume designed to impress a potential employer, client or investor. Prepare a brochure on the products or services you offer.

- If you want to entice others to do business with you, upgrade your manners and appearance. Shed weight if you are overweight, improve your grooming and be charming.

- Self-made millionaires are generally persons who are well-disciplined, enthusiastic knowledgeable and dedicated to high achievement. Are you prepared to devote your energy to these ideals?

- Accept your true place in life. Remind your subconscious of your right to riches and success. Keep your mind focused on your goal to succeed, to be rich, healthy and happy.

HOW TO FOLLOW
THE PATH OF
THE MEGA RICH

FORMULA **14**

THE AGE OF MILLIONAIRESHIP

We are in an age of prosperity and you are entitled through your efforts to be rich. The USA is a great bastion of free enterprise. People who decide they want to work hard and succeed are encouraged to do so. The system works. In 1991, statistics revealed that the number of millionaires had peaked the one million mark. Over the past two decades, the moderately wealthy have become rich, the rich have become super rich and the super rich have become mega rich. The personal wealth-list grows rapidly day-by-day.

Becoming a Great Gatsby may seem difficult to some — particularly in these seemingly-tough economic times. But tough times are when fortunes are made. Gamblers fell during the depression years but during that same period millionaires were made. In this age of expanding millionaireship, the clever person latches onto ideas and ventures capable of money growth. Waiting for a miracle to occur and lazily floating through life is the reason so many people are financial losers. Look at what the rich are doing and chase them. Activate a work plan which encourages you to become a financial winner. The time is right. It is *now.*

INVEST TODAY FOR TOMORROW

Society offers us a choice. We can choose to live for today and hope tomorrow will be better or we can plan today and take action to bring about a prosperous tomorrow. Get your priorities in order. It may be necessary to put off doing today what you'd like to do in order to accomplish what you must do if you want to grow rich.

DON'T DISSIPATE WHAT YOU HAVE

Some people who come into money quickly make a concerted effort to spend it quickly — often on useless pursuits and unnecessary luxuries. They choose the tie today rather than the suit tomorrow. It's a trap to avoid. Make what you have — no matter how small — work for you. Put profits to work. Compound the money you earn via sound investment in a workable venture. You don't have to be miserly but you should avoid *wasting* the money you earn on unnecessary possessions and questionable ventures. Sound investment of what you have guarantees a sound future as your investments grows. When you have accumulated a reasonable bank balance you can afford to spend on and enjoy a few luxuries.

HOW TO CHALLENGE YOURSELF TO BECOME RICH

Millionaires often borrow 'to-the-hilt' as much to put themselves on-the-line as to finance a business venture. Going into 'hock' commits them to winning at all costs. It's an act of daring which often pays-off. However, borrowing to the hilt can be dangerous. Fluctuating interest rates can spell disaster. In recent times, some well-known names have gone-to-the-wall due to heavy borrowings and rising interest rates. They found that their incomes couldn't service their debts.

The chief consideration when borrowing is to establish your ability to carry the interest charges should they take a giant leap upward. And, be sure that the hoped-for gain outweighs the risk involved in borrowing a large sum of money.

SOME QUALITIES THE RICH SHARE

A mega rich friend who made his fortune buying old buildings, refurbishing them and then renting them as offices, told me that he has noticed among all of his wealthy friends and business associates five common success qualities. They are:

1: Rich people view life as a great opportunity to achieve.
2: Rich people are always specific in what they want to do in life.
3: Rich people place an importance on compounding money.
4: Rich people see bad times as opportunity times.
5: Rich people temporarily forego some things they'd like to do to go after the things the know they *have* to do.

Another important factor of wealth accumulation according to my friend, is the ability to *visualize* the end result of venture strategies, to 'see' them unfolding and succeeding. 'It comes from an affirmative, highly-creative imagination which I've noticed rich people seem to possess,' he told me.

SOME OTHER CHARACTERISTICS OF THE MEGA RICH

The average millionaire is in his/her late 50s. About 20-percent are in retirement and 70-percent are self employed. Most millionaires have their money invested in real estate and in their companies. They are hard workers, ambitious, frugal, disciplined and self confident. Most are married, conservative, fiercely independent who have made it to the top on their own. Despite their wealth, most rich entrepreneurs do not exploit their position by living lavishly, Dynasty-style. In America, more millionaires live in California than anywhere else, which says something about Horace Creely's advice to 'go west young man'.

MARRIAGE HELPS ROAD TO RICHES

Behind every wealthy person is a supporting and clever mate. Marriage, it seems, is a pretty good start to the accrual of money. Approximately one in every 100 US homes is a millionaire household, according to research conducted by Dr. Thomas J. Stanley, a professor of marketing at Georgia State University in Atlanta. Most millionaires are men, but women are gaining ground fast and are likely to even-the-score in the next decade or so. In millionaire households, more than 80-percent are composed of a married couple and two children. It's interesting to note that women generally outlive men, so millionaires' wives tend to outlive their mates.

It has been said that you can't have a successful family relationship *and* a career which is demanding of time and energy. I believe you can have both — even if both partners work — if you carefully plan for it. The big hurdle is integrating family and work so that neither suffers. *Priorities* need to be established. *Time* requires analysis and a satisfactory *schedule* established. Careful lifestyle restructuring can bring the balance needed to succeed in business and in the home.

A POOR BOY CAN STILL MAKE IT TO THE TOP

From the early 1900s onward, fortunes were founded on merchandising, steel, oil, banking and railroads. The names Henry Ford, John D. Rockefeller, Andrew Carnegie, F.W. Woolworth, J.P. Morgan and H.L. Hunt are synonymous with the great economic dynasties of America. Most of these men built their fortunes from scratch. They were singular-minded individuals who worked hard, knew what they wanted to achieve and were tough in their dealings with others. But times have changed and so have the conditions which faced entrepreneurs like Ford and Carnegie.

Fortunately, opportunity still exists to accrue wealth and attain fame. Today, a fortune hunter doesn't need to start a railroad or build a steel mill but should look to commonplace goods and services which fit the needs of present-day society. Seize profit-making ideas and develop profit-making habits. It's the way to start from scratch and build a large personal nest egg.

HOW TO JOIN THE MEGA RICH

Wealth-makers are where the action is. That is where *you* must be if you want to become mega rich. There is a wealth-making arena you must enter and it is packed with challenges to be taken on and won. Once you enter the arena, you need to bravely take calculated risks and boldly ride challenges to victory. The stronger your resolve to achieve, the easier will be your path to victory.

Your wealth-making aspirations need to be supported by a certain boldness, a strength of consciousness, a brave mentality. You cannot afford to be timid, apologetic, weak-minded, — a wimp — or you will be scared to face challenges. This puts you outside the arena and thus, outside the area of money-making opportunity.

One of the secrets of wealth accumulation is the ability to confront challenges in a tough, often brash way. The mega rich thrive on danger, difficult situations and acts of daring. They engage in risky behavior for the excitement it produces as much as for the financial benefit. Warren Avis, rent-a-car entrepreneur, once told a reporter: 'What's the point of getting up in the morning unless there's excitement to experience, a challenge to take on, something to achieve'. The Avis attitude is worth thinking about if you want to become *number one*.

THE DIFFERENCE BETWEEN TIMID AND BOLD PEOPLE

There is a great difference between timid people and bold people. The bold convert fear into excitement, exploit opportunity, thrive on a crisis and are strong-minded. Timid people hate making decisions, refuse to take action on opportunity unless a guarantee is given of success and buckle when confronted by a crisis. The two are miles apart in attitude which clearly reflects in their vastly-different lifestyles.

It isn't necessary to live dangerously to succeed, but you've got to be prepared to take a few chances, to gamble on your hunches and grasp opportunity where others run from it. The best advice is to play the wealth-making game as *safely* as you can but not to the point where you refuse to take action because you fear failure. Be bold and brave danger now and then. Learn to thrive on a crisis. Allow excitement to penetrate your life. The mark of the entrepreneur is *boldness*.

A BENEFIT OF BOLDNESS

One of the many benefits of boldly taking on challenges is that you are never plagued by 'what ifs'. Getting into the thick of it — win, lose or draw — let's you know exactly where you stand. It eliminates the frustration of wondering what the outcome of a venture might have been had you tried. There's no guarantee that every hunch you play or every chance you take will be a winner. One hundred-percent success in every goal you set is unrealistic. However, it's important that you enter the race with optimism and keep entering it *expecting* to win.

SALES ABILITY AND INSURANCE BUSINESS BROUGHT RICHES

W. Clement Stone started his career with a mere $100. When he reached the age of 80, Mr. Stone had amassed $400 million. He made every cent selling insurance. According to the super salesman, 'anyone' can be a millionaire. 'You can turn a miserable failure into an outstanding success through PMA,' he maintains. PMA — positive mental attitude — features strongly in the three books Mr. Stone has written. He's applied it all through his working life and has his company, Combined Insurance Company of America, other substantial assets and his huge bank balance to show for it.

Wealth, according to Mr. Stone, doesn't come easy. It makes a lot of demands. 'You must generate a magnificent obsession for the things you want. You've got to do twice what the other fellow does and do it better. The majority of people won't pay the price success demands. All they want to do is dream of spending the money,' he says. This dynamic money-maker also offers this advice: 'Don't be hazy about how much you want to earn. Be specific. Get your goals straight. Don't lose time. Get started now.'

One of the aspects of success which Clement Stone possesses is that he sees money-making as a worthwhile exercise. He always *wanted* to make money. He began his rise to fame and fortune with a millionaire mentality, believing that it is easier to become rich if you start with the assumption that you are going to *be* rich.

DISCOVERING WHERE THE MONEY IS

In my studies of many successful people and how they attained wealth, it is my belief that *big* money is made through shrewd real estate deals and ventures. Acquiring good property does not always require a huge bank balance. Some super rich property developers have told me they started out with a bank balance of only a few thousand dollars. Some with only a few hundred dollars. They took options on land, in some cases paying as little as a $100 deposit. Through clever marketing plans, they enticed people with money to invest and back them. In some instances, banks were the backers.

Owning property as an investment is a sound way to get where the money is and to build on your investment through the acquisition of bigger and better properties as your money base expands. Start in a small way. Purchase a parcel of land or a housing block. Sell it at a profit and buy again. Purchase a run-down house or building. Do a clean-up or refurbishment, get it back on the market with an added profit. Keep building your property base so that your profits compound as your business expands. If you think acquiring riches from a low-income base is a pipe-dream, remember that, for the most part, America's richest entrepreneurs have built their fortunes from scratch.

TURNED SMALL MONEY GIFT INTO A FORTUNE

Two brothers, both friends of mine, received an inheritance gift of $3,000. One of the brothers used the money to buy clothes and a set of golf clubs. The other brother made the rounds of real estate offices and put a deposit on a run-down house. He obtained a mortgage for the balance and then on weekends used his time to clean it up and re-paint it. Three months later he placed a small advertisement in his local paper and sold the house. He made a profit of $20,000. With his capital increase, he bought another house and repeated the exercise.

Over the next four years, this enterprising young man followed this simple formula until he had accumulated over $150,000. He went into partnership with a realtor and they opened their own office. He is now well on his way to millionaireship — all due to taking a calculated risk, hard work and a desire to advance his position in life.

The different attitude of the first brother verses the second one is that the first wanted instant benefit and pleasure. The second was willing to wait and go for bigger stakes. The first brother wanted to *appear* rich, the second brother wanted to *be* rich, to exploit his abilities and enhance his life.

FOLLOW THE HENRY FORD ADVICE

The previous example of opportunity lost and opportunity gained is reflected in the advice Henry Ford offered: 'Money is like a limb. Use it or lose it.' Many people are frightened to commit their savings because they might lose them. Others take what savings they have and spend them unwisely on items they could well do without. Whether spendthrift or miser, don't expect your future to be bright. Be an investor, a doer. Get your mind and bank account — small or large — into *action*. Strive to be a capitalist. The person who creates wealth is in a position to help a neighbor, the community and the nation through employment, investment and taxes. J. Paul Getty once said: 'The best form of charity I know is meeting a payroll.'

HOW TO USE A CURRENT ASSET TO GET STARTED

George worked as a real estate salesman. 'I want to be rich, but the opportunity isn't there,' he told me. George had a bank balance of $7,327. He had put every other cent into the purchase of an expensive sports car. 'Sell it,' I suggested. 'Sell it and use the money to open your own office. Put your money to work and in time you'll have enough to buy a dozen luxury cars.'

George sold the car and replaced it with an inexpensive model which he bought second-hand from a friend. That was five years ago. Today, George drives a Rolls-Royce and runs four real estate offices. Sometimes it is wise to sell a personal asset — no matter how much it may hurt — in order to give yourself a stake in the future.

GET THE LAW OF AVERAGES ON YOUR SIDE

The more irons in the fire you have, the more chances you have of succeeding. The more opportunities you grab, the more challenges you take on, the more likely you are to hit a home run. The secret is to expand your opportunity-base without spreading your time and energy too thinly. Don't take on dubious ventures or high-risk, low-gain propositions. When assessing opportunities, look for the ones that have the most built-in benefits. When you get the law of averages on your side, your success rate increases.

HOW TO BENEFIT FROM INVESTMENT

It is surprising how many people refuse to place their money in a bank where it is relatively safe and can earn interest. Whatever the reason, they prefer to keep it hidden at home. Money under the mattress doesn't do itself or its owner any good. Some people do put their money into banks, but in a low-interest or non-interest bearing account where inflation eats away at its purchasing power. Whatever funds you have available — small or large — get them into a solid investment which guarantees a safe, better than inflation rate of return.

ADVICE OF MEGA-RICH INDUSTRIALIST ON INVESTMENT

A mega-rich industrialist once told me: 'If you want money to grow, don't stifle its potential by sitting on it. The purchasing power of money decreases each year. Its value shrinks. A prudent investor of money always seeks a proposition that brings a return far greater than the rate of inflation. Unless you can achieve high capital growth, you will be losing out to inflation.'

ESTABLISH YOUR PERSONAL CRITERIA

Before you can achieve worthwhile investment goals they need to be specified in terms of what you desire to accomplish. Think about what your investment returns are to be used for. Do you seek funds for a future business or ownership of a property or just comfortable retirement and financial independence? Be specific as to *when* you wish to accomplish financial goals and the *amount* of funds required.

INVESTMENT STRATEGIES TO FOLLOW

Every person has individual and specific needs that will affect his or her investment strategy. As a general rule-of-thumb, there are three considerations: *inflation, taxation* and *personal need*. Further considerations are:

- SECURITY OF INVESTMENT
- FLEXIBILITY OF INVESTMENT
- SPREAD OF INVESTMENT
- LIQUIDITY OF INVESTMENT

GLOBAL INVESTMENT

Some countries offer good investment opportunities. The global investment market is worth investigating. A professional consultant, ethical, with a proven background should be consulted. Don't let promises of huge profits sway your decision. Know what you are getting into. Remember, a fool and his money are *soon* parted.

Different countries offer varying rates of interest on bank-invested funds. Australia, for instance, has for the past decade, paid interest in double figures. Switzerland's banks, during this same period, have offered much lower rates, mostly in single figures. With the experience of corporate crashes around the world in recent times, investment advice of the experts is: *act carefully.* Find an established, respected money institution you feel is worthy of your trust. Spread your investment monies over various markets and with various *solid* institutions.

A SIMPLE INVESTMENT FORMULA TO MAKE A MILLION DOLLARS

Banks, insurance companies, governments (state and federal), private institutions, all offer some form of investment opportunity. One safe and sure way to make a million dollars is through a fixed-income investment with a bank or money institution. As an example, if you invest $1,000 today at 15-percent per annum compound, you will attain your million in 50 years. If you wish to have your million in 25 years, you would need to invest $32,000 today. The greater the capital invested, the sooner you reach your goal of one million dollars.

If you invest at a low-interest rate of say 5-percent compound, your principal doubles in 15 years. At 10-percent in 7½ years and at 20-percent in four years. The objective is to find the safest, highest interest rate available and to invest as much capital as practical, allowing capital and interest to compound.

SHORT-TERM OR LONG-TERM INVESTMENT?

Personally, I am not in favor of long-term fixed investments. It restricts the use of money should an investment opportunity too-good-to-miss come up. Locking your money away puts you at a disadvantage should business or career problems arise. Yes, it's possible to borrow funds on the strength of your assets, but at what price? There are short-term money-market opportunities offered over periods of 30, 60, 90 and 180 days. In most instances, the rates of interest are higher than longer-term offerings, the money is as safe and you have ready access to your funds. The choice of short or long-term investment is really a matter of your personal and business needs, requirements and expectations.

DON'T WAIT FOR THE TOOTH FAIRY TO DROP RICHES IN YOUR LAP

As I conclude this chapter, I am reminded of a seminar on entrepreneurship I conducted for a group of business executives. Except for one, they were a pretty smart bunch. His name was Herbert. He'd been promoted into the job by his brother-in-law. Nepotism can be a dangerous thing. Herbert kept asking throughout the program how to make money. Initially, I ignored the question. He was so persistent I decided to give him an answer. 'The only way to *make* money is to print it. But that's illegal. The only other way I know is to *earn* it.' Herbert didn't much like my answer. 'I thought you'd have a magic formula. I'm disappointed in you,' he said.

When I was a kid, I remember my parents telling me I'd get a visit from the tooth fairy and she'd bring me money for my dropped-out tooth. Herbert, like a lot of dreamers, still believes in the tooth fairy. As I've suggested in an earlier chapter, life doesn't give you a free success ride. In some way, you've got to *pay* for it. You do this through exploiting talents and skills, the time and energy expended on personal development and the contribution you make to life in general. You have to build the attitude that you are really in business for yourself and if you desire to live successfully and profitably, you have to be a good manager of your mind, your skills and talents and your time and energy. In short, you've got to take care of your *own* life and *make* things happen. Don't wait for the tooth fairy to show up.

LIFT YOUR CONSCIOUSNESS TO MEGA RICHES

Get smart. Lift your wealth-gathering goals high-up in your consciousness. Influence your mind to *act* on your dreams, to discover opportunities which pave the way to the prosperity you seek. Go for the substance of your aspirations. Forget the way things were or are. Head in the direction of the way things *can* be. Dream about the future by all means, but don't let it stop there. Live your dreams on the inside, then make them happen on the outside. You do this through belief in the *possibility* of things. Lean on your imagination. Stretch it. Entice the images in your mind to drive you to the place you want to be, the prosperity you want to achieve and the happiness and creativity you wish to experience. You are good. But you won't know *how* good until you challenge yourself to follow the path of the mega rich.

> *Thrust in they sickle and reap: for the time is come for thee to reap; for the harvest of the earth is ripe.*
>
> −REV. 14:5

PERSONAL CHECK LIST OF ACHIEVEMENT STOPPERS

Tick each 'achievement stopper' which applies to you and set about changing it.

- [ ] I AM SATISFIED WITH WHATEVER LIFE OFFERS ME.
- [ ] I DESIRE TO BE RICH BUT LACK A WORKABLE PLAN TO ACHIEVE WEALTH.
- [ ] I DESIRE CAREER IMPROVEMENT BUT LACK THE NECESSARY SKILLS TO WARRANT IT.
- [ ] I HAVE MANY PROBLEMS WHICH I CANNOT COME TO GRIPS WITH.
- [ ] I SEEK NEW COMPANIONS BUT CAN'T SEEM TO GET ALONG WITH PEOPLE
- [ ] I DESIRE PEACE OF MIND. I CAN'T SLEEP AT NIGHT. I AM FEARFUL OF THE FUTURE.
- [ ] I SUPPOSE I COULD BEGIN MY OWN BUSINESS BUT WHO WOULD BACK ME?
- [ ] I BELIEVE IN FATE.
- [ ] I ALWAYS FEEL INSECURE WHEN DOING BUSINESS WITH OTHERS.
- [ ] I HAVE BEEN TOLD THAT MONEY IS THE ROOT OF ALL EVIL. I BELIEVE IT.
- [ ] I AM A RELIGIOUS FANATIC. I HAVE PREJUDICES AGAINST CERTAIN PEOPLES.
- [ ] I DO NOT BELIEVE IN THE FREE-ENTERPRISE SYSTEM.
- [ ] I NEVER GET BREAKS OR HAVE OPPORTUNITIES HANDED TO ME.
- [ ] I CANNOT EXPRESS MYSELF WITH CONFIDENCE.
- [ ] I DO NOT BELIEVE IN SHARING GOOD FORTUNE WITH OTHERS.
- [ ] I LISTEN TO THE OPINIONS OF OTHERS AND CAN BE SWAYED BY OTHERS.
- [ ] I HAVE STRONG DESIRES BUT I DO NOT BELIEVE I CAN ATTAIN SUCCESS.
- [ ] I FRET, FUSS AND FUME WHEN I DO NOT GET MY WAY.
- [ ] I PROCRASTINATE. IT IS DIFFICULT TO MAKE DECISIONS.
- [ ] I FEAR TAKING A CHANCE ON IDEAS I HAVE.
- [ ] I DO NOT READ VERY MUCH. I'M NOT REALLY UP-TO-DATE ON CURRENT EVENTS.
- [ ] I AM UNHAPPY MOST OF THE TIME. I GET EASILY DEPRESSED.
- [ ] I AM BORED WITH MY LIFE. I CAN'T SEEM TO CHANGE THINGS FOR THE BETTER.
- [ ] I FAIL AT MOST THINGS I ATTEMPT. WHAT'S THE POINT IN TRYING AGAIN?

BECOME FREE AND RICH

You are the judge in your own court of life. You sentence yourself.

You allow others to sentence you via the acceptance of their viewpoints, persuasions and intimidations.

Free yourself from unfair judgments, restraints and indoctrinations.

Be a free-thinker, a person capable of making your own evaluations, arriving at your own decisions and taking your own initiatives.

Cease transferring your power of mind to others. Retain control over your life.

Crowd out of your mind all fears, self doubts, worries and frustrations.

Your desire for prosperity is the Creative Intelligence within prodding you to go forth and conquer.

Expand, unfold and achieve. If the urge is there then the capability is there to accomplish your desires.

Release yourself from the prison of your mind. Step into the wonderment of rich living: peace, harmony, joy, love, happiness, creative accomplishment and prosperity.

Life extends to you success and wealth. Claim them, *now*.

FORMULAS TO GROW RICH

- We are in an age of prosperity and you are entitled through your efforts to be rich. While some may tell you that times are tough, it's a time many see as an opportunity to get rich.

- Don't waste the resources you currently possess. No matter how small, put them to work. Don't waste money on unnecessary luxuries until you are in a position to afford them. Money *makes* money. Use your money wisely.

- The mega rich thrive on danger, excitement and acts of daring. You must boldly take on challenges without becoming reckless. When you *try* to succeed, you are never plagued by 'what-ifs'. You always know where you stand.

- Discover 'where the money is' and go after it. Many people become rich through the buying and selling of real estate. Others through saleable ideas, viable business enterprises.

- The more irons in the fire you have the greater the chance *one* or more will succeed. Get the law of averages working for you. But don't take on more than you can handle. Forget dubious ventures or high-risk low-return propositions. Look for opportunities with the most built-in benefits.

- If you want your current bank account to grow, invest available funds so that the interest earned exceeds the rate of inflation.

- The short-term money market offers a better return than a bank savings account and $1,000 invested today at 15-percent per annum compound will return $1,000,000 in 50 years. A long time into the future perhaps, but not a bad return.

- Don't tie-up large sums of money for lengthy periods in case of an emergency which may require instant cash. Always have some liquid funds available.

- Don't wait for the tooth fairy to drop-in and present you with riches. Take care of your own life. They money you seek must be earned by using your talents and skills, your time and sweat, blood and tears.

- *Lift* your consciousness. Influence your mind to *act* on your dreams. You are good. You won't know *how* good until you challenge yourself to follow the path of the mega rich.

HOW TO ENJOY
AND RETAIN
MILLIONAIRESHIP

FORMULA **15**

HOW TO AVOID THE FAUST SYNDROME IN YOUR QUEST FOR WEALTH

The story goes that Faust was willing to give over his soul to the Devil in exchange for 24 years of unlimited power, fame and pleasure. Since the middle ages, the Faustian theme has been worked on by playwrights, composers, novelists and poets. In recent times, the theme has been used in television and film dramas. The Faust legend strikes home hard in this age of power-hungry, greedy and pleasure-seeking entrepreneurs prepared to 'sell out' to accomplish aims.

Selling your soul to the Devil in social, personal and business relationships may attract short-term gain, but long-term, you are likely to be asked to make full restitution for what you've won. The penalty could be severe.

Life is a precious gift. The value of this gift should be assessed by every human being before making a decision to give it away. It is a wise person indeed who takes the time to ponder why success is desired, what degree of success is required and what level of ethical behavior is to be followed. Regardless of your personal push for fame, no matter how much money you wish to earn, refuse to strike a deal with the Devil — negative forces — and you will have no consequences to suffer, no guilt feelings to overcome. Your self esteem, confidence and pride will be untouched and you will live triumphantly.

ADHERE TO LOFTY PRINCIPLES AND YOU WILL WIN AND BE HAPPY

In 1987, in the US, Dennis Levine pleaded guilty to charges related to insider trading. To his credit, he made full restitution of the $11.5 million in trading profits he made. After spending 18 months in prison, Dennis toured colleges and universities giving speeches on the evils of insider trading. He wanted to deter overly-ambitious business students from the temptation of unethical business dealings. He espoused the benefits of adhering to lofty principles, maintaining that lasting happiness and success cannot be had through dishonesty. The advice is sound. Consider your own business practices and if they are unethical, *change* them.

TOUGH TIMES REQUIRE PLENTY OF SELF CONFIDENCE

Many of the world's wealthiest businessmen and women have lost millions and in some cases hundreds of million of dollars on personal investments in the companies they run. With each stock market slump comes massive drops in shareholdings. Some high-fliers of recent times have not survived the traumas of business failure. Two prominent entrepreneurs come to mind. Both committed suicide rather than face an uncertain future. The strain and stress of failure can bring horrendous bouts of self pity and self punishment. It is a time to call on the mind to respond firmly, favorably and confidently, to give the subsconsious *life-giving* thought forms and images rather than life-taking ideas.

Tough times come and tough times go. It's a fact of life that must be faced and a contingency plan made ready if and when a downside comes. Coping with problems is an essential ingredient empire-builders need to possess. They must cast-off negative vibes when times aren't good and do the best they can to survive. Whining, crying, being morbid and fearful won't convert failure into success. It isn't an intelligent approach to personal and business recovery. Self confidence, affirmative thought and imagery, faith in victory are the inner convictions capable of bringing improvement to outer conditions. Exalt the best in you. Value and praise what you are. Deep-down in your heart say to yourself, 'I have the strength to withstand any loss, any hurt. I am confident in my capacity to succeed.'

YOUR BUSINESS PROSPERITY AND HAPPINESS STEM FROM YOUR CONVICTIONS

Your business and career are an outward expression of yourself. If your concepts and motivations are negative, you can't expect your business to prosper. Negativity is a poison. It kills ambition, shatters self confidence and slays the soul. It puts an end to worthy empire-building aspirations and actions. Stabilize your thinking. Generate bold, uplifting ideas which penetrate the deeper mind bringing about unshakable faith in your ability to ride-through any storm. When your emotions remain buoyant, they harden against thoughts of self denial and self destruction. They support you every step of the way. A tough conviction to be happy and grow rich will cause you to prosper.

HOW TO FACE UP TO BAD NEWS AND TOUGH TIMES AND REMAIN UNAFFECTED

Several business people I know refuse to read stories in the press which relate to depressed business conditions or turn-downs in the economy. They won't engage in conversations where there is any talk of 'bad times'. They feel that negative news is too depressing and not conducive to staying 'on top' when things are tough. 'I close my eyes and ears to junk news in newspapers and on the radio. Hearing about business bankruptcies, national debt, unemployment, high-interest rates and other rubbish is too much for me. I can't cop it. It makes me nervous,' a real estate broker told me. I explained to him that good and bad business news needs to be studied to learn what's happening in the marketplace. The secret to staying unaffected by it is to be analytical about it. Sift-through information. Absorb what is beneficial, use it and *discard* the rest.

Take a sensible, rational and practical attitude to what's going on around you. You've got to stay *fully* informed about current business trends or rivals will walk on top of you. You need day-to-day, up-to-date information in order to plot a course of action and if necessary, revise goals, budgets and strategies. You cannot make sensible decisions, take appropriate actions and generally, stay successful unless you are aware of what is going on in the world. Bad news and tough times are a fact of life. You can't avoid them but you can *adjust* to them, *handle* them and take *advantage* of them.

DON'T PLAY THE OSTRICH GAME

In business, you cannot afford to play the Ostrich game — bury your head, close your eyes and ears to the world. As an entrepreneur, you need to be knowledgeable and ahead of trends, not trailing them. Your *attitude* to people, places, things and events and the *information* you have of these things can make or break you. It is of foremost importance that you face-up to the real world and learn to cope with the situations, events and conditions — good or bad — as they occur. Bad news and tough times can often be more interesting, more opportunistic than you might have imagined. The key to surviving them is to remember: it is your *reaction* to events that counts, *not* the events themselves.

THE TRUMP CARD

Entrepreneur Donald Trump feels that business people should look for 'opportunity' during tough times. 'The bad times, while they are tougher, can be more exciting and challenging than the good times. I see far more chances for making good when things are down than when things are going well. There are opportunities galore,' Mr. Trump maintains.

HOW A TYCOON USED TOUGH TIMES TO ADVANTAGE

Sir Alexander Korda, the Hungarian who transformed the British film industry and made a fortune along the way, had this advice for those hit by tough times: 'Keep up appearances when things are bleak. Don't give-in to defeatism. If you think you're beaten you'll look like you're beaten and people will spot it immediately. It won't help you in the least. If you act as though you are rich and look like you are enjoying success, money will come to you. It doesn't come to losers. Living well is the best revenge for lean times.'

Sir Alex followed his own advice. He always dined in the best restaurants, left substantial tips, even when things were grim. He dressed well and presented a bright personality. Discover the joy of living in contemplation of better times, greater success. Feel inspired and excited about what's ahead. *Remember*, you become what you contemplate.

HOW A LONDONER CONTEMPLATED EXPANDED FORTUNES AND WON

Stuart Wilde, at the age of 20, was earning over $20,000 a week as a clothing manufacturer in London. That was in 1972. He was unhappy at the way his life was progressing. 'Even though I lived well, I was miserable. I wanted more from life than just money,' he said. Stuart learned how to rechannel his money, to use it in a positive way to make more money, but more importantly, how to enjoy it. In 1978, after contemplating his future, he decided to head for the USA where he began teaching richness-of-living seekers how to make money and be happy. 'There's no point having wealth if you don't spend it wisely and enjoy the benefits money can bring. Properly-earned and properly-dispersed money can bring a great deal of happiness,' Stuart teaches.

DON'T MAKE A DIME DO FOR A DOLLAR

I was watching a late-night film on television, *City of Conquest* and a line from the film caught my attention. 'Don't make a dime do for a dollar,' Ann Sheridan said to Jimmy Cagney. As the character, she was admonishing her boyfriend because he was content to struggle through life when, with ambition and effort, he could earn more and live better. Many people are like the character played by James Cagney. They are content to make a dime do when, with concerted effort, they could make a dollar and be happier.

Dissatisfaction with life is your starting point. You must turn things around — your attitudes and actions — and concentrate your attention on acquiring some of the limitless riches available to you. Convert your dime mentality into a million dollar mentality. Behold the possibility of wealth, financial security and happiness and you will bring forth rich results.

DO WHAT YOUR HEART TELLS YOU TO DO

Mike Nesmith, a few years ago, was one of the biggest rock music idols in the world. As a star of the group, The Monkees, he earned $3 million in two years. He lived in a mansion, collected a fleet of expensive cars, hired servants to cater to his every whim. He went into debt, then lost his luxury lifestyle and says he's the happiest he's ever been.

'The happiest day of my life was when I surrendered my cars and the mansion and called my creditors. I couldn't handle the overnight fame and wealth achieved through the music scene. I spent like crazy. I was recognized everywhere and given instant credit. I bought everything I saw,' he said. Nesmith believes that he had a subconscious desire to get rid of his money and its problems because he felt trapped and uncomfortable.

Having wealth and fame suits many people. They revel in it. Some people are content to experience life's riches in a different way. Financial security from a steady income or retirement investments could be the limit of their money ambitions. Enjoying life without the penalty of responsibility and commitment may be all that is required. In the final analysis, it is *your* decision that counts. You must do what your heart *tells* you to do. Don't force yourself into a lifestyle which makes you unhappy. The degree of your ambition must be set according to the degree of lifestyle you expect and hope to achieve. It would make little sense to become the wealthiest person alive and then spend your life totally miserable because of your wealth. Creative fulfillment in life is important, so too is peace of mind, well-being and happiness. Add to this list *wealth* if it has a part to play in the lifestyle you desire.

BEING A BENEFACTOR MAKES ENTREPRENEUR HAPPY

Paul Mellon acquired wealth from his father, banker Andrew Mellon. He left his son one of the great fortunes in American history. Paul's nest egg is estimated at $1 billion. He has been giving away millions of dollars through his family and their foundations to art museums, universities, wildlife sanctuaries, historical societies and mental-health programs. Instead of chasing business ventures, Mr. Mellon has chosen to devote his time to disbursing the family fortune to worthy causes and it gives him great satisfaction and happiness to do so. It is a prime example of doing what the heart indicates you *must* do and finding happiness because of it.

CANTANKEROUS SKINFLINT REAPED HAPPINESS LATE IN LIFE

John D. Rockefeller was known as a miserly person. Some called him a 'cantankerous skinflint'. Stubborn and penny-pinching, Rockefeller's wealth caused him much suffering, worry and sickness. For a time, his diet consisted mainly of crackers and milk. He wasn't able to enjoy a hearty meal. Late in life, Rockefeller began to share his money with those who were less fortunate and gave generously to charity organizations and worthy causes. Friends noticed that the old man was now smiling, friendly and experiencing better health and happiness. Rockefeller admitted that he should have been 'more open' and 'giving' earlier in life. 'I would have been all the better for it,' he is reported as saying.

SPREAD A LITTLE KINDNESS IN THE WORLD

When it comes your time to assist others in some way, do it graciously, sincerely and generously. Acts of kindness and generosity are mentally, emotionally, physically and spiritually therapeutic. You hold the key to the storehouse of happiness, peace and contentment. It resides in your *attitude* to people, places and things. When you uplift the hearts of others, you are prospered in many wonderful ways.

SMILE AND THE WORLD SMILES WITH YOU

Those who have met J. Paul Getty and have written about him, say that for a person who was earning more than $300,000 per day from his holdings in oil, art, real estate and stocks and bonds, he seemed to experience 'little joy' in life. A reporter once asked him if he had time for fun. 'Not much,' Getty answered. 'When I interviewed him, he was cheerless, poker-faced and lacked warmth. For all Getty's millions and vast holdings, he seemed to me to be an unhappy man,' the reporter commented.

A joyous heart promotes good health, beautifies the face, preserves peace in the soul, keeps us in high-spirits and good-humor. Making money should be a noble and happy pursuit. Through selfishness it can produce resentment, hostility, suspicion and irritability causing physical ailments. Along your path to entrepreneurship and wealth-accumulation — *smile*. Just remember to stay happy. Reflect on what you are doing and why. Don't allow your ambitions to sour your disposition.

YOU DON'T HAVE TO SUFFER ON THE ROAD TO RICHES

People wonder why their lives are filled with suffering, heartache and failure, while others are happy, prosperous and successful. Very few people travel through life without some degree of suffering, inconvenience and failure. However, to spend a lifetime experiencing misery and destructive experience, is not only life-wasting, it is unnecessary and idiotic.

You live in your mind and that is where you *first* experience heartache or happiness, poverty or riches. It is where you first become thief or honorable person. Your happiness and success materialize when you relax, let go and allow the power resident in your mind to work *minus* obstruction. Gutter-thinking can only produce gutter circumstances, conditions and events, the very things you don't want. Help yourself to life's riches through affirmative re-conditioning of your thoughts, feelings and beliefs.

DON'T DENY YOURSELF RICH LIVING

Denying yourself a chance to share life's riches is silly when you could easily be enjoying an opportunity-rich, exciting and creatively-rewarding lifestyle. There are people who, because of religious beliefs, guilt-feelings or ignorance, practice self denial. This is illogical behavior. Nature doesn't offer riches then tell us we cannot have them when we seek to experience them. Nor are we asked to forsake them as a form of self punishment. It is within our power and earthly right to *claim* wealth, to *enjoy* success and to *experience* life's infinite riches.

GIVE YOURSELF A PROMOTION

Promote yourself a notch or two. Rise from corporal to general, from failure to achiever, from poor person to rich person, from morose person to happy person. A mental promotion of your status, your *self image*, improves your 'on-show' personality, your physical demeanor and your overall view of life. Take yourself up the success ladder. Focus your attention on your *true* potential, your ability to become great, wealthy and happy.

WHEN YOU ACHIEVE FAME AND FORTUNE RETAIN YOUR IDEALS

Refuse to bend to race-mind thinking which, on the whole, is negative by nature. You *can* reach success and retain it through the wisdom and power of your faculties. Lasting riches are yours to have and to hold. They are yours to enjoy and to share. The law of mind is that whatever is continuously believed to be true comes true. Keep your consciousness spiritually pure. Retain high ideals. Identify with the principles of harmony, peace, joy and perfection and you will attract into your existence these qualities and benefits.

DON'T STAY DOWN WHEN YOU CAN GET UP AND WIN

A boxer doesn't lose a fight going to the canvas. He loses it by *staying* there. You are going to hit the canvas many times on your journey to success. Get up. Hit back. Try again. You won't find satisfaction in failure, in losing, in poverty. Life by its very nature wants you to grow, develop and partake all the blessings it offers. When you are happy, healthy, creatively *self* satisfied and financially content, you are experiencing the reality of success. Success means successful living, doing what you love to do, freely, harmoniously, nobly and rewardingly.

PURSUE EXCELLENCE

The pursuit of social and career excellence, striving to become number one, to eliminate mediocrity and to exploit your personal creativity should be high priorities on your goals list. Don't work your fingers to the bone just for the sake of amassing wealth. Pure materialism is a sure way to attract disillusionment and unhappiness. Work to have *fun*, to bring benefit to yourself and to the world around you.

Elitism in some areas of society is a negative aspiration and is frowned upon. People who aren't into excellence often resent those who are. If you want to get ahead, to compete successfully, to be efficient in business and to become a stand-out performer, it is necessary to promote the *best* you have to offer. You must continually go after being best at what you do. Elitism is a good thing when it improves your position in life and you use your position to help others to find their true place.

SUCCESS IS YOURS NOW

People climb mountains because they want to. People succeed in business, in marriage, in sports contests and in personal achievement because they *want* to. I've never heard of a person succeeding because he or she didn't want to. High-achievers become successful, not by accident, but by design, through seeking excellence and believing in their ability to succeed. This is the attitude you must take as you track down the things you want in life.

From this day forth, picture yourself in the role you wish to play, see the environment and conditions you desire and feel the reality of the events you want to take place. Determine that you *will* prosper, you *will* exploit your talents and skills and you *will* experience happiness and well-being along the way. Remain faithful to your ideas and ideals. Persevere to the end. Use your inner power to thrust you into the sphere of life's fabulous riches and magnificent aura. Remember, you go where your vision is, where your thoughts, feelings and beliefs are. Your destiny is to *grow rich* with your million dollar mind.

BEGIN IT NOW

*Whatever
you can do*

*Or dream you can,
Begin it.*

*Boldness has genius,
power and magic in it.
Begin it now.*

GOETHE

Note: Brian Adams is available as a seminar or keynote speaker. Contact Image Book Company Box A133 Sydney South NSW 2000 Australia.

FORMULAS TO GROW RICH

- Faust was willing to sell his soul to the Devil in exchange for 24 years of unlimited power, fame and pleasure. Selling your soul may attract immediate gains but in the long run you will have to make restitution. The penalty could be severe. Life is a gift. Don't give it away in a moment of weakness. Be a person of high moral standing, an ethical person and you will have no guilt feelings to overcome.

- You will face tough times in life. Difficult times come and go. Self confidence is your support element when things don't go as smoothly as you would like. Hold onto your inner convictions, your faith in victory, your ability to sell yourself and your talents.

- Turn bad news and tough times into an advantage. Don't let adverse news affect you. Use it to gather up valuable information on what's happening in the world. Don't drop out of the achievement race when tough times appear. Difficult times often present more opportunity for success than good times and they are often more exciting and challenging.

- Don't make a dime do for a dollar. Strive to go after *greater* success so that you can do the things you dream of doing and enjoy the life you seek.

- Do what your heart tells you to do. If making lots of money is on your agenda then go after money. If a simple lifestyle is all you want then that's ok, too. Go after it. Do what makes you happy, gives you satisfaction and peace of mind. Don't force yourself into ventures and commitments likely to make you unhappy.

- Be kind to others and be generous in your assistance to them. When you uplift the hearts of others, you are prospered in many wonderful ways.

- Give yourself a promotion. Lift your life. Don't deny yourself the riches that are available to you. Focus your attention on your true potential and reach for it.

- Refuse to bend to race-mind thinking which, on the whole, is negative. The law of mind is the law of belief. What do you believe about yourself, your ambitions, your talents and your future?

- A boxer doesn't lose a fight going to the canvas. He loses it by staying there. When facing adversity on your success journey, get up on your feet and hit back. You *can* win.

- Strive for excellence — elitism. Start climbing your mountain, *now.* From this day forth, picture yourself in the role you wish to play, the environment you desire and feel the reality of the events you want to take place. Your destiny is to grow rich. Do it!

THINK . . .
IDEAS HELP PRODUCE

As you were reading, what ideas did you identify as being of specific value to you?

1: _____

2: _____

3: _____

4: _____

5: _____

6: _____

7: _____

8: _____

9: _____

10: _____

THINK . . .
IDEAS HELP PRODUCE

As you were reading, what ideas did you identify as being of specific value to you?

1: _____

2: _____

3: _____

4: _____

5: _____

6: _____

7: _____

8: _____

9: _____

10: _____

THINK . . .
IDEAS HELP PRODUCE

As you were reading, what ideas did you identify as being of specific value to you?

1: _____

_____

2: _____

_____

3: _____

_____

4: _____

_____

5: _____

_____

6: _____

_____

7: _____

_____

8: _____

_____

9: _____

_____

10: _____

_____

A PERSONAL WORD FROM MELVIN POWERS, PUBLISHER, WILSHIRE BOOK COMPANY

My goal is to publish interesting, informative, and inspirational books. You can help me to accomplish this by sending me your answers to the following questions:

Did you enjoy reading this book? Why?

What ideas in the book impressed you most? Have you applied them to your daily life? How?

Is there a chapter that could serve as a theme for an entire book? Explain.

Would you like to read similar books? What additional information would you like them to contain?

If you have an idea for a book, I would welcome discussing it with you. If you have a manuscript in progress, write or call me concerning possible publication.

Melvin Powers
12015 Sherman Road
North Hollywood, California 91605

(818) 765-8579

MELVIN POWERS SELF-IMPROVEMENT LIBRARY

ASTROLOGY
____ASTROLOGY—HOW TO CHART YOUR HOROSCOPE Max Heindel 7.00
____ASTROLOGY AND SEXUAL ANALYSIS Morris C. Goodman 10.00
____ASTROLOGY AND YOU Carroll Righter 5.00
____ASTROLOGY MADE EASY Astarte 7.00
____ASTROLOGY, ROMANCE, YOU AND THE STARS Anthony Norvell 10.00
____MY WORLD OF ASTROLOGY Sydney Omarr 10.00
____THOUGHT DIAL Sydney Omarr 7.00
____WHAT THE STARS REVEAL ABOUT THE MEN IN YOUR LIFE Thelma White 3.00

BRIDGE
____BRIDGE BIDDING MADE EASY Edwin B. Kantar 15.00
____BRIDGE CONVENTIONS Edwin B. Kantar 10.00
____COMPETITIVE BIDDING IN MODERN BRIDGE Edgar Kaplan 7.00
____DEFENSIVE BRIDGE PLAY COMPLETE Edwin B Kantar 20.00
____GAMESMAN BRIDGE—PLAY BETTER WITH KANTAR Edwin B. Kantar 7.00
____HOW TO IMPROVE YOUR BRIDGE Alfred Sheinwold 7.00
____IMPROVING YOUR BIDDING SKILLS Edwin B. Kantar 10.00
____INTRODUCTION TO DECLARER'S PLAY Edwin B. Kantar 10.00
____INTRODUCTION TO DEFENDER'S PLAY Edwin B. Kantar 10.00
____KANTAR FOR THE DEFENSE Edwin B. Kantar 10.00
____KANTAR FOR THE DEFENSE VOLUME 2 Edwin B. Kantar 10.00
____TEST YOUR BRIDGE PLAY Edwin B. Kantar 10.00
____VOLUME 2—TEST YOUR BRIDGE PLAY Edwin B. Kantar 10.00
____WINNING DECLARER PLAY Dorothy Hayden Truscott 10.00

BUSINESS, STUDY & REFERENCE
____BRAINSTORMING Charles Clark 10.00
____CONVERSATION MADE EASY Elliot Russell 5.00
____EXAM SECRET Dennis B. Jackson 7.00
____FIX-IT BOOK Arthur Symons 2.00
____HOW TO DEVELOP A BETTER SPEAKING VOICE M. Hellier 5.00
____HOW TO SAVE 50% ON GAS & CAR EXPENSES Ken Stansbie 5.00
____HOW TO SELF-PUBLISH YOUR BOOK & MAKE IT A BEST SELLER Melvin Powers 20.00
____INCREASE YOUR LEARNING POWER Geoffrey A. Dudley 5.00
____PRACTICAL GUIDE TO BETTER CONCENTRATION Melvin Powers 5.00
____PUBLIC SPEAKING MADE EASY Thomas Montalbo 10.00
____7 DAYS TO FASTER READING William S. Schaill 7.00
____SONGWRITER'S RHYMING DICTIONARY Jane Shaw Whitfield 10.00
____SPELLING MADE EASY Lester D. Basch & Dr. Milton Finkelstein 3.00
____STUDENT'S GUIDE TO BETTER GRADES J.A. Rickard 3.00
____YOUR WILL & WHAT TO DO ABOUT IT Attorney Samuel G. King 7.00

CALLIGRAPHY
____ADVANCED CALLIGRAPHY Katherine Jeffares 7.00
____CALLIGRAPHY—THE ART OF BEAUTIFUL WRITING Katherine Jeffares 7.00
____CALLIGRAPHY FOR FUN & PROFIT Anne Leptich & Jacque Evans 10.00
____CALLIGRAPHY MADE EASY Tina Serafini 7.00

CHESS & CHECKERS
____BEGINNER'S GUIDE TO WINNING CHESS Fred Reinfeld 10.00
____CHESS IN TEN EASY LESSONS Larry Evans 10.00
____CHESS MADE EASY Milton L. Hanauer 5.00
____CHESS PROBLEMS FOR BEGINNERS Edited by Fred Reinfeld 7.00

___ CHESS TACTICS FOR BEGINNERS Edited by Fred Reinfeld 10.00
___ HOW TO WIN AT CHECKERS Fred Reinfeld 7.00
___ 1001 BRILLIANT WAYS TO CHECKMATE Fred Reinfeld 10.00
___ 1001 WINNING CHESS SACRIFICES & COMBINATIONS Fred Reinfeld 10.00

COOKERY & HERBS

___ CULPEPER'S HERBAL REMEDIES Dr. Nicholas Culpeper 5.00
___ FAST GOURMET COOKBOOK Poppy Cannon 2.50
___ HEALING POWER OF HERBS May Bethel 5.00
___ HEALING POWER OF NATURAL FOODS May Bethel 7.00
___ HERBS FOR HEALTH—HOW TO GROW & USE THEM Louise Evans Doole 7.00
___ HOME GARDEN COOKBOOK—DELICIOUS NATURAL FOOD RECIPES Ken Kraft . 3.00
___ MEATLESS MEAL GUIDE Tomi Ryan & James H. Ryan, M.D. 4.00
___ VEGETABLE GARDENING FOR BEGINNERS Hugh Wilberg 2.00
___ VEGETABLES FOR TODAY'S GARDENS R. Milton Carleton 2.00
___ VEGETARIAN COOKERY Janet Walker 10.00
___ VEGETARIAN COOKING MADE EASY & DELECTABLE Veronica Vezza 3.00

GAMBLING & POKER

___ HOW TO WIN AT POKER Terence Reese & Anthony T. Watkins 10.00
___ SCARNE ON DICE John Scarne 15.00
___ WINNING AT CRAPS Dr. Lloyd T. Commins 10.00
___ WINNING AT GIN Chester Wander & Cy Rice 10.00
___ WINNING AT POKER—AN EXPERT'S GUIDE John Archer 10.00
___ WINNING AT 21—AN EXPERT'S GUIDE John Archer 10.00
___ WINNING POKER SYSTEMS Norman Zadeh 10.00

HEALTH

___ BEE POLLEN Lynda Lyngheim & Jack Scagnetti 5.00
___ COPING WITH ALZHEIMER'S Rose Oliver, Ph.D. & Francis Bock, Ph.D. 10.00
___ HELP YOURSELF TO BETTER SIGHT Margaret Darst Corbett 10.00
___ HOW YOU CAN STOP SMOKING PERMANENTLY Ernest Caldwell 5.00
___ NATURE'S WAY TO NUTRITION & VIBRANT HEALTH Robert J. Scrutton 3.00
___ NEW CARBOHYDRATE DIET COUNTER Patti Lopez-Pereira 2.00
___ REFLEXOLOGY Dr. Maybelle Segal 7.00
___ REFLEXOLOGY FOR GOOD HEALTH Anna Kaye & Don C. Matchan 10.00
___ YOU CAN LEARN TO RELAX Dr. Samuel Gutwirth 5.00

HOBBIES

___ BEACHCOMBING FOR BEGINNERS Norman Hickin 2.00
___ BLACKSTONE'S MODERN CARD TRICKS Harry Blackstone 7.00
___ BLACKSTONE'S SECRETS OF MAGIC Harry Blackstone 7.00
___ COIN COLLECTING FOR BEGINNERS Burton Hobson & Fred Reinfeld 7.00
___ ENTERTAINING WITH ESP Tony 'Doc' Shiels 2.00
___ 400 FASCINATING MAGIC TRICKS YOU CAN DO Howard Thurston 10.00
___ HOW I TURN JUNK INTO FUN AND PROFIT Sari 3.00
___ HOW TO WRITE A HIT SONG AND SELL IT Tommy Boyce 10.00
___ MAGIC FOR ALL AGES Walter Gibson 10.00
___ PLANTING A TREE TreePeople with Andy & Katie Lipkis 13.00
___ STAMP COLLECTING FOR BEGINNERS Burton Hobson 3.00

HORSE PLAYERS' WINNING GUIDES

___ BETTING HORSES TO WIN Les Conklin 10.00
___ ELIMINATE THE LOSERS Bob McKnight 5.00
___ HOW TO PICK WINNING HORSES Bob McKnight 5.00
___ HOW TO WIN AT THE RACES Sam (The Genius) Lewin 5.00
___ HOW YOU CAN BEAT THE RACES Jack Kavanagh 5.00

_____ MAKING MONEY AT THE RACES David Barr 7.00
_____ PAYDAY AT THE RACES Les Conklin 7.00
_____ SMART HANDICAPPING MADE EASY William Bauman 5.00
_____ SUCCESS AT THE HARNESS RACES Barry Meadow 7.00

HUMOR

_____ HOW TO FLATTEN YOUR TUSH Coach Marge Reardon 2.00
_____ JOKE TELLER'S HANDBOOK Bob Orben 10.00
_____ JOKES FOR ALL OCCASIONS Al Schock 7.00
_____ 2,000 NEW LAUGHS FOR SPEAKERS Bob Orben 7.00
_____ 2,400 JOKES TO BRIGHTEN YOUR SPEECHES Robert Orben 10.00
_____ 2,500 JOKES TO START'EM LAUGHING Bob Orben 10.00

HYPNOTISM

_____ CHILDBIRTH WITH HYPNOSIS William S. Kroger, M.D. 5.00
_____ HOW YOU CAN BOWL BETTER USING SELF-HYPNOSIS Jack Heise 7.00
_____ HOW YOU CAN PLAY BETTER GOLF USING SELF-HYPNOSIS Jack Heise 3.00
_____ HYPNOSIS AND SELF-HYPNOSIS Bernard Hollander, M.D. 7.00
_____ HYPNOTISM (Originally published 1893) Carl Sextus 5.00
_____ HYPNOTISM MADE EASY Dr. Ralph Winn 10.00
_____ HYPNOTISM MADE PRACTICAL Louis Orton 5.00
_____ MODERN HYPNOSIS Lesley Kuhn & Salvatore Russo, Ph.D. 5.00
_____ NEW CONCEPTS OF HYPNOSIS Bernard C. Gindes, M.D. 10.00
_____ NEW SELF-HYPNOSIS Paul Adams 10.00
_____ POST-HYPNOTIC INSTRUCTIONS—SUGGESTIONS FOR THERAPY Arnold Furst 10.00
_____ PRACTICAL GUIDE TO SELF-HYPNOSIS Melvin Powers 10.00
_____ PRACTICAL HYPNOTISM Philip Magonet, M.D. 3.00
_____ SECRETS OF HYPNOTISM S.J. Van Pelt, M.D. 5.00
_____ SELF-HYPNOSIS—A CONDITIONED-RESPONSE TECHNIQUE Laurence Sparks . 7.00
_____ SELF-HYPNOSIS—ITS THEORY, TECHNIQUE & APPLICATION Melvin Powers ... 7.00
_____ THERAPY THROUGH HYPNOSIS Edited by Raphael H. Rhodes 5.00

JUDAICA

_____ SERVICE OF THE HEART Evelyn Garfiel, Ph.D. 10.00
_____ STORY OF ISRAEL IN COINS Jean & Maurice Gould 2.00
_____ STORY OF ISRAEL IN STAMPS Maxim & Gabriel Shamir 1.00
_____ TONGUE OF THE PROPHETS Robert St. John 10.00

JUST FOR WOMEN

_____ COSMOPOLITAN'S GUIDE TO MARVELOUS MEN Foreword by Helen Gurley Brown 3.00
_____ COSMOPOLITAN'S HANG-UP HANDBOOK Foreword by Helen Gurley Brown 4.00
_____ COSMOPOLITAN'S LOVE BOOK—A GUIDE TO ECSTASY IN BED 7.00
_____ COSMOPOLITAN'S NEW ETIQUETTE GUIDE Foreword by Helen Gurley Brown ... 4.00
_____ I AM A COMPLEAT WOMAN Doris Hagopian & Karen O'Connor Sweeney 3.00
_____ JUST FOR WOMEN—A GUIDE TO THE FEMALE BODY Richard E. Sand M.D. 5.00
_____ NEW APPROACHES TO SEX IN MARRIAGE John E. Eichenlaub, M.D. 3.00
_____ SEXUALLY ADEQUATE FEMALE Frank S. Caprio, M.D. 3.00
_____ SEXUALLY FULFILLED WOMAN Dr. Rachel Copelan 5.00

MARRIAGE, SEX & PARENTHOOD

_____ ABILITY TO LOVE Dr. Allan Fromme 7.00
_____ GUIDE TO SUCCESSFUL MARRIAGE Drs. Albert Ellis & Robert Harper 10.00
_____ HOW TO RAISE AN EMOTIONALLY HEALTHY, HAPPY CHILD Albert Ellis, Ph.D. . 10.00
_____ PARENT SURVIVAL TRAINING Marvin Silverman, Ed.D. & David Lustig, Ph.D. 15.00
_____ POTENCY MIRACLE Uri P. Peles, M.D. 10.00
_____ SEX WITHOUT GUILT Albert Ellis, Ph.D. 7.00
_____ SEXUALLY ADEQUATE MALE Frank S. Caprio, M.D. 3.00

___ I WILL Ben Sweetland 10.00
___ KNIGHT IN RUSTY ARMOR Robert Fisher 5.00
___ MAGIC IN YOUR MIND U.S. Andersen 15.00
___ MAGIC OF THINKING SUCCESS Dr. David J. Schwartz 10.00
___ MAGIC POWER OF YOUR MIND Walter M. Germain 10.00
___ NEVER UNDERESTIMATE THE SELLING POWER OF A WOMAN Dottie Walters . . 7.00
___ PRINCESS WHO BELIEVED IN FAIRY TALES Marcia Grad 10.00
___ PSYCHO-CYBERNETICS Maxwell Maltz, M.D. 10.00
___ PSYCHOLOGY OF HANDWRITING Nadya Olyanova 10.00
___ SALES CYBERNETICS Brian Adams 10.00
___ SECRET OF SECRETS U.S. Andersen 10.00
___ SECRET POWER OF THE PYRAMIDS U.S. Andersen 7.00
___ SELF-THERAPY FOR THE STUTTERER Malcolm Frazer 3.00
___ STOP COMMITTING VOICE SUICIDE Morton Cooper, Ph.D. 10.00
___ SUCCESS CYBERNETICS U.S. Andersen 10.00
___ 10 DAYS TO A GREAT NEW LIFE William E. Edwards 3.00
___ THINK AND GROW RICH Napoleon Hill 10.00
___ THINK LIKE A WINNER Walter Doyle Staples, Ph.D. 15.00
___ THREE MAGIC WORDS U.S. Andersen 12.00
___ TREASURY OF COMFORT Edited by Rabbi Sidney Greenberg 10.00
___ TREASURY OF THE ART OF LIVING Edited by Rabbi Sidney Greenberg 10.00
___ WHAT YOUR HANDWRITING REVEALS Albert E. Hughes 4.00
___ WINNING WITH YOUR VOICE Morton Cooper, Ph.D. 10.00
___ YOUR SUBCONSCIOUS POWER Charles M. Simmons 7.00

SPORTS

___ BILLIARDS—POCKET • CAROM • THREE CUSHION Clive Cottingham, Jr. 10.00
___ COMPLETE GUIDE TO FISHING Vlad Evanoff 2.00
___ HOW TO IMPROVE YOUR RACQUETBALL Lubarsky, Kaufman & Scagnetti 5.00
___ HOW TO WIN AT POCKET BILLIARDS Edward D. Knuchell 10.00
___ JOY OF WALKING Jack Scagnetti 3.00
___ RACQUETBALL FOR WOMEN Toni Hudson, Jack Scagnetti & Vince Rondone 3.00
___ SECRET OF BOWLING STRIKES Dawson Taylor 5.00
___ SOCCER—THE GAME & HOW TO PLAY IT Gary Rosenthal 7.00
___ STARTING SOCCER Edward F Dolan, Jr. 5.00

TENNIS LOVERS' LIBRARY

___ HOW TO BEAT BETTER TENNIS PLAYERS Loring Fiske 4.00
___ PSYCH YOURSELF TO BETTER TENNIS Dr. Walter A. Luszki 2.00
___ TENNIS FOR BEGINNERS Dr. H.A. Murray 2.00
___ WEEKEND TENNIS—HOW TO HAVE FUN & WIN AT THE SAME TIME Bill Talbert . 3.00

WILSHIRE PET LIBRARY

___ DOG TRAINING MADE EASY & FUN John W. Kellogg 5.00
___ HOW TO BRING UP YOUR PET DOG Kurt Unkelbach 2.00
___ HOW TO RAISE & TRAIN YOUR PUPPY Jeff Griffen 5.00

Available from your bookstore or directly from Melvin Powers.
Please add $2.00 shipping and handling for each book ordered.

Melvin Powers
12015 Sherman Road
No. Hollywood, California 91605

For our complete catalog, visit our Web site at http://www.mpowers.com.

WILSHIRE HORSE LOVERS' LIBRARY

___AMATEUR HORSE BREEDER A.C. Leighton Hardman 5.00
___AMERICAN QUARTER HORSE IN PICTURES Margaret Cabel Self 5.00
___APPALOOSA HORSE Donna & Bill Richardson 7.00
___ARABIAN HORSE Reginald S. Summerhays 7.00
___ART OF WESTERN RIDING Suzanne Norton Jones 10.00
___BASIC DRESSAGE Jean Froissard 7.00
___BEGINNER'S GUIDE TO HORSEBACK RIDING Sheila Wall 5.00
___BITS—THEIR HISTORY, USE AND MISUSE Louis Taylor 10.00
___BREAKING & TRAINING THE DRIVING HORSE Doris Ganton 10.00
___BREAKING YOUR HORSE'S BAD HABITS W. Dayton Sumner 10.00
___COMPLETE TRAINING OF HORSE AND RIDER Colonel Alois Podhajsky 15.00
___DISORDERS OF THE HORSE & WHAT TO DO ABOUT THEM E. Hanauer 5.00
___DOG TRAINING MADE EASY AND FUN John W. Kellogg 5.00
___DRESSAGE—A STUDY OF THE FINER POINTS IN RIDING Henry Wynmalen 15.00
___DRIVE ON Doris Ganton 7.00
___DRIVING HORSES Sallie Walrond 7.00
___EQUITATION Jean Froissard 7.00
___FIRST AID FOR HORSES Dr. Charles H. Denning, Jr. 7.00
___FUN ON HORSEBACK Margaret Cabell Self 4.00
___HORSE OWNER'S CONCISE GUIDE Elsie V. Hanauer 5.00
___HORSE SELECTION & CARE FOR BEGINNERS George H. Conn 10.00
___HORSEBACK RIDING FOR BEGINNERS Louis Taylor 10.00
___HORSEBACK RIDING MADE EASY & FUN Sue Henderson Coen 10.00
___HORSES—THEIR SELECTION, CARE & HANDLING Margaret Cabell Self 5.00
___HOW TO CURE BEHAVIOR PROBLEMS IN HORSES Susan McBane 15.00
___HUNTER IN PICTURES Margaret Cabell Self 2.00
___ILLUSTRATED BOOK OF THE HORSE S. Sidney (8½" x 11") 10.00
___ILLUSTRATED HORSEBACK RIDING FOR BEGINNERS Jeanne Mellin 5.00
___KNOW ALL ABOUT HORSES Harry Disston 5.00
___LAME HORSE—CAUSES, SYMPTOMS & TREATMENT Dr. James R. Rooney 15.00
___POLICE HORSES Judith Campbell 2.00
___PRACTICAL GUIDE TO HORSESHOEING 5.00
___PRACTICAL HORSE PSYCHOLOGY Moyra Williams 10.00
___PROBLEM HORSES—CURING SERIOUS BEHAVIOR HABITS Summerhays 5.00
___REINSMAN OF THE WEST—BRIDLES & BITS Ed Connell 10.00
___RIDE WESTERN Louis Taylor 7.00
___SCHOOLING YOUR YOUNG HORSE George Wheatley 7.00
___STABLE MANAGEMENT FOR THE OWNER—GROOM George Wheatley 7.00
___STALLION MANAGEMENT—A GUIDE FOR STUD OWNERS A.C. Hardman 5.00
___YOU AND YOUR PONY Pepper Mainwaring Healey (8½" x 11") 6.00
___YOUR PONY BOOK Hermann Wiederhold 2.00

Available from your bookstore or directly from Melvin Powers.
Please add $2.00 shipping and handling for each book ordered.

Melvin Powers
12015 Sherman Road
No. Hollywood, California 91605

For our complete catalog, visit our Web site at http://www.mpowers.com.

Books by Melvin Powers

HOW TO GET RICH IN MAIL ORDER

1. How to Develop Your Mail Order Expertise 2. How to Find a Unique Product or Service to Sell 3. How to Make Money with Classified Ads 4. How to Make Money with Display Ads 5. The Unlimited Potential for Making Money with Direct Mail 6. How to Copycat Successful Mail Order Operations 7. How I Created a Bestseller Using the Copycat Technique 8. How to Start and Run a Profitable Mail Order Special Interest Book Business 9. I Enjoy Selling Books by Mail—Some of My Successful Ads 10. Five of My Most Successful Direct Mail Pieces That Sold and Are Selling Millions of Dollars' Worth of Books 11. Melvin Powers's Mail Order Success Strategy—Follow it and You'll Become a Millionaire 12. How to Sell Your Products to Mail Order Companies, Retail Outlets, Jobbers, and Fund Raisers for Maximum Distribution and Profit 13. How to Get Free Display Ads and Publicity that Will Put You on the Road to Riches 14. How to Make Your Advertising Copy Sizzle 15. Questions and Answers to Help You Get Started Making Money 16. A Personal Word from Melvin Powers 17. How to Get Started 18. Selling Products on Television   8½" x 11½" — 352 Pages . . . $20.00

MAKING MONEY WITH CLASSIFIED ADS

1. Getting Started with Classified Ads 2. Everyone Loves to Read Classified Ads 3. How to Find a Money-Making Product 4. How to Write Classified Ads that Make Money 5. What I've Learned from Running Thousands of Classified Ads 6. Classified Ads Can Help You Make Big Money in Multi-Level Programs 7. Two-Step Classified Ads Made Me a Multi-Millionaire—They Can Do the Same for You! 8. One-Inch Display Ads Can Work Wonders 9. Display Ads Can Make You a Fortune Overnight 10. Although I Live in California, I Buy My Grapefruit from Florida 11. Nuts and Bolts of Mail Order Success 12. What if You Can't Get Your Business Running Successfully? What's Wrong? How to Correct it 13. Strategy for Mail Order Success   8½" x 11½" — 240 Pages . . . $20.00

HOW TO SELF-PUBLISH YOUR BOOK AND HAVE THE FUN AND EXCITEMENT OF BEING A BEST-SELLING AUTHOR

1. Who is Melvin Powers? 2. What is the Motivation Behind Your Decision to Publish Your Book? 3. Why You Should Read This Chapter Even if You Already Have an Idea for a Book 4. How to Test the Salability of Your Book Before You Write One Word 5. How I Achieved Sales Totaling $2,000,000 on My Book *How to Get Rich in Mail Order* 6. How to Develop a Second Career by Using Your Expertise 7. How to Choose an Enticing Book Title 8. Marketing Strategy 9. Success Stories 10. How to Copyright Your Book 11. How to Write a Winning Advertisement 12. Advertising that Money Can't Buy 13. Questions and Answers to Help You Get Started 14. Self-Publishing and the Midas Touch
8½" x 11½" — 240 Pages . . . $20.00

A PRACTICAL GUIDE TO SELF-HYPNOSIS

1. What You Should Know about Self-Hypnosis 2. What about the Dangers of Hypnosis? 3. Is Hypnosis the Answer? 4. How Does Self-Hypnosis Work? 5. How to Arouse Yourself From the Self-Hypnotic State 6. How to Attain Self-Hypnosis 7. Deepening the Self-Hypnotic State 8. What You Should Know about Becoming an Excellent Subject 9. Techniques for Reaching the Somnambulistic State 10. A New Approach to Self-Hypnosis 11. Psychological Aids and Their Function 12. Practical Applications of Self-Hypnosis
144 Pages . . . $10.00

Available at your bookstore or directly from Melvin Powers.
Please add $2.00 shipping and handling for each book ordered.

Melvin Powers
12015 Sherman Road, No. Hollywood, California 91605

For our complete catalog, visit our Web site at http://www.mpowers.com.

A Personal Invitation from the Publisher, Melvin Powers...

Since we first published *The Knight in Rusty Armor,* we've received an unprecedented number of calls and letters from readers praising its powerful insights and entertaining style. It is a memorable fun-filled story, rich in wit and humor, that has changed thousands of lives for the better.

The Knight is one of our most popular titles and has been published in numerous languages. I feel so strongly about this unusual book that I'm personally extending an invitation for you to read it.

The Knight in Rusty Armor

The Knight in Rusty Armor is a lighthearted tale of a desperate knight in search of his true self. It's guaranteed to captivate your imagination as it helps you discover the secret of what is most important in life.

Join the knight as he faces a life-changing dilemma upon discovering that he is trapped in his shining armor, as *we* may find that we are trapped in *our* armor—an invisible kind that we use to protect ourselves from various aspects of life.

As the knight searches for a way to free himself, he receives guidance from the wise sage Merlin the Magician, who encourages the knight to embark on the most difficult crusade of his life. The knight takes up the challenge and travels the Path of Truth, where he meets his real self for the first time and confronts the Universal Truths that govern his life—and ours.

The knight's journey reflects our own, filled with hope and despair, belief and disillusionment, laughter and tears. His insights become our insights as we follow along on this intriguing adventure of self-discovery. Anyone who has ever struggled with the meaning of life and love will discover profound wisdom and truth as this delightful fantasy unfolds. *The Knight in Rusty Armor* is an experience that will expand your mind, touch your heart, and nourish your soul.

The author, Robert Fisher, has enjoyed a long and distinguished career writing for such comedy greats as Groucho Marx, Bob Hope, George Burns, Jack Benny, Red Skelton, and Lucille Ball. Mr. Fisher has also written hundreds of comedic radio and television shows.

Available at all bookstores, or send $5.00 (CA res. $5.41) plus $2.00 S/H to Wilshire Book Company, 12015 Sherman Road, No. Hollywood, CA 91605.
For our complete catalog, visit our web site at http://www.mpowers.com.

NEW... by Marcia Grad
Author of *Charisma: How to get that "special magic"*

THE PRINCESS WHO BELIEVED
IN
FAIRY TALES

"Here is a very special book that will guide you lovingly into a new way of thinking about yourself and your life so that the future will be filled with hope and love and song."

OG MANDINO
Author, *The Greatest Salesman in the World*

The Princess Who Believed in Fairy Tales is a personal growth book of the rarest kind. It is a delightful, humor-filled story you will experience so deeply that it can literally change your feelings about yourself, your relationships, and your life.

The princess' journey of self-discovery on the Path of Truth is an eye-opening, inspiring, empowering psychological and spiritual journey that symbolizes the one we all take through life as we sort out illusion from reality, come to terms with our childhood dreams and pain, and discover who we really are and how life works.

If you have struggled with childhood pain, with feelings of not being good enough, with the loss of your dreams, or if you have been disappointed in your relationships, *The Princess Who Believed in Fairy Tales* will prove to you that happy endings—and new beginnings—are always possible. Or if you simply want to get closer to your own truth, the princess will guide you.

You will experience the princess' journey as your own. You will laugh with her and cry with her, learn with her and grow with her, and if you are in pain, you will begin to heal with her.

The universal appeal to both men and women of *The Princess Who Believed in Fairy Tales* has resulted in its translation into numerous languages.

Excerpts from Readers' Heartfelt Letters

"*The Princess* is truly a gem! Though I've read a zillion self-help and spiritual books, I got more out of this one than from any other one I've ever read. It is just too illuminating and full of wisdom to ever be able to thank you enough."

"Your loving story tells my story and many other women's so beautifully. I related to each page for different reasons. Thank you for putting my experience into words for me.... I've been waiting to read this book my entire life."

Available at bookstores, or send $10.00 (CA res. $10.83) plus $2.00 S/H to Wilshire Book Company, 12015 Sherman Road, No. Hollywood, CA 91605.
For our complete catalog, visit our web site at http://www.mpowers.com.

NOTES